Aspirations of Young Adults in Urban Asia

Asian Anthropologies

General Editors:
Hans Steinmüller, London School of Economics
Dolores Martinez, SOAS, University of London

Founding Editors:
Shinji Yamashita, The University of Tokyo
J.S. Eades, Emeritus Professor, Ritsumeikan Asia Pacific University

For a full volume listing, please see the series page on our website: https://www.berghahn-books.com/series/asian-anthropologies

ASPIRATIONS OF YOUNG ADULTS IN URBAN ASIA

Values, Family and Identity

❧

Edited by
Mariske Westendorp, Désirée Remmert and Kenneth Finis

berghahn
NEW YORK · OXFORD
www.berghahnbooks.com

First published in 2021 by
Berghahn Books
www.berghahnbooks.com

© 2021, 2024 Mariske Westendorp, Désirée Remmert and Kenneth Finis
First paperback edition published in 2024

Library of Congress Cataloging-in-Publication Data

Names: Westendorp, Mariske, editor. | Remmert, Désirée, editor. | Finis, Kenneth, editor.
Title: Aspirations of young adults in urban Asia : values, family, and identity / edited by
  Mariske Westendorp, Désirée Remmert and Kenneth Finis.
Description: New York : Berghahn Books, 2021. | Series: Asian anthropologies ;
  volume 11 | Includes bibliographical references and index.
Identifiers: LCCN 2020017770 (print) | LCCN 2020017771 (ebook) |
  ISBN 9781789208955 (hardback) | ISBN 9781789208962 (ebook)
Subjects: LCSH: Young adults—Asia—Social conditions—21st century. | Young adults—
  Asia—Conduct of life. | Urban youth—Asia—Social conditions—21st century. |
  Urban youth—Asia—Conduct of life. | Social values—Asia.
Classification: LCC HQ799.8.A75 A76 2021 (print) | LCC HQ799.8.A75 (ebook) |
  DDC 305.235095/091732—dc23
LC record available at https://lccn.loc.gov/2020017770
LC ebook record available at https://lccn.loc.gov/2020017771

British Library Cataloguing in Publication Data

A catalogue record for this book is available from the British Library

ISBN 978-1-78920-895-5 hardback
ISBN 978-1-80539-147-0 paperback
ISBN 978-1-80539-562-1 epub
ISBN 978-1-78920-896-2 web pdf

https://doi.org/10.3167/9781789208955

CONTENTS

ACKNOWLEDGEMENTS

Editing and publishing this collection on aspirations has for a number of years been an aspiration of our own. As young academics, we hoped to find venues to share our research, ideas and insights. Now this aspiration has finally come to fruition.

The three of us first started discussing the idea for this project in July 2017. We had each been working on papers relating to young people in urban sites in Asia – Mariske on Buddhist beliefs and political aspirations in post-Umbrella Movement Hong Kong, Désirée on a comparison between national identity and future outlook among highly educated urban youth in China and Taiwan, and Kenneth on aspirations, uneven development and culture change for young underprivileged Cambodians in Phnom Penh. Upon hearing about each other's research, we quickly saw a strong connecting theme: a clear emphasis on youth aspirations came to the fore.

In the months that followed, we crafted a call for chapters for a book tentatively entitled *Aspirations of Young Adults in Urban Asia*. In the initial call, we were primarily interested in contributions from other early-career scholars. As our hope was to have the edited volume go beyond Western-centric appraisals, we encouraged scholars from Asian contexts to contribute. In short, we wanted to produce a book written by people who could contemporaneously understand the lifeworlds of their research participants: to be young, urban and most likely a member of the middle class, and be constructing ambitions, life goals and hopes for a future as yet uncertain. A careful selection process and a number of years of work by both editors and contributors alike has produced a volume of ethnographically informed studies that we believe speaks well to this theme and in turn has been the realisation of our own initial aspirations for this project.

We have aimed to produce a book in which the chapters not only speak to the general theoretical framework of aspirations but also to each other. To make this possible, we have asked quite a lot from our contributors, from multiple rounds of revision to reviewing and engaging with each other's work. We are extremely grateful for their continuous efforts. We would also like to thank Tom Bonnington from Berghahn Books for his supervision and guidance through the publication process. Lastly, we thank all those who we have encountered on our young career paths and who have inspired us in one way or another to produce this book.

INTRODUCTION

A Theoretical Framework for Exploring Aspirations of Youth in Urban Asia

Mariske Westendorp, Désirée Remmert and Kenneth Finis

Navigating daily life in a highly urbanised environment has become a challenge that a majority of the global population now faces. As of 2018, over half of the world's population live in cities, a figure that is expected to rise to 68% by 2050. While Asia still experiences a relatively low level of urbanisation, it is home to 54% of the world's urban population as well as to many of today's megacities, such as Tokyo, New Delhi and Shanghai (UN 2018). Many of those sprawling metropoles that seem to pop up on the map out of nowhere impress because of the speed at which they grow, as well as the modern architectural designs and technological advances that govern life in these cities. The transformed physical environment of urbanising societies has not only altered mundane everyday procedures, but has also left a deep imprint on how people define national identity, the distribution of wealth and economic power, religion, family, nature and so forth. Thus, the quickly changing landscapes of modern cities are sites of reimagination and the creation of new concepts that influence the political, social and spiritual life not only of their urban inhabitants but also, as new trends of thought are carried to the urban peripheries, of rural dwellers.

Looking back at some of the major political movements that have arisen in Asian urban environments in the last decade – such as the 2014 Taiwanese Sunflower Movement, the 2014 Hong Kong Umbrella Movement and later the 2019 Hong Kong Protests, the 2014 hunger strikes in Seoul or the 2018 Bangladesh Quota Reform Movement – it becomes obvious that urban youth play a pivotal role in influencing both city and national politics. They not only challenge notions of national identity and the authority of the state, but are also willing to take considerable risks in spreading their message and exerting pressure on political leaders in order to achieve their goals. The aspirations that these youths hold for a better, fairer society are closely connected to grievances about their personal futures that have arisen from bleak prospects on the labour market, political oppression and social expectations. This is not to say that the aspirations of young people are always or even primarily political in nature. Aspirations can relate to different desires for things like education, career trajectory, close relationships or finding a fulfilling way of life. Indeed, in the city young people are often at the forefront of emerging sets of lifestyle ideas. Hungry for change, they explore new ways to live in the city; inspired by trends brought to them by the digital media as well as their studies and travels, they try to find new compromises between the lives they ought to live and the ones they want to live.

This volume explores some of these intricacies by analysing the aspirations of youth and young adults who are navigating life and imagining futures in various cities across Asia. By bringing together contributions from scholars studying different geographical and thematic contexts and inviting them to read and reflect on each other's work in the process, we hope to create a broader theoretical framework for the study of emerging economic, sociocultural and political aspirations of youth and young adults in urban Asian environments. By exploring such aspirations from a comparative perspective, we hope to uncover different understandings of what constitutes the 'good life' or 'a life worth living' across Asia's urban centres. We will look at youth aspirations through an ethnographic lens to interpret our contributors' 'thick' descriptions of how their adolescent and young adult respondents perceive the topic at hand. Ethnographic descriptions provide an opportunity to obtain an insight into how young urbanites conceptualise their aspirations, as well as the societal background against which these emerge. However, this approach raises some important empirical questions: in Asian urban contexts, what precisely defines young adults' aspirations? Are they intricately bound to the hopes and desires that shape the future visions of their Western urban peers and thus more a phenomenon of a particular technological generation than a specific geographical or ideological environment? Or, if not, to what extent do their aspirations reflect the yearning for a future that emerges distinctively in the specific urban Asian lifeworlds in which our young interlocutors have come of age? Finally, what general lessons can we draw from the study of the aspirations of young urbanites in Asia that will also help us understand youth in other geographical regions and sociocultural environments?

Before delving into the rich accounts given by the contributors to this volume, it is important to note that definitions of the main concepts that frame the ethnographies presented in this volume – 'urban', 'youth' or 'young adults' and 'aspirations' – are not necessarily self-evident and require some discussion. For this purpose, we will begin by presenting our interpretation of these concepts and will then briefly elaborate on the specifics of studying aspirations in urban Asian contexts.

Urban Aspirations

Defining the 'urban' implies a comparison with its polar opposite, the rural. In fact, the rural–urban divide is one of the traditional pieties in social science and has been of particular interest in the sociology and anthropology of East Asia in recent decades (see Gaetano and Jacka 2004; Pun 2016). Differences between villages and cities are not only related to scale, complexity and the associated demographic effects, but are also reflected in political, economic and legal areas such as social welfare, housing, land ownership and citizen rights (van der Veer 2015). However, various studies globally have empirically demonstrated that the traditional divide between urban and rural does not hold fast. Increasing mobility, online communication and networking technologies cause a blurring of the boundaries between rural and urban areas by connecting them through a steady flow of people and information (Inda and Rosaldo 2008; Jensen 2006; Nonini 2014). Asian cities have become exceptionally large and continue expanding, displaying the porosity of borders and the flexibility of urban social structures. In this context, the term 'city', which can seem to suggest a static or fixed state, becomes somewhat problematic. Expressions such as 'urban societies', 'city regions' or even 'city states' appear to express the material and social outlines of these modern phenomena more aptly.

Even though a strict divide between the rural and the urban is made difficult by the intense interrelations between villages and cities, we assert that the latter are distinct in their particular multilayered interplay of structures, functions, power networks, hegemonies, politics and ethics. While such aspects certainly also exist in rural areas, the scale and sheer volume of such competing systems in an urban environment make them unique stages of study. The city environment prompts increasingly complex processes of contestation, identification and symbolisation to take place. In addition: 'Under urban circumstances people experience, more than anywhere else, the rapidity of cultural change, the hiatus of social inequalities, the consequences of the human impact on nature and the tangible power of political authorities' (Burchardt and Becci 2013: 17–18). This acceleration of social and cultural change forms the backdrop against which we analyse the hopes and desires of youth in the following chapters. Looking at different ways of imagining the future and the ways in which young people pursue their aspirations will expose these complex processes to scrutiny.

Scholarly attention to the concept of 'aspirations' began most notably with Arjun Appadurai's theorising of the future. Humans are, Appadurai states, 'future-makers' (2013: 285). With the future playing a pivotal role in the construction of culture as well as collective and individual identity, he calls into question anthropology's tendency to frame culture as a form of 'pastness'. This retrospective view, he writes, narrows down the research scope of anthropology to phenomena that entail an orientation to the past, such as 'habit, custom, heritage, tradition' (2013: 180). Moreover, being limited to mostly archival sources to tackle these past-oriented issues presents the anthropologist with further problems. Appadurai notes that archival documents often originate from official sources and thus might present a biased account of the past; as such, they reflect the agenda of the ruling elite and are instrumental in reinforcing and legitimising the power of the state. Instead, he suggests that anthropologists should explore 'personal, familial and community archives', which he describes as 'critical sites for negotiating paths to dignity, recognition and politically feasible maps for the future' (2013: 288). Considering these points, he suggests that anthropologists must aim at condensing their knowledge of how people anticipate the future into a more general theory of humans as future-oriented beings and the future as a 'cultural fact' (2013: 285). He stresses that anthropological analyses must zoom in on the perspectives and experiences of individuals, which form maps to navigate the future and also shape those futures at the same time (2013: 288).

Appadurai is not alone in his call for an 'ethnography of the future'. Clammer (2012) also criticises anthropologists' habit of restricting themselves to researching issues of the past and the present. However, whereas Appadurai laments anthropologists' neglect of the future as a subject of study, Clammer criticises them for not using their ethnographic findings as a basis for making informed predictions about socioeconomic trends, as is done in other disciplines. These alternative principles, he suggests, could counter dominant economic models that currently form the framework of how we anticipate the future:

> Up until now this has been rarely attempted – the ethnographic present or the past providing a safe environment for anthropologists to ply their priestly rather than prophetic functions – as keepers of the knowledge rather than as adventurous speculators of what might be done with that knowledge given the range of social, economic and environmental crises that we have ourselves induced. (Clammer 2012: 129–30)

By focusing our attention on the aspirations of urban youths, a demographic that often sets trends for powerful social and political movements, we are exploring future-oriented cultural capacities related to wants, preferences, choices and calculations as they emerge to become transformative forces. However, we are not suggesting a total shift away from the focus on habit, custom, heritage and tradition. Instead, we perceive the past and present to be integral to the future (see

Bunnell and Goh 2018). The present redefines the past and shapes the aspirations people hold for themselves and their community.

Our study of youth aspirations will also shed light on the fundamental ideas and beliefs that motivate these aspirations and keep them alive; these beliefs include those about 'life and death, the nature of worldly possessions, the significance of material assets over social relations, the relative illusion of social permanence for a society, the value of peace or war' (Appadurai 2004: 68). Aspirations, which promise the realisation of core values held by individuals and groups, can thus give meaning to the future. They involve the arduous work of *becoming*, of trying to live a life that one deems worthwhile and of becoming the person that one desires (Fischer 2014). They involve pleasures and pains, experiences and struggles. As Benoit de L'Estoile (2014) has argued, orientations to the future are epitomised by the verb *esperar*, which means equally to wait, to hope and to expect – already indicating the different attitudes one can have regarding aspirations and the capability of making aspirations a reality.

Aspirations determine a person's wants and wishes for 'commodities', such as physical goods, marriage, work, leisure, respectability, friendship and health (Appadurai 2004). 'Living up to the expectations of particular values', Fischer notes, 'is in many ways the stock and trade of human existence; and it is this forward-looking, aspirational quality that gives meaning to much of what we do, affluent and impoverished alike' (2014: 6). We should nevertheless be careful not to reduce the scope of aspirations to material conditions alone. Aspirations maintain a key nonmaterial quality; although sometimes related to or influenced by the economic market, they often transcend it. Aspirations may determine the way in which a person leads every aspect of their life and can create the potential to provide the empowerment needed to construct a life that one values.

Moreover, aspirations are not merely individual. Economist Debraj Ray (2006) points out that aspirations are a part of larger ethical and metaphysical ideas, formed in interaction with social life, or 'the cognitive neighborhood of [a] person' (2006: 409). Aspirations orient on social norms and expectations, as well as on communally held hopes and desires. Referring to Appadurai, Ray holds that aspirations, which are deeply embedded in the local culture and social fabric, are shaped by power hierarchies and access to material resources. He illustrates how limited access to power diminishes people's ability to achieve their aspirations, leaving them frustrated or in despair and susceptible to engagement in political action. He argues that in order for aspirations to form and be effectively realised, several conditions must be met. Crucially, an individual's environment must allow for suitable role models whose background is relatable and whose achievements appear relevant. Socioeconomic closeness to role models reassures those who follow in their steps that a reward for their efforts is likely and that risks are not taken in vain: 'Looking at the experiences of individuals similar to me is like running an experiment with better controls and therefore has better content in informing my decisions – and by extension – my aspirations' (Ray 2006: 411). Further, a perceived degree of social mobility in society is necessary to foster motivation and open up paths to pursue and realise ambitions. The higher the perceived degree of social mobility, the greater the 'aspirations window'; that is, the opportunities people see as worth pursuing (2006). The strategies individuals apply to realise their aspirations and the risks they are willing to take to close aspiration gaps ('the difference between the standard of living that's aspired to and the standard of living that one already has' – Ray 2006: 412) are thus importantly shaped by the individual's specific sociocultural, economic and political lifeworlds. Having seen that individual aspirations and local power structures are closely interwoven, it becomes clear why reframing 'aspirations' as a cultural category seems more helpful in their analysis than merely defining them as an individual trait.

Appadurai describes the capacity to aspire as the ability to read 'a map of a journey into the future' (2004: 76). A map can be an inscrutable document covered in unfamiliar symbols and words unless we are supplied with the information and experiences required to interpret it. Aspirations themselves are complex understandings of the future pathways available to people; courses drawn to guide oneself through unfamiliar terrain. The direction of these aspirations will be determined by the limits of possibilities that young people see presented by the lives of those around them or to which they are exposed. In order for young people to develop their capacity to aspire, their families, local community members and those they encounter in their daily lives must have experience of navigating particular fields and routes. Regarding this navigational aspect, Bunnell, Gillen and Ho (2017) rightfully state that aspiration should not be taken as a fixed destination or endpoint, but rather as both a noun and a verb. As a noun, it evokes 'a mental image of the future'; as a verb, it suggests 'practices of seeking, searching – and the possibility of finding opportunities not only different from a priori imaginings but beyond what had previously even been imaginable or deemed possible' (2017: 37). Thus, aspirations are not static, but are responsive to and have functional value for facing the situations and needs of the present as much as the future.

Responding flexibly to new needs and ideals in society, aspirations might change over time and, being closely tied to local values and norms, these transformations might not always play out smoothly. A plethora of anthropological work in recent years has explored how the globalisation of values and the change of aspirations they bring about has influenced family dynamics and complicated intergenerational relationships (Fong 2004; Hong Fincher 2014; Kelsky 2001). Increased access to higher education and Western philosophical thought, as well as widespread access to social media, have played a role in changing attitudes and expectations, especially of younger generations. The growing focus on individualised goals and aspirations tied to self-realisation and personal independence that has emerged in Asia has had a significant impact on intergenerational relations. Decisions on matters such as career, marriage and location of residence, which used to be made communally or were under the authority of parents or the state, are now claimed by a younger generation who want to be in charge of their own life. This increased emphasis on individual preferences and goals also affects young people's notion of their personal capacity to realise their aspirations. Agency 'denotes the freedom to act on behalf of what one values and has reason to value' (Fischer 2014: 11). It contrasts with oppression or passivity. Agency, as the following chapters will illustrate, can be claimed in decisions pertaining to family life in order to assert one's position as a self-responsible individual with one's own hopes and desires against the expectation of parents and the wider society. It can also be used to assert one's status as a group against political, religious or other social authorities. Importantly, however, notions of individual and collective agency are connected by the environment they emerged from and may inform each other in significant ways. Referring back to Appadurai and Ray's outline of the embeddedness of aspirations in societal structures, it becomes clear that not only individual and collective hopes and desires but also perceptions of one's capacity to achieve these are significantly shaped by one's surroundings.

According to Appadurai (2004), whereas all humans have the capacity to aspire, it is the social, cultural and economic framework that informs the content of these aspirations as well as individuals' and groups' sense of efficacy in realising them. Exploring the notion of aspiration as a cultural capacity, rather than an individual motivational trait, enables an understanding of the effects of the unequal distribution of social, cultural and economic capital on the capacity to aspire. For this reason, aspirations have often been studied in marginalised groups, such as ethnic minorities or those living in poverty. At the same time, we recognise the potential for using the concept of aspirations when focusing on members of the middle and upper classes too. The effects of significant sociocultural, political and economic changes, as well as the challenges of rapid urbanisation and development, are not exclusive to those of lower socioeconomic means and are felt to varying degrees across all strata of society. It is therefore important to take other sections of society into consideration when researching aspirations.

Aspirations come in many different forms. Some of them can seem almost utopian in nature. These include aspirations that are religiously or ideologically inspired, such as to create a Kingdom of God on earth, or the nationalistic aspiration for sovereignty. Others are neither utopian nor long-term. They might be practically oriented, such as the aspiration for homeownership. Certain aspirations can be an end goal (e.g. becoming a business owner), or a means to a longer-term goal (e.g. becoming a business owner so that a house can be bought).

This diversity in the nature of aspirations leads to the question of how to empirically study them. In this regard, we find the heuristic model proposed by Paolo

Boccagni (2017) insightful. Whereas Boccagni applies this analytical framework to dissect migrant workers' aspirations, we believe that it is useful beyond this social demographic to explore aspirations in general. Boccagni's framework is developed around three key dimensions. First, he directs our attention to the contents of aspirations: to what do people aspire? This dimension highlights the necessity of studying aspirations with regards to specific, subjectively meaningful objectives, which are in turn embedded in specific sets of values, interests and rights. The second dimension questions the relation reference of aspirations; that is, who the aspirations benefit. One can cultivate aspirations involving oneself as much as significant others and this relational reference is important to take into account. Lastly, he addresses the 'where' and the 'when' of aspirational goals by applying terms of space-time horizons. Aspirations are embedded in complex spatial and temporal frameworks. They can develop in relation to more or less idealised places, as short-term or long-term projects, or even as temporally undetermined projects. The directions to which aspirations call our attention are crucial in terms of understanding their spatiality. Taking these three dimensions into account will facilitate an ethnographically inspired and comprehensive analysis of aspirations.

Urban Aspirations in Asian Contexts: From the Contemporary Mundane to the Transcendent Future

A comparison between such diverse Asian contexts as Japan, Malaysia, China and Sri Lanka might appear odd, as these places seem to share little in common beyond their continental positioning. We have seen so far that while we are united by our ability to aspire, we differ considerably in terms of the aspirations we hold, in the perception of our capacity to realise those aspirations and in how we pursue them. Moreover, our conceptualisations of our aspirations are not only laden with deeply held, culturally specific values, but they are also constantly in flux as they integrate new values and ideas that are incessantly supplied by a globalised media and social network platforms. Focusing on cities across Asia and exploring how aspirations form under such diverse influences and against the backdrop of cultural and demographic specifics may help to illuminate threads of confluence and influence, as well as divergence, among geographically close neighbours in this dynamic and rapidly rising region.

Some of the aspirations that will emerge in this volume might seem trivial, mundane, ridiculous, uninspiring or even concerning; others might seem fantastical or beyond the scope of an individual's own life. We will not assign an assessment of worth to these aspirations, as we are not interested in developing normative definitions about what is, or is not, an appropriate aspiration. Rather, we see aspirations as frameworks, emerging out of cultural contexts, that can make us aware of the cultural diversities and similarities that exist within and between Asian cities. They emerge through affective and evaluative engagements with things that are present in the world. Therefore, by researching aspirations, we gain an insight not only into what people value, but also into the culturally diverse frames and strategies in which these values are embedded.

Despite the variety of aspirations that are likely to emerge, in this volume we aim to explore whether notable similarities can be detected. Young adults in different Asian contexts are confronted with a shared global future, involving uncertainties, unpredictability and possible ecological catastrophes, not to mention the ever-present threat of yet another political or economic crisis. It could be that these might translate into similar aspirations. Similarities in young people's aspirations might also be related to changing traditions in urban spaces, the emergence of climate change, as well as political uprisings that result from the fundamentalisms and activisms that often erupt in urban centres. Through a cross-case comparison, we can reach an understanding of patterns and dissimilarities concerning the aspirations and opportunities people have to effectively pursue their vision of the future. Towards that end, this volume brings together studies from a diverse range of contexts to explore how aspirations are conceptualised and pursued in very different places, while also allowing us to focus on commonalities.

The contributors to this volume have taken Appadurai's concept of 'aspirations' as an analytical lens through which to investigate and analyse the actions, behaviours, values and attitudes of their research participants. The result is a colourful collection of chapters based on empirical data. As the chapters in this volume will show, precise aspirations are not always immediately identifiable in the mundanity of everyday life. However, in most cases longer-term research based on ethnographic methods can allow aspirations to be deduced more clearly. Such methods also reveal that the concept of aspirations is highly specific and divergent from context to context and sometimes even within the same context. Differences between the aspirations presented in these chapters therefore abound.

Regardless, certain similarities bring these case studies together. First, the chapters presented are all based on contemporary data, gathered between 2012 and 2018. Consequently, the aspirations presented are very timely. They relate to current events and changes taking place on the Asian continent, as well as to changes in gendered perspectives, technological potential, urbanisation rates, and international and national migration patterns. The aspirations are therefore reflections of changing demographics and political ideologies (see e.g. the chapters by Remmert and Westendorp), globalisation patterns (Huang and Grant), socioeconomics (Huang and Param), urbanisation rates (Camellia), gendered norms (Camellia and Suzuki) and violence (Andersen).

In addition, almost all the chapters (except for the chapter by Grant) concern members or aspiring members of Asia's middle class. Middle-classness in this case is concurrently an economic opportunity, a political position, an ideology and an identity. It is a position that one occupies, that one aspires to (Andersen) or that one aims to 'talk back' to (Param). It can represent freedom and economic independence or can be felt as a constraint to reaching these same goals (see e.g. Param, Suzuki and Landgraf).

Lastly, the chapters paint pictures of the experience of young people growing up and making a life for themselves in urban cities in Asia. These include adolescents (see Param) who still live under the wings of their parents, young adults who are studying or finishing their studies (Andersen, Grant and Camellia) and young adults who are struggling with questions of family life and careers (Remmert, Huang, Landgraf, Suzuki and Westendorp).

An Overview of the Chapters

This volume consists of nine chapters. We place these chapters along a 'continuum' from the here and now to the transcendent future; from more mundane and personalised aspirations to aspirations that are transcendental and idealistic. The former include aspirations towards a middle-class lifestyle, marriage and having a family and career prospects. The latter include nationalistic and religious aspirations that are temporally and spatially transcendent. Arranging the chapters in this way shows that aspirations are not only material or 'mundane', but can just as easily relate to larger frameworks.

In Chapter 1, Remmert presents a clear emphasis on aspirations as not only economic but also ideological, demographic and generational. She shows how individuals are confronted with various aspirational maps that they negotiate based on personal values and objectives. The aspirational maps presented by young Chinese and Taiwanese women are not only obstructed by the socioeconomic and political constraints of their home societies, but are themselves also a reflection of complex maps of filial obligations that are difficult to synchronise with personal goals. In Chapter 2, Huang takes a similar approach, but with a clear emphasis on the improvement of individuals' lives. As she shows, migration experience and anticipation shape the identities and aspirations of the young adults in her study. She indicates how an action (migration) can shape aspirations, with urban overseas experiences affecting future aspirations and intentions.

The emphasis in Chapter 3 by Landgraf shifts to normative ideas about how one *should* live and the good life one *should* be able to have. In her chapter, the 'good life' is conceptualised by young South Koreans with regard to middle-class standards for education, life and marriage. It is a negotiation and balance of different values and practices that are considered 'right' and 'good'. In addition, the chapter suggests that a simple dichotomy between 'tradition' and 'modernity' thus falls short, as 'traditional' values are constantly reinvented and 'modern' values, ideas and ethics keep changing. In Chapter 4, Camellia likewise considers more present-worldly aspirations that can be achieved in a person's individual life. However, she approaches this mainly from the strategic choices one makes to navigate life towards these aspirations. The growing global trend towards educating girls coupled with the local belief that marriage is central to a woman's wellbeing has shaped individual young women's aspirations in Dhaka. Many no longer want to be stay-at-home-wives, but rather want economic independence. Interestingly, Camellia shows how they try to reach this aspiration through embodied practices, namely appearance. In Chapter 5, Suzuki builds upon similar ideas to show how the embodied practice of international migration from Japan to Ireland leads to a different, normatively better, lifestyle. Here, international migration is a self-oriented approach to life, reflecting changing relations to family and work. Suzuki's informants seek a sense of self-fulfilment beyond the constraints of personal relations by travelling away from the confines and securities of home.

In the remaining chapters, the emphasis shifts from aspiring to a good life in the here and now to aspirations that reach beyond the individual to a larger national, international or even transnational community. In Chapter 6, Param shows how aspirations can break open existing norms regarding individuality and careers. The personalised aspirations of middle-class Indians in Malaysia question definitions of success and wellbeing and talk back to existing frameworks of achievement and kinship-based relationships in the predominant discourses of middle-classness within that community. In Chapter 7, Andersen describes how the aspirations of young lawyers-to-be in Sri Lanka intersect with common notions of accomplishment in a situation of heightened political tensions. He describes individuals engaging in careers that are not necessarily beneficial primarily to themselves but rather that relate to the future of the country at large. This transformative focus has echoes in Chapter 8 by Grant, in which she shows how coffee baristas in Vietnam are aiming to paint a different picture of their nation as an authentic coffee-producing country on the world stage. She introduces her research participants as young adults who identify strongly with a global coffee community. Lastly, in Chapter 9, Westendorp takes this approach one step further. By focusing on religious orientations of young Hong Kong Buddhists, she argues how we might move beyond the present concept of aspirations in total, seeing it stretch beyond temporal and spatial boundaries.

Taking all these chapters together, we will discover how aspirations are alternately material and immaterial, subjective and communally constructed, practical and utopian, normative, individual and universal. They are situated between 'should' and 'want to' and sometimes even 'have to'. As the chapters will show, they are neither fixed nor always easily identifiable, but their influence on the course and personal interpretation of a young person's experience can be profound.

Mariske Westendorp is an anthropologist and religious studies scholar. She was awarded her Ph.D. in anthropology in 2016; her dissertation was entitled 'In the Eye of the Typhoon: Aspirations of Buddhists and Catholics in Turbulent Hong Kong'. Her research interests include the anthropology of religion, urban anthropology, Buddhism and the study of death in contemporary urban societies.

Désirée Remmert obtained her Ph.D. in Anthropology from the London School of Economics and Political Science (LSE), United Kingdom. She subsequently conducted postdoctoral research at the University of Tübingen in Germany, Academia Sinica in Taiwan and at the LSE in the United Kingdom. She specialises in cognitive anthropology, urban ethnography and multisited comparative research with a regional focus on East Asia.

Kenneth Finis is a Ph.D. candidate with the Anthropology Department of Macquarie University in Australia. His current research focuses on the question of the intergenerational transmission of trauma, exploring how young people in Cambodia today see themselves in relation to the past, their family and their society. He has a professional background in social work, having practised in both community youth work and clinical settings.

References

Appadurai, Arjun. 2004. 'The Capacity to Aspire: Culture and the Terms of Recognition', in Vijayendra Rao and Michael Walton (eds), *Culture and Public Action*. Stanford: Stanford University Press, pp. 59–84.

———. 2013. *The Future as Cultural Fact: Essays on the Global Condition*. London: Verso.

Boccagni, Paolo. 2017. 'Aspirations and the Subjective Future of Migration: Comparing Views and Desires of the "Time Ahead" through the Narratives of Immigrant Domestic Workers', *Comparative Migration Studies* 5(4): 1–18.

Bunnell, Tim, Jamie Gillen and Elaine Lynn-Ee Ho. 2017. 'The Prospect of Elsewhere: Engaging the Future through Aspirations in Asia', *Annuals of the American Association of Geographers* 108(1): 35–51.

Bunnell, Tim, and Daniel Goh (eds). 2018. *Urban Asias: Essays on Futurity Past and Present*. Berlin: Jovis.

Burchardt, Marian, and Irene Becci. 2013. 'Introduction: Religion Takes Place: Producing Urban Locality', in Irene Becci, Marian Burchardt and José Casanova (eds), *Topographies of Faith: Religion in Urban Spaces*. Leiden: Brill, pp. 1–21.

Clammer, John. 2012. *Culture, Development and Social Theory: Towards an Integrated Social Development*. London: Zed Books.

De L'Estoile, Benoit. 2014. 'Money Is Good, But a Friend Is Better', *Current Anthropology* 55(9): S62–S73.

Fischer, Edward F. 2014. *The Good Life: Aspiration, Dignity and the Anthropology of Wellbeing*. Stanford: Stanford University Press.

Fong, Vanessa. 2004. *Only Hope: Coming of Age under China's One-Child Policy*. Stanford: Stanford University Press.

Gaetano, Arianne M., and Tamara Jacka. 2004. *On the Move: Women and Rural-to-Urban Migration in Contemporary China*. New York: Columbia University Press.

Hong Fincher, Leta. 2014. *Leftover Women: The Resurgence of Gender Inequality in China*. London: Zed Books.

Inda, Jonathan Xavier, and Renato Rosaldo. 2008. 'Tracking Global Flows', in Jonathan Xavier Inda and Renato Rosaldo (eds), *The Anthropology of Globalization: A Reader*, 2nd edn. Chichester: Wiley-Blackwell, pp. 3–46.

Jensen, Ole. 2006. '"Facework", Flow and the City: Simmel, Goffman and Mobility in the Contemporary City', *Mobilities* 1(2): 143–65.

Kelsky, Karen. 2001. *Women on the Verge: Japanese Women, Western Dreams*. Durham, NC: Duke University Press.

Nonini, Donald (ed.). 2014. *A Companion to Urban Anthropology*. Chichester: Wiley-Blackwell.

Pun, Ngai. 2016. *Migrant Labor in China: Post-socialist Transformations*. Cambridge: Polity Press.

Ray, Debraj. 2006. 'Aspirations, Poverty and Economic Change', in Abhijit Banerjee, Roland Bénabou and Dilip Mookherjee (eds), *Understanding Poverty*. Oxford: Oxford University Press, pp. 409–21.

UN. 2018. '68% of the World Population Projected to Live in Urban Areas by 2050, Says UN', Department of Economic and Social Affairs, 16 May. Retrieved 17 March 2020 from https://www.un.org/development/desa/en/news/population/2018-revision-of-world-urbanization-prospects.html.

Van der Veer, Peter (ed.). 2015. *Handbook of Religion and the Asian City: Aspiration and Urbanization in the Twenty-First Century*. Berkeley: University of California Press.

1

FEMALE FILIALITY RECONFIGURED

Integrating Parental Expectations and Personal Aspirations in Beijing and Taipei

Désirée Remmert

In early March 2018, one month after I had returned to London from my second period of fieldwork in Taipei, I received a phone call from Yu-ching,[1] a young Taiwanese woman who I had already known for several years. She sounded exasperated when she told me that she needed advice. Despite being in her early thirties, she had only recently moved out of her parental home in one of Taipei's exclusive neighbourhoods into a small apartment in a less expensive part of the city. Her parents had not been fond of her decision, but, after long discussions, they let her leave. Yu-ching had pondered living on her own for years as she felt constricted by her parents' frequent questions about her private life and by the strict rules she had to obey at home. Yet, assuming her parents would only accept her moving out after getting married, she had repeatedly abandoned the plan. Moreover, she was unsure if she wanted to give up her comfortable home in an upscale neighbourhood for a less luxurious place. Like many of her peers, she would not be able to sustain the lifestyle she enjoyed at the parental home once she lived on her own. Entry-level salaries for graduates in Taiwan had not risen since the 1990s and the overpriced housing marked in Taipei made it difficult to find an affordable apartment (Chan and Yang 2015: 301).

However, a range of different events eventually triggered Yu-ching's decision to go through with her plan. First, she had been on and off work for several months and did not seem to be able to find employment that suited her. Only

Endnotes for this chapter begin on page 31.

recently, she had lost her job in the legal department of a local company that had initially appeared to be promising. Her parents were concerned about her repeated phases of unemployment and felt disappointed that she had not managed to establish a career yet, despite obtaining several degrees from universities in Taiwan and North America in sought-after fields. As such, they increased their pressure on her to find a new job. Accordingly, the atmosphere at home was tense and she avoided spending more time with her parents than necessary. At the same time, she had secretly started dating a young man and feared the watchful eyes of her parents, who took a rather conservative stance on premarital relationships.

When I visited Yu-ching at her new place shortly before I left Taiwan, she still appeared elated, despite the obvious shortcomings of the damp and rather drab-looking room she had rented near a noisy street market. Moving away from home, she stressed, had been her 'declaration of independence'. Her parents had never acknowledged her as a grown woman with her own needs and aspirations. After moving into the new apartment, she had told them: 'You think you know me, but there is another person existing besides your daughter that is also Yu-ching.' Radiating with confidence, she hoped that without her parents' constant (often contradictory) reminders that she should develop her career and find a husband in order to start a family, her life would take a turn for the better.

Yet, when Yu-ching called me on that morning in March, her anticipation for a new, self-determined life had given way to anxious apprehensions of the future. Her blossoming relationship had failed, which left her feeling devastated and lonely, longing for the warmth and security of her parental home. She now pondered moving back to her parents' house. Yet she feared their judgement, as her emotional turmoil had distracted her from advancing her professional career, which had been stalled for a while by that time. Her father grew more and more impatient and had recently complained that she, unlike other young Taiwanese, had not yet offered her parents financial support. Young adults with similar educational backgrounds usually transferred a symbolic sum of money to their parents each month to demonstrate their filial care. Yu-ching's father argued that he had worked all his life and made many sacrifices, yet she appeared to have wasted the opportunities he had offered her. She admitted that she was indeed not very ambitious and had mostly concentrated on her love life. After all, her parents had been pressuring her for years to get married.

The antagonistic expectation that daughters should meet rather conservative gendered norms like marriage and childbirth, while simultaneously succeeding in their academic and professional lives, was not uncommon among the parents of my Taiwanese interlocutors. Despite the significant socioeconomic and demographic changes in recent decades that were accompanied by a constant rise in female labour force participation, the notion that women were selfless carers of children and elderly family members had not lost much of its impact in modern

Taiwanese society (Ministry of Labor 2019). However, the dramatically decreasing birth rate and the resulting higher investment into daughters' education raised parents' expectations of their academic and professional achievements and, by extension, their future economic support, especially in the absence of sons. Like Yu-ching's experience, many of my female Taiwanese interlocutors complained that their families anticipated academic and professional excellence from them, while at the same time expecting them to be present at home to keep their parents company. Furthermore, they were encouraged to marry and have children within a socially accepted timeframe, which also correlated with those years that were most important to build a professional career. Consequently, normative expectations on women's expression of filiality curtailed their scope in terms of realising their personal career and lifestyle aspirations.

Comparative research has shown that Taiwan, as opposed to China, has retained a surprisingly traditional Confucian gender and family ideology, considering its modern economy, high degree of urbanisation and level of education (Chu and Yu 2010; Whyte 2004, 2005). This phenomenon is rooted in a complex interplay of socioeconomic and political factors that I will discuss in more detail below. However, traditional notions of filiality have recently been challenged by substantial demographic and socioeconomic transitions. Yu-ching's experience is thus typical of a generation of young Taiwanese women who have been raised to accommodate expectations of female filiality that have been extended beyond the traditional notion of a woman as a caregiver to her children and parents-in-law. Women's obligations now include physical care responsibilities towards their own parents as well as the task of providing economic safety and social status. However, whereas this adjustment of traditional concepts of filiality has been adopted by many Taiwanese parents, what features less obviously in parent's future plans is an acknowledgement of women's increased professional opportunities and the accompanying wish to realise personal ambitions. Due to this unilateral reconceptualisation of the concept of filial care, many of my Taiwanese interlocutors felt torn between their sense of obligation towards their parents and their wish to realise their aspirations for a career and a more autonomous lifestyle.

Earlier I mentioned that comparative studies have suggested that urban-based families in China adhere to a less traditional concept of filiality; this appears to be a consequence of the particular structure of the labour market as well as social policies and ideological campaigns during the Mao era whose repercussions are still palpable today (Whyte 2004). Indeed, I was stunned by the relative freedom my interlocutors in Beijing had, not only in their daily lives but also in confidently adjusting the fulfilment of their filial obligations to their particular circumstances. A memorable conversation, due to its stark contrast with the phone call with Yu-ching described above, was one I had with Sun, a young Chinese woman in her mid-twenties in Beijing in the autumn of 2013. Sun had grown up in Shaanxi

Province and only rarely saw her parents. Slightly younger than Yu-ching, she made an independent living in Beijing and thought about starting her own business. During one of our meetings, she mischievously told me her strategy to mitigate the fact that she had moved in with her new boyfriend following her mother's visit to Beijing. Her mother had long worried about her still being single, yet Sun had not told her about her new relationship before her arrival: '[M]y boyfriend and I went to the train station to see my mother. It was a big surprise for her. I did not tell her before.' Counting on her mother's relief, she had hoped that she would not be angry about the fact that she had already moved in with her new boyfriend: 'My mother accepted it, she was also happy, because before that, she was worried that I didn't have a boyfriend . . . I think she saw I was happy with my boyfriend and she found it was OK.' Compared to Yu-ching, not living in the same city as her parents gave Sun significant leeway in pursuing a more liberal lifestyle without their knowledge. Like many of her Chinese peers, she had left her parental home as a teenager to attend boarding high school and her educational career took her even further away from her parental home in the following years. Her parents had thus become used to her absence from home and accepted it as necessary for the development of her career.

However, Taiwanese interlocutors whose families lived in other parts of the island rarely challenged parental authority in a comparable way, fearing the impact that such violation of social norms would have on the family's reputation. Moreover, due to the small size of Taiwan and the fast communication channels among members of the close-knit family networks, news about their behaviour would soon reach relatives even in remote locations and provoke parents' anger.

The cases of Yu-ching and Sun give an impression of how various structural specifics of Taiwan and China affect the scope within which young women could strategise to win their parents' approval and realise personal aspirations. In order to understand these regional differences in attitudes towards filiality, particularly the greater emphasis on the physical presence of adult daughters in the parental home in Taiwan as compared to China, a more detailed look at the particular demographic, socioeconomic and politico-ideological landscapes of the two locales is necessary.

In the following, I will first discuss the Confucian concept of filial piety with a focus on the new role of women as caregivers as well as providers of social status and economic support. This will be followed by a brief historical overview of the socioeconomic and political trajectories of China and Taiwan and how they are reflected in notions of filial care. Referring to Appadurai's concept of 'maps of aspirations' (2004), I will suggest that these have to be synchronised with complex maps of obligations towards family members that significantly affect the scope within which young adults form and pursue their aspirations in China and Taiwan. Two case studies from Beijing and Taipei will be given to will illustrate how differing attitudes towards the expression of filiality, particularly regarding adult daughters' obligations in the parental home, have impacted how young women negotiate the pursuit of personal aspirations with their duties towards their parents.

Most of the data I draw on in this chapter was gathered during eighteen months of ethnographic research in Taipei and Beijing in 2012–13. This material will be supplemented by follow-up interviews I conducted during twelve months of research in Taipei in 2017–18. My methodology comprised participant observation, structured and semi-structured interviews and a survey. In each field site I interviewed approximately thirty young adults in their early twenties to early thirties. I chose to conduct the study among students and young graduates, as I hypothesised that their academic credentials would provide them with a wide range of professional choices that might not always be easily integrated with parental interests.

Filial Piety in China and Taiwan

Despite the major changes that could be observed in China and Taiwan over the last seventy years, the concept of filial piety (*xiao* 孝), a key aspect of Chinese ethics since the pre-imperial era, is still at the centre of the parent–child relationship (Chan and Tan 2004: 1–2; Fei 1992 [1948]: 43–44). *Xiao*, Yan emphasises, is 'the ultimate responsibility of every individual and the moral trait that distinguishes human beings from animals' (Yan 2003: 173). The term connotes a host of moral and ethical interpretations, but at its core lies a reciprocal element that is commonly understood as the obligation of parents to provide their offspring with material and emotional care during childhood and the duty of children to assist their parents in old age and to perform rituals that guarantee a pleasant afterlife. Traditionally, the eldest son was responsible for the provision of economic support as well as for the ritual aspects of *xiao*, whereas the burden of daily care mostly fell on daughters-in-law (Chan and Tan 2004; Stafford 2000a: 60–62; Tan 2004: 226–27). However, the concept of filial piety has been subject to reinterpretation throughout the centuries, responding to the specific concerns of each era and its practicality in everyday life. For example, Stafford observed in rural China and Taiwan that women are often not only meeting the normative expectation of providing everyday support for their parents-in-law, but that they are also deeply involved in the emotional and practical care of their own ageing parents (2000a, 2000b). This double responsibility, often combined with household and childcare duties, can put a heavy strain on women's physical and emotional wellbeing and can complicate relationships with spouses and children.

Although Confucian values of obedience to parents had been called into question by the May Fourth Movement as early as 1919–25, they were much more fiercely attacked from the 1950s onwards as the Chinese Communist Party (CCP) introduced political reforms aimed at dissolving family ties and intergenerational obligations in order to strengthen Party rule (Harrison 2001: 170–75; Yan 2003). The restructuring of the workplace and the growing popularity of political youth groups might have been the most effective measures that the Party took in this context. During the Cultural Revolution, many young people joined activist groups and with the growing influence of youth leaders, parents' authority diminished (Chan 1985: 68–79). Moreover, to those young people who worked on family farms and businesses prior to collectivisation, the new working conditions in the communes and work units (*danwei* 單位) not only opened up a new space free from parental supervision, but the individualised income also granted them some financial independence that further contributed to parents' loss of control (Yan 2003: 52; cf. Yan 2009). In the Chinese cities, where workers were assigned accommodation in compounds that belonged to their work unit and family structures were eclipsed by those of the *danwei*, children's independence from parental control was fostered at a much earlier age by the provision of day care facilities and the strong bonds formed with peers in the new living arrangements (Liu 2007). The assignment of workplaces, housing and childcare facilities, combined with other social benefits in urban areas, thus helped young couples to start married life without depending heavily on their parents (Evans 2010). In addition, the rustication programme, during which urban youths were assigned agricultural work in rural areas, played a key role in increasing children's independence from parents (Rene 2013: 90). Though it is disputed as to how successful the campaigns and policy reforms of the Mao era were in dissolving family bonds in the long term, comparative research has shown that at least in Chinese cities, nuclear households with more flexible intergenerational support patterns became increasingly common in the reform era (Davis and Harrell 1993; Whyte 2004; Whyte et al. 2003).

Whereas the abolition of state welfare measures in the reform era gradually reversed the dissolution of intra-family dependencies created during the Mao era in China, in Taiwan filial values have never been contested by the state. The Kuomintang (KMT) instrumentalised Confucian ideology to legitimise its rule and reinforce Taiwan's role as the repository of authentic Chinese culture (Fetzer and Soper 2013: 20). During this movement, the KMT introduced 'a conservative, moralistic Confucianism' into the curriculum in order to instil obedience to superiors in the Taiwanese from an early age (Fetzer and Soper 2013: 20). Unlike the CCP, the KMT in Taiwan used the image of the family as an instrument to instil in its population a sense of duty towards the nation (Stafford 1995: 117). In an effort to Sinicize the populace, the KMT also introduced the reading of the Confucian classics into Taiwanese classrooms, especially emphasising those works that stressed filial virtues and the recognition of natural hierarchies (Fetzer and Soper 2013: 21–25). At the same time, the KMT's export-oriented strategy of industrialisation induced a flourishing of family businesses, which reinforced economic dependencies among family members (Whyte 2004). It is difficult to determine whether the more conservative attitude towards filial obligations in Taiwan was preserved largely by ideological inculcation or the structures of the labour market, especially the prevalence of women employed in the informal sector. Either way, the KMT's endorsement of the concept did not imply any strict break with Taiwanese family life, but instead highlighted the Confucian roots of existing practices in order to foster an identification with Chinese culture in the population (Fetzer and Soper 2013: 47–48).

In China, the importance of filial support came to the fore again as the CCP successively abolished social benefits in the reform era and, losing the prospect of secure pensions, parents again grew increasingly dependent on their offspring for old-age support. Moreover, with the introduction of the one-child policy in the late 1970s, the burden to care for ageing parents now fell increasingly on unmarried individuals (Fong 2004). At the same time, in Taiwan a naturally decreasing birth rate combined with a growing trend for neolocal postmarital residence and female full-time employment has complicated the continuation of traditional care practices in old age (Hsu 2007; Lee et al. 1994).

The current young generations of China and Taiwan thus both grew up with an awareness that not only their personal but also their family's wellbeing is dependent on their academic and professional achievements. For this reason, it is not surprising that considerations of future financial, physical and emotional care obligations have a major impact on young people's life choices. Whereas its core value of filial respect for elders remained largely unchanged, the expression of care and support has altered in tandem with new demands that have emerged in modern society. Hence, in both urban China and Taiwan, the practice of *xiao* has taken on new forms that respond to the major societal changes that have occurred over the last century (Ikels 2004). This is particularly reflected in the expectations on women who assume an increasingly important role as providers of economic security and social status in their families. In the next section I will take a closer look at how absence from the parental home is perceived to be a legitimate filial act in some cases, yet not in others, and how this affects women's mobility in pursuing their aspirations, particularly with regard to education and career.

Changing Notions of Female Filiality in China and Taiwan

Sangren notes that 'the embedded value that most defines the Chinese family system, "filial piety", is a concept whose content and consequences register very differently for sons and daughters and (not to be overlooked) for mothers and fathers' (Sangren 2017: 65). Sangren remarks that daughters, who are expected to be better behaved and more obedient than sons, are considered as more reliable providers of elderly care by many Chinese parents: 'The fact that adult daughters are often more solicitous of their parents than are their brothers seems to be viewed as a natural extension of these gender stereotypes, outweighing implicitly recognised patrilineal imperatives' (2017: 249). However, Fong observed in the northern Chinese city of Dalian that parents' expectations on daughters went beyond female gender stereotypes that typically centre on aspects like emotional nurture and care and included an increasing appreciation of daughters as being more studious and conscientious than sons and thus more likely to improve the family's economic and social status (Fong 2004). This was a central concern, particularly in urban areas, where the one-child policy was more strictly enforced and parents' hopes for old age security were pinned on one child only (Fong 2004). Sangren points out that 'a striving for academic distinction' is an important tenet of filial piety (2017: 65). Whereas academic success had formerly been solely expected of sons, daughters are now often held to the same standards. Bilateral care obligations towards parents and in-laws, combined with new expectations placed on daughters' academic and professional performance, add to the pressure on young women. Moreover, as the short vignettes at the beginning of this chapter highlighted, integrating parents' conservative expectations and realising personal goals that emerged precisely out of daughters' higher academic credentials often proved difficult for young women. Many young women I talked to in China and Taiwan worried about how they would be able to pursue their career goals while taking care of their obligations towards parents and in-laws (see Fong 2011). Leaving the parental home for a certain period of time in order to achieve success and increase the family's 'face' (*mianzi* 面子) has been considered integral to a son's demonstration of filiality for centuries. Stafford notes that 'even "impossible" separations (e.g. between fathers and sons) are sometimes very desirable indeed, while others (e.g. between parents and daughters) are seen, however unwanted, to be socially necessary' (Stafford 2000a: 3). The separations between parents and daughters that Stafford alludes to concern a daughter's move to her husband's family upon marriage due to the widely practised exogamy in China and Taiwan. Sons, however, are expected to 'become dragons' (*cheng long* 成龍) and are allowed to leave the parental home (at least for a while) to seek success in places with better opportunities (Stafford 2000a: 97). Likewise, Johnston (2013) observed among male students in Anhui Province that even though they struggled to negotiate their parents' conflicting expectations, their families appeared to accept that at least a temporary absence from home was necessary to create the academic and financial foundation upon which their ability to fulfil their filial obligations in the future would be based.

However, among my female interlocutors in Taipei and to a certain degree also in Beijing, I observed that unmarried daughters' absence from home was regarded with a higher degree of ambiguity than was the absence of sons. Even though daughters were expected to leave the parental home after getting married, Taiwanese parents appeared to be especially cautious about their prolonged absence before that, in particular as they approached marriageable age. 'Filial piety', Sangren argues, 'is clearly bound up with patriliny' (Sangren 2017: 64), and one of the most effective ways to assert agency and to consolidate a position of power as a woman has long been her bearing sons (Wolf 1972). However, the increasing importance of women to their natal families as providers of economic, practical and emotional care was accompanied by the challenging of patrilineal power structures. Women, as Sangren asserts, 'are no less possessed of an ego-focused logic of desire than are men, [and] it is unlikely that a "system" that denies this fact (by "determining" identification) will succeed altogether in orienting women's actual desires or actions' (Sangren 2017: 250). Indeed, my female interlocutors grew increasingly stressed by the prospect of either having to violate gendered norms upon which their own and their families' reputation rested or having to abandon personal aspirations that did not align with their families' interests. The assertion of personal desires turned out to be particularly complicated in Taiwan, as the next section will illustrate, where a patriarchal system had long been buttressed by state ideology and local economic structures. Yet also in China, where gender and family ideology tended to be less traditional in practice, young women's quest for personal autonomy was complicated by parental expectations that were still inspired by Confucian notions of filiality.

Appadurai notes that 'it is in culture that ideas of the future, as much as of those about the past, are embedded and nurtured' (2004: 59). The problems surrounding the concept of filiality in urban life illustrate how aspirations and the struggles that accompany them emerge out of shared metaphysical and ethical ideals. They are thus a product of social life that connects the past, the present and the future (Appadurai 2004: 67). However, relating to his research among housing activists in Mumbai, Appadurai (2004) points out that structural constraints might restrict an individual's 'capacity to aspire' – that is, the ability to assert one's position in society and to conceive of strategic pathways to pursue goals that are believed to lie beyond one's reach. Likewise, Fischer, drawing on his research among Guatemalan coffee farmers, highlights the 'complex dynamic between aspirations, structural opportunity and agency' (2014: 158). Whereas urban slum dwellers in Mumbai and Guatemalan coffee farmers might be confronted with more precarious economic constraints than my interlocutors in Taipei and Beijing, the following case studies will nevertheless demonstrate that economic constraints play a vital role not only in the strategies young adults apply in the pursuit of their goals, but also in the compromises their families are willing to make in terms of the fulfilment of traditional filial norms. According to Appadurai, the 'capacity to aspire is . . . a navigational capacity' that is shaped by the particular socioeconomic and political constraints that an individual or a group faces (Appadurai 2004: 69). He explains: 'If the map of aspirations . . . is seen to consist of a dense combination of nodes and pathways, relative poverty means a smaller number of aspirational nodes and a thinner, weaker sense of the pathways from concrete wants to intermediate contexts to general norms and back again' (2004: 69). However, my data from urban China and Taiwan suggest that while economic factors certainly had a significant influence, ideological factors pertaining to gender and family ideals played an equally important part in how my young female interlocutors perceived their opportunities and their efficacy in reaching their goals. Young adults in China and Taiwan must synchronise 'aspirational maps' with complex maps of obligations that mark particular social expectations as they pass each biographical landmark and that, at times, might lead in opposite directions. In the next section, two case studies from Taipei and Beijing will show how young women tried to align these two maps, while the particular difficulties they encountered in the pursuit of their paths wear the specific imprints of the different urban environments of China and Taiwan.

Pursuing Aspirations in Taipei and Beijing: Two Case Studies

A few weeks after I received Yu-ching's panicked phone call, she let me know that she had moved back into her parental home in the city centre of Taipei. However, I wondered if her decision to return would indeed improve their tense relationship. From the time I had come to know her during my doctoral research in Taipei in 2012, the pressure her parents exerted on her to excel professionally as well as in her role as a filial daughter had steadily increased.

Yu-ching found herself in the rare situation of being her parents' only hope in terms of filial care, despite having grown up with two siblings – an older sister and a younger brother. Due to a string of tragic events, she now faced the prospect of having to fulfil both the hopes her parents formerly had for the academic and professional career of their only son as well as their expectation that their daughters would marry into prestigious affluent families. Yu-ching's younger brother died from complications during a childhood disease. Helpless in the face of her parents' grief, as she told me, she decided to make up for the loss of her brother by realising the dreams her parents had invested in him. However, her elder sister reacted in a very different way in response to her brother's death and started to rebel against their parents' strictness. As a teenager, she left the family home and, soon after, became pregnant out of wedlock. Yu-ching's parents were devastated and even though they continued to support their eldest daughter financially, they broke off contact with her almost entirely. Yu-ching, by contrast, had an exceptionally close relationship with her parents, in particular her father, and at times, her life seemed to revolve around her urge to realise the hopes they had placed in her.

Yu-ching told me that since her older sister had derailed from the path her parents had laid out for her, they had been particularly cautious about guarding her own development. Afraid that she would attract 'bad company' at a regular school, they had sent her to an expensive private high school. Her parents owned a successful company in Taipei and were thus affluent enough to invest in her private education. When Yu-ching was fifteen years old, she and her parents decided that she would continue her education in North America. After having completed high school, she studied an undergraduate degree abroad. She originally wanted to become a veterinarian, but her mother suggested that she should study economics instead. Assuming that this would be a safer choice, Yu-ching agreed. She ended up not particularly liking this subject area and returned home to Taiwan after her graduation. She often mentioned that she felt troubled at the thought of making decisions on her own without asking for her parents' advice. As a consequence, this not only granted her parents a considerate amount of authority over her career and partner choices, but also forced her to quickly resume her role as a reliable and dutiful daughter upon her return.

Struggling to find employment, Yu-ching's mother used her vast network of Taiwanese business families and obtained a job for her. After working for a few years, Yu-ching decided to study for a degree in law. Her parents, relieved to see their daughter showing academic ambitions again, were happy to support this decision. Attending a local university this time allowed her to remain living at home. This was a decision many of my interlocutors also made due to the high rent prices in Taipei and the notoriously poor condition of university dorms, which often extended parental authority over their children far into adulthood.

In the years after her graduation, Yu-ching repeatedly tried to pass the national bar exam to become a licensed lawyer, yet, to her parents' disappointment, she remained unsuccessful. At the same time, she frequently changed jobs and appeared to become increasingly insecure about which career path she should take. Her indecision was compounded by her growing wish to marry and to have a family. She entered a string of unsuccessful relationships, which she largely kept secret from her parents – a tricky endeavour as her parents kept a watchful eye over her comings and goings. Her mother, unaware of any details about her past relationships, even expected her daughter to still be a virgin and to remain so until marriage. If Yu-ching lost her virginity before wedlock, her mother had warned her, she would 'break her legs'. During one of my visits at their family home, Yu-ching's mother confided in me that she believed women became socially awkward or 'strange' (*guai* 怪) if they married too late. Her concern for her daughter to find a husband thus appeared to be both founded in fears for the family's reputation as well as in her worries about Yu-ching's emotional wellbeing in the future.

After a string of disappointing experiences with men, Yu-ching's mother, now growing increasingly impatient, arranged several dates for her daughter. I met Yu-ching after one of these introductory meetings where her family and the family of the young man had both been present. At the restaurant, the parents had shared a table while Yu-Ching and the young man were placed at a separate table in order to have the opportunity to get to know each other in more privacy. However, as Yu-ching told me with some annoyance, her mother had overheard their conversation and criticised her afterwards for her frequent, noisy laughing. On a first date, she expected a more demure demeanour from her daughter. Yu-ching attributed her difficulty in finding a partner to her perceived lack of gentleness or 'cute' (*ke'ai* 可愛) appearance, which her ex-partners had already criticised her for. She complained that her previous dating mishaps had only confirmed her inability to 'entertain' men. Indeed, one of her ex-boyfriends whom I met several times during my fieldwork repeatedly stressed his rather conservative outlook on relationships, including his preference for Japanese women, who he assumed to be more docile, caring and 'family-focused' than Taiwanese women. For this reason, Yu-ching told me, her mother had recently advised her to 'just obey' her dating partner and not to be too opinionated if a controversial topic came up.

In the winter of the same year, it appeared as if Yu-ching had found a suitable match. Yu-ching almost became engaged to a young man she had met at a self-improvement seminar. Yet, following the advice of her parents, she ended the relationship. They were concerned that the young man was not as sincere and hard-working as they had hoped and they worried that he might not provide Yu-ching with the guidance and support they desired. I was not surprised about this development: Yu-ching's mother had once mentioned to me in a conversation that she hoped that her daughter's future husband would be as reliable and attentive to his family's material needs (*gujia* 顧家) as her own husband. Every mother, she explained, would be anxious (*danxin* 擔心) about her daughter getting married (at this point, she wondered how my parents felt about this issue, astonished to hear that they were rather unfazed about me being unmarried in my late twenties). However, once Yu-ching was married, she stressed, the responsibility for her wellbeing would be with her in-laws. Unbeknownst to her at this point, Yu-ching was pondering going abroad again in order to study another degree. When she told her mother about her plans a few months later, her mother replied that marriage should be Yu-ching's top priority now. If her husband subsequently supported her aspirations, she could still realise that dream.

At the end of our phone call that morning in March, several years after the above events had taken place, Yu-ching told me that despite the high level of education she had received and the career opportunities that were open to her, she still did not feel very ambitious in terms of pursuing this path further. Instead, all she longed for was to get married and to have children. When she told her mother about this wish, the latter replied that this desire was only 'natural'.[2]

Yu-ching's case resembled the stories of several others of my female Taiwanese interlocutors whose families lived in Taipei. Even though many of them
had spent several years abroad pursuing degrees or work experience, once they
returned to Taipei – which appeared to be expected by many parents once their
daughters approached marriageable age – their parents tried to exert an equal
amount of authority over their daughters as they had during their teenage years.
I vividly remember the case of a young woman who had moved back in with her
parents after she had completed a degree in Europe. She started a professional
career in Taipei and would have been able to support herself while living on her
own. However, she explained that her parents might not approve of her moving
out, arguing that instead of paying rent to a stranger and thus supplementing his
mortgage, she should rather hand this money over to her parents for monthly support. Her relationship with her father had always been tense and once she started
going out with a young man she had met on an online dating app, her father controlled all of her moves. He once searched through her room when she was not at
home and found a pregnancy test she had hidden carelessly in a drawer. When she
returned home, she had to endure his angry outburst about her no longer being a
virgin. He would have expected her to be chaste (*zhenjie* 貞潔) and to behave 'like
a lady', she explained to me, hardly able to suppress her laughter. He would have
expected her to fall on her knees and beg for his forgiveness, as you see in TV
dramas, she continued. Her arguing back only increased his rage and she decided
to keep a distance from him for a while.

Whyte notes in his comparative study of urban families that in Taiwan, patrilocal
residence and cohabitation of parents with a married child (usually a son) were
still the norm in the 1990s, whereas in China 'networked families' (*wangluo
jiating* 網絡家庭) who supported each other in various ways, yet did not share
a residence, were more common (Whyte 2004; 2005; cf. Chu and Yu 2010; Chu
et al. 2011). The above cases illustrate that even in the 2010s, the repercussions
of the KMT traditionalist family ideology of the 1960s and 1970s and the simul-
taneous strategy of strengthening family businesses are still palpable in many
Taiwanese parents' rather conservative expectations on premarital and postmarital
living arrangements and gendered behavioural norms. At the same time, however,
the decreasing number of children has transferred certain traditionally male filial
duties to women. This shift is compounded by women's extended education,
which, under the premise that they live with their parents until marriage, subjects
them to parental authority even longer than previous generations of women. Further, the tight housing market in Taipei and the relatively low entry-level salaries
for graduates increase young people's economic dependence on their parents,
which in turn increases the latter's leverage on their decisions even in the cases of
children who live independently. In Beijing, as I have already alluded to above, the

situation of my female interlocutors was markedly different. A specific interplay of demographic, economic and ideological factors resulted in parents adopting a more accepting stance in relation to their daughters' independence and prolonged absence from home (which, in certain cases, was even actively encouraged). For these reasons, as the following case study will outline, my young interlocutors in Beijing had more leeway in pursuing personal goals and asserting their agency in making important decisions in terms of their choice of partner and residence.

One evening in the autumn of 2013, I met Sun and her colleague Ming for dinner. They were working for the same event management company and shared a passion for theatre, having quickly become friends. Ming, like Sun, was in her mid-twenties and came across as an energetic individual. Over dinner, our discussion soon turned towards their plans for the future. Sun explained with a sour face that her boyfriend's parents, who were from the south and thus had a more traditional (*chuantong* 傳統) mindset than her parents, had pushed them to marry as her boyfriend was already thirty-three years old. She had eventually agreed and would travel to his hometown for the ceremony in the following month. However, she stressed, they kept it as small as possible. Sun was not keen on changing her current lifestyle, but as his parents had no insight into their rather bohemian life in Beijing, she did not appear to fear any intervention from their side after the wedding.

Ming led a similarly liberal lifestyle to Sun. She explained that she had recently moved into a flatshare with several friends. Her parents, who also lived in Beijing, had not been happy about her decision to move out, but she had craved more independence and pushed her wish through. I was curious to know more about her relationship with her parents, which, like Sun's relationship with her family, seemed to be surprisingly different from the close-knit families of my Taiwanese interlocutors. A few weeks later, I met Ming alone at a tea store where she told me more of her story. Ming was an only child and had spent her childhood in Xi'an until her father relocated to Beijing for a job. Growing up in a big factory compound where both her parents worked, she had spent more time with her friends, whose parents were employed in the same work unit, than with her parents. She attended the kindergarten and elementary school adjacent to their *danwei* until they moved to Beijing when she was in fifth grade. Ming spent only a few years with her parents in the capital before she was sent back to attend senior high school (*gaozhong* 高中) in Xi'an, as this was the place of her household registration (*hukou* 戶口) and where she would also have to take the national higher education entrance exam (*gaokao* 高考). Eager to gain more independence, she decided against moving in with her grandparents and instead lived in the school dormitory. She spent only the weekends with family members. However, Ming did not like the strict rules that restricted her movement outside of the school grounds and, like many other of my Chinese interlocutors, found it difficult to adjust to the low living standards of the high school dormitory. She recounted: 'I think you should try everything, just maybe not too long . . . finding out what you like . . . Some of my classmates cried a lot because they missed their families and felt the pressure, but I was not very serious about my studies.' Indeed, she did not score as high as her parents had hoped in the *gaokao*, which excluded her from the top-tier universities in Beijing. Accordingly, her parents suggested that she continue her education in Xi'an, where she would be able to enter a higher-ranking university than in the capital. However, Ming did not want to hear anything about this as she longed to return to Beijing, where she found life more exciting. She would eventually convince her parents to let her return. She remembers that even though her parents let her choose her subject fairly independently, her choice was restricted by her relatively low score. She was eventually accepted on to a psychology programme at a Beijing university. During her studies, she lived at the student dormitory, as her family home was too remote for a daily commute. The absence of parental control also enabled her to express her homosexuality more freely and during this time she started a relationship with another student.

Having spent a significant part of her adolescence living in dormitories might explain why Ming perceived living in the parental household as stressful and thus decided to move into a flatshare. In the autumn when we met, she pondered studying a master's degree abroad: 'I think I should try some place different, I don't want to stay in the same place for too long.' She could not imagine having an office job in the future and dreamt of a more adventurous lifestyle. I asked what her parents thought about her rather unconventional plans – would they not want her to get married soon? Ming had a girlfriend at the time I came to know her, a fact she concealed from her parents. 'They think I am single', she explained. Of course, they wanted her to get married, but at the moment she felt no pressure from them. She thus felt no rush to reveal to them that she was homosexual, even though she expected her parents to be relatively tolerant. Interestingly, Ming found herself in a similar situation to Yu-ching, entering marriageable age (which starts a few years earlier in China than in Taiwan), yet not having a stable heterosexual partnership. Ming mentioned that her mother sometimes tried to arrange a date for her (*xiangqin* 相親), but so far she had successfully rejected this offer. Yu-ching, living together with her parents in a single household, found it more difficult to counter her parents' pressure. I asked Ming about her parents' expectations; she was their only child, so surely they wanted to live close to her in the future? Initially they had planned to move close to where she lived, Ming explained. However, when they told her about this, she let them know that she was not keen on their plans: 'I said no and they said we will [at least] visit you a lot [laughs]. Then that is OK.' Like many of her Chinese peers, Ming did not expect to demonstrate her filiality by a continuous presence in the parental home. 'People who work with me don't visit their parents often, maybe once a year', she argued – they supported their parents financially, but could not afford to bring them to Beijing. Like Sun, Ming saw no urgency in changing her current lifestyle in order to fulfil her filial duties to her parents. In her eyes, both parties had to show a certain degree of flexibility in the future to integrate their different needs.

The cases of Ming and Sun illustrate how the model of the 'networked family' in urban China is a result of the complex interaction of demographic, socioeconomic and ideological factors that have a direct impact on how young adults realise their obligations towards parents (see Whyte et al. 2003; Whyte 2004). Due to the prevalence of boarding education in China compared to Taiwan, many of my interlocutors left the parental home upon entry into senior high school at the latest; some started boarding education much earlier, depending on their parents' occupation (see Hansen 2015). Further, many of their parents had already grown up relatively independent due to having been sent to the countryside during the rustication movement or due to their busy working life in the agricultural communes or work units during the Mao era (see Liu 2007). For this reason, they might have been less concerned about granting their children a certain amount of independence in their decisions on their personal lives. Moreover, many families like those of Ming and Sun had long histories of migration caused by the multiple wars that ravaged China in the twentieth century, as well as due to a frequent relocation of their workplaces. The families of my Taiwanese interlocutors tended to be more closely tied to a geographical place. Even though many had moved to the cities, they frequently used to visit their parents in the countryside and felt a deep connection to their ancestral places. Despite the decreasing number of family businesses in Taiwan, many families I knew still owned a business and often expected their children to take it over in the future. Further, I would argue that there was still a stronger economic necessity among my interlocutors in China to establish their careers in the city in order to financially support their parents in old age than for families in the comparatively affluent Taiwan. Knowing that their future livelihood depended on it, mainland parents might have been more tolerant of their children's long absence from home than those of their Taiwanese peers.[3] In Taipei, by contrast, generational relationships appeared to be reversed, with adult children in their twenties still being financially dependent on their (comparatively affluent) parents due to wage stagnation and the high real estate prices in the city (see Lai and Tung 2015). Due to all these factors, my female interlocutors in Beijing found themselves in a situation in which they could make decisions on their career, partner and residence with far fewer restrictions created by parental control than the young women I interviewed in Taipei.

Conclusion

The trend outlined above wherein women in both Beijing and Taipei are increasingly expected to take over filial duties of daughters *and* sons while also (particularly in Taiwan) being held to traditional standards of female demeanour complicates their pursuit of personal aspirations. How far my young interlocutors could follow their 'aspirational maps' was thus highly dependent on how well they could synchronise these with their lifelong obligations towards their parents, as well as to a future husband and children. While most of the highly educated young women I interviewed had concrete ideas of the pathways of their 'aspirational maps' regardless of their socioeconomic background, I observed significant differences in terms of how they perceived their efficacy in pursuing these goals while also meeting their social obligations towards family members – another complex map that connected each biographical landmark with specific duties (see Appadurai 2004). The paths that these two maps delineated were not only constantly modified along with the transformations of the landscapes they were meant to guide through, but they might at certain points lead in two opposite directions. The young women whose cases I have described above found themselves at exactly these intersections, which required a decision on which path to follow, not knowing whether or not these courses might merge again in the future. However, the scope within which these young women were able to make independent decisions and accept risks was decisively influenced by the different urban locales in which they were situated.

It must be noted that my study is a snapshot of a particular group of people at a specific point in time, in two extremely fast-paced environments. Peers only a few years younger than them might have had very different experiences coming of age – this applies especially to youth in China, who have witnessed rapid societal changes in the last few decades. Moreover, the students and young professionals I interviewed had all been relatively successful in navigating the educational system and socioeconomic constraints up to the point where they felt restricted by parental demands. Young adults with lower educational degrees and a more limited range of future options might relate to their filial duties in very different ways. Nevertheless, the above cases illustrate a direct connection between societal changes and young people's vision of the future. As Bunnell and colleagues note: 'At a variety of scales, shifting geographies of uneven development are bound up with shifting senses of where the future lies' (Bunnell et al. 2018: 47). My comparative study of students and professionals in Taipei and Beijing illustrates how differently similar cultural factors can play out in locales with drastically different economic and political trajectories. Shifting state ideologies, demographics and strategies of economic development had a direct, yet very different, effect on young women's aspirations and where they locate their futures. How well the obligation of being a filial daughter, often an aspiration in itself, could be integrated into the pursuit of self-fulfilment was thus dependent to a significant degree on the space that these differing urban environments had opened up for it.

Désirée Remmert obtained her Ph.D. in Anthropology from the London School of Economics and Political Science (LSE), United Kingdom. She subsequently conducted postdoctoral research at the University of Tübingen in Germany, Academia Sinica in Taiwan and at the LSE in the United Kingdom. She specialises in cognitive anthropology, urban ethnography and multisited comparative research with a regional focus on East Asia.

Notes

1. To maintain anonymity, all the names of the interviewees quoted in this chapter have been changed. I also do not disclose details about their professions or academic degrees in those cases in which these could reveal the identity of my interlocutors.
2. Diamond (1973) illustrates how women who came of age in the 1950s and 1960s in Taiwan were encouraged to aspire to a middle-class ideal that depicted the man as the breadwinner and the woman as a homemaker who devoted her time to the raising of children and to household tasks. This allocation of gender roles thus transferred Confucian-inspired gender models into urban nuclear families in Taiwan. Against this background, the notion of the 'naturalness' of conventional gender roles could be preserved.
3. However, for the same reasons, parents in China seemed to be more willing to leave their home places and to join their children in the city. Thus, it would be interesting to conduct a follow-up study once my interlocutors have established their careers in order to see how they negotiate their parents' expectations once living together becomes a possibility.

References

Appadurai, Arjun. 2004. 'The Capacity to Aspire: Culture and the Terms of Recognition', in Vijayendra Rao and Michael Walton (eds), *Culture and Public Action*. Stanford: Stanford University Press, pp. 59–84.

Bunnell, Tim, Jamie Gillen and Elaine Lynn-Ee Ho. 2018. 'The Prospect of Elsewhere: Engaging the Future through Aspirations in Asia', *Annals of the American Association of Geographers* 108(1): 35–51.

Chan, Alan K., and Sor-hoon Tan. 2004. 'Introduction', in Alan K. Chan and Sor-hoon Tan (eds), *Filial Piety in Chinese Thought and History*. New York: Routledge Curzon, pp. 1–11.

Chan, Anita. 1985. *Children of Mao: Personality Development and Political Activism in the Red Guard Generation*. London: Macmillan.

Chan, Sheng-Ju, and Chi-Hua Yang. 2015. 'The Employment of the College Graduate: Changing Wages in Mass Higher Education', in Jung Cheol Shin, Gerard A. Postiglione and Futao Huang (eds), *Mass Higher Education Development in East Asia: Strategy, Quality and Challenges*. Cham: Springer, pp. 289–306.

Chen, Fen-Ling. 2000. *Working Women and State Policies in Taiwan*. Basingstoke: Palgrave Macmillan.

Chu, C.Y. Cyrus, and Ruoh-Rong Yu. 2010. *Understanding Chinese Families: A Comparative Study of Taiwan and Southeast China*. Oxford: Oxford University Press.

Chu, C.Y. Cyrus, Yu Xie and Ruoh Rong Yu. 2011. 'Coresidence with Elderly Parents: A Comparative Study of Southeast China and Taiwan', *Journal of Marriage and Family* 73: 120–35.

Davis, Deborah, and Stevan Harrell. 1993. 'Introduction: The Impact of Post-Mao Reforms on Family Life', in Deborah Davis and Stevan Harrell (eds), *Chinese Families in the Post-Mao Era*. Berkeley: University of California Press, pp. 1–22.

Diamond, Norma. 1973. 'The Middle Class Family Model in Taiwan: Women's Place Is in the Home', *Asian Survey* 13(9): 853–72.

Evans, Harriet. 2010. 'The Gender of Communication: Changing Expectations of Mothers and Daughters in Urban China.' *The China Quarterly*, 980–1000.

Fei, Xiaotong. 1992 [1948]. *From the Soil: The Foundations of Chinese Society*. Berkeley and London: University of California Press.

Fetzer, Joel S., and J. Christopher Soper. 2013. *Confucianism, Democratization and Human Rights in Taiwan*. Plymouth: Lexington Books.

Fischer, Edward. 2014. *The Good Life: Aspiration, Dignity and the Anthropology of Well-being*. Stanford: Stanford University Press.

Fong, Vanessa L. 2004. *Only Hope: Coming of Age under China's One-Child Policy*. Stanford: Stanford University Press.

———. 2011. *Paradise Redefined: Transnational Chinese Students and the Quest for Flexible Citizenship in the Developed World*. Stanford: Stanford University Press.

Hansen, Mette Halskov. 2015. *Educating the Chinese Individual: Life in a Rural Boarding School*. Seattle: University of Washington Press.

Harrison, Henrietta. 2001. *China: Inventing the Nation*. London: Arnold.

Johnston, James. 2013. 'Filial Paths and the Ordinary Ethics of Movement', in Charles Stafford (ed.), *Ordinary Ethics in China*. London: Bloomsbury, pp. 45–65.

Lai, Nicole Mun Sim, and An-Chi Tung. 2015. 'Who Supports the Elderly? The Changing Economic Lifestyle Reallocation, 1985 and 2005.' *The Journal of the Economics of Ageing* Vol. 5: 63–68.

Liu, Jieyu. 2007. *Gender and Work in Urban China: Women Workers of the Unlucky Generation*. Abingdon: Routledge.

Ministry of Labor, Republic of China (Taiwan). 2019. 'Labor Force Participation Rate by Sex', International Gender Statistics. Accessed May 18, 2020. https://english.mol.gov.tw/media/76938/table14.pdf

Rene, Helena K. 2013. *China's Sent-Down Generation: Public Administration and the Legacies of Mao's Rustication Program*. Washington DC: Georgetown University Press.

Sangren, Steven P. 2017. *Filial Obsessions: Chinese Patriliny and Its Discontents*. London: Palgrave Macmillan.

Stafford, Charles. 1995. *The Roads of Chinese Childhood: Learning and Identification in Angang*. Cambridge: Cambridge University Press.

———. 2000a. *Separation and Reunion in Modern China*. Cambridge: Cambridge University Press.

———. 2000b. 'Chinese Patriliny and the Cycles of Yang and Laiwang', in Janet Carsten (ed.), *Cultures of Relatedness: New Approaches to the Study of Kinship*. Cambridge: Cambridge University Press, pp. 35–54.

Tan, Soor-hon. 2004. 'Filial Daughters-in-Law: Questioning Confucian Filiality', in Alan K. Chan and Sor-hoon Tan (eds), *Filial Piety in Chinese Thought and History*. London: Routledge Curzon, pp. 226–40.

Whyte, Martin K. 2004. 'Filial Obligations in Chinese Families: Paradoxes of Modernization', in Charlotte Ikels (ed.), *Filial Piety: Practice and Discourse in Contemporary East Asia*. Stanford: Stanford University Press, pp. 106–27.

———. 2005. 'Continuity and Change in Urban Chinese Family Life', *China Journal* 53: 9–33.

Whyte, Martin King, Albert I. Hermelin and Mary Beth Ofstedal. 2003. 'Intergenerational Relations in Two Chinese Societies', in Martin King Whyte (ed.), *China's Revolutions and Intergenerational Relations*. Ann Arbor: Center for Chinese Studies, University of Michigan, pp. 225–54.

Wolf, Margery. 1972. *Women and the Family in Rural Taiwan*. Stanford CA: Stanford University Press.

Yan, Yunxiang. 2003. *Private Life under Socialism: Love, Intimacy and Family Change in a Chinese Village, 1949–1999*. Stanford: Stanford University Press.

——. 2009. *The Individualization of Chinese Society*. Oxford: Berg.

2

A JOURNEY FROM TAIPEI TO SHANGHAI

The Impact of Migration Experience on Taiwanese Young Adults' Aspirations and Identities in an Asian Global City

Chia-Yuan Huang

In August 2016, in a large coffee shop in a creative park in Pudong, Shanghai, I attended an alumni gathering organised by a group of local Taiwanese. Over a hundred people attended the event, with the majority of attendees being young people aged between twenty and thirty. A number of them had recently graduated from university in June of that year. All attendees included several older people who had already been in Shanghai for many years and had built successful careers for themselves. While this group of aspiring young Taiwanese exchanged business cards, the content of their conversation consisted of questions such as 'How long have you been in Shanghai?' 'Which company do you work for now?' and 'How did you find this job?' The 'brain drain' problem that Taiwan is currently facing was all too evident to me when witnessing this scene. At the same time, I saw in the faces of these young Taiwanese that Shanghai represented a great opportunity for success and the chance of a bright future. In the same month I attended a party, also hosted by local Taiwanese in Shanghai. Most of the guests were Taiwanese people who had been in Shanghai for different lengths of time. The organiser had invited a guest speaker to give strategies in stress management and advise attendees on how best to settle into their new life in Shanghai. These exchanges led me to believe that the goals and aspirations of these longer-term young Taiwanese expatriates had changed compared to when they had first arrived.

In contrast to the economic boom of the late twentieth century, Taiwan has more recently become a land of talent exodus. Numerous news outlets have picked up this story, with headlines such as: 'As Taiwan's Workers Flock to China, Concerns about Economy Grow' (Ramzy 2016), 'Brain Drain: A Serious Problem in Taiwan' (Chiu and Lin 2015), 'If You Are Young and Talented, Don't Stay in Taipei' (Huang 2013) and 'If I Stay in Taiwan, I May Not Have a Job' (Jang-Chun Lin 2010) becoming common. At the 2010 National Security Council, Taiwan's former President Ma Ying-Jeou even stated that: 'Brain drain has become a serious national security issue that Taiwan cannot afford to ignore' (Chen 2011). This attention has led the research community to focus more on the reasons behind this 'youth exodus', such as Taiwan's current economic recession and development stagnation and the diversity of recent transnational movements and practices. This underlined to me the necessity of conducting this research in order to better understand individual mobility behaviours of aspiring young people, whilst simultaneously exploring how these migration experiences have shaped their aspirations and identities.

First, this study can reveal entanglements on both sides of the strait in terms of Taiwanese young people's identities. It contributes to an emerging interest in Taiwanese young people's identities and what contributes to their sense of belonging. Second, it considers the different ways in which these Taiwanese young people are incorporated into the labour market, paying attention to how their nonlocal status affects their everyday workplace experiences. As transborder workers, they are maintaining networks located between their origin and destination. Third, this study also investigates how their overseas urban experiences affect their future intentions and aspirations.

According to statistical data released by the Executive Yuan in 2017, the number of Taiwanese overseas workers has grown rapidly, more than doubling from 340,000 to 724,000 between 2005 and 2015. Another factor that has changed over the last decade is the age of the workers. In the past, overseas Taiwanese workers were typically thirty years or older, but now young people aged twenty-five to twenty-nine comprise the highest percentage. The number of overseas Taiwanese working in China has also increased from 290,000 to 420,000 in the ten years between 2005 and 2015, a proportion that now accounts for 58% of all Taiwanese overseas workers worldwide (Directorate-General of Budget, Accounting and Statistics, Executive Yuan of Taiwan 2017). Among those who moved to China to access work opportunities, Shanghai is their number-one destination (Morgan Philips Executive Search 2017; MRI China Group 2013). Shanghai has a reputation as a 'global city', which is highly attractive to educated and skilled migrants; global cities are seen as the preferred destination of aspiring Taiwanese young adults (Taylor 2006; Tseng 2011; Wu 2000; Yeoh and Khoo 1998). I chose Shanghai as a study site for two main reasons: first, because Shanghai is the main destination for a large number of young Taiwanese professionals (Lin and Teng 2014; MRI China Group 2013). Second, Shanghai's position as a 'global city' makes it suitable to examine globalisation as a major driving force behind individual migration behaviour. Taiwanese migrants moving to nearby global cities usually have at least a university degree and normally work for an enterprise or institution that requires professional skills (Chang 2012; Chiang and Huang 2014; Ping Lin 2010).

This study found that although political tensions continues to exist on both sides of the Taiwan Strait, aspiring young Taiwanese are nevertheless willing to overlook this and move to China for the sake of work. The main driving force behind this is that Taiwanese companies are often unable to provide young people with higher salaries and promotion opportunities, while Shanghai is able to offer financial incentives and enjoys a cosmopolitan reputation. The second finding revealed an identity dynamic. As Shanghai is a modern global city, many people living there have also moved from other cities in China. In light of this, Taiwanese young people who work in Shanghai do not consider that there is that much of a difference between Taiwanese and mainland Chinese, but rather that there is a difference between Shanghai locals and non-Shanghai locals. The third finding was that Taiwan-funded companies based in China are increasingly unappealing to Taiwanese young people, who are now more interested in working for international companies or mainland Chinese enterprises. Nowadays, many Taiwanese young people use job search websites to seek employment opportunities independently. How these Taiwanese jobseekers identify employment opportunities and ascertain salary levels is more or less the same as the process that mainland Chinese jobseekers use. If they are working in a mainland Chinese enterprise, localisation begins to play a major part as local employers often prefer to employ mainland Chinese workers over Taiwanese workers when presented with job candidates who have the same credentials. Taiwanese people no longer have competitive advantages. Therefore, Taiwanese young people have had to force themselves to integrate into local society and life, as well as striving to understand the Shanghai dialect and local idioms.

I will begin with a review of the pertinent literature as it relates to the recent migratory context, the emergence of young skilled workers and the formation of migrants' identity. Although my empirical findings are centred on the Taiwanese case study, this research has broader implications for theoretical formulations of aspirations and identities of young adults in urban Asia.

Recent Movements of Taiwanese to Mainland China

Since the 1990s, Taiwanese people have moved to China in large numbers. With this wave of emigrants from Taiwan has come increased Taiwanese economic investment in China, along with a relaxation of Chinese regulations concerning Taiwanese migration, including work and residence rights. Greater employment opportunities have attracted those who either were unsatisfied with their current jobs in Taiwan or who had been unable to find suitable employment (Tseng 2014). Since Taiwanese migrants arrived in China under specific macroeconomic circumstances, most related research has emphasised political-economic themes (e.g. Hsing 1996; Hsiao, Kung and Wang 2010; Keng and Schubert 2010; Ong, Cheng and Evans 1992; Tsai and Chang 2010). Up until the last decade, little attention has been paid to Taiwanese migrants' personal experiences related to employment (Tseng 2014), residential patterns (Lin 2009) and relationships with local people (Kung 2005; Ping Lin 2010, 2011).

Of all the destinations in China where Taiwanese migration takes place, Shanghai has become the most-favoured host city. In fact, Shanghai offers more job opportunities for Taiwanese people than the whole of Taiwan. Although the earliest waves of Taiwanese migrants were mostly expatriates sent by Taiwanese companies, many young Taiwanese in Shanghai have proactively sought overseas job opportunities independently instead of waiting for overseas assignments. Many come to find jobs or entrepreneurial opportunities on their own, while even those who initially migrated as employees of Taiwanese companies tend to find other jobs or become business owners or self-employed once their assignment ends. Nowadays, Taiwanese young people can find potential jobs on various online employment sites whose sole purpose is to match Taiwanese workers with opportunities in major Chinese cities. Shanghai has accelerated its industrial restructuring and has shifted from manufacturing to professional services in recent years. At the same time, Shanghai's internationalisation is accelerating. This is the most important reason why Taiwanese young people dream of Shanghai. After the financial crash of 2008, the employment market in Europe and the United States experienced a sharp decline. In contrast, Shanghai's opportunities have not reduced and it has naturally become a great attraction for young international and Taiwanese skilled workers.

While economic factors are a key driving force behind this wave of migration, complex social and cultural aspects of living and working overseas are also important considerations. Tseng (2011) has found that the lifestyle of skilled Taiwanese in the Shanghai displays several distinctive characteristics in comparison to their counterparts based in other cities. For example, the local concentration of transnational corporations' regional headquarters has allowed Shanghai to build an infrastructure and lifestyle that appeals to young people such as comfortable apartments, stores stocked with Western food, an English-speaking working environment and so on.

Young Skilled Workers in a Global City

Conradson and Latham (2005) pointed out that living abroad temporarily during early adulthood is in part about developing one's life through geographical mobility, as well as exploring both personal and professional possibilities. This has arisen due to economic and cultural globalisation, technological advances in communication and a continuing drift towards societal individualisation. In addition, Fränberg (2014) has stated that going abroad to live, work or study for a period when one is young has long been part of the transition to adulthood among certain privileged social groups.

It is quite possible that youth migration is related to skilled migrants, as the population involved tends to be well-educated, young, fertile and taxpaying, as in south–north migration (Beaverstock and Hall 2012). Most studies on skilled migration explain their choice of research sites in terms of the career development opportunities of occupations provided by industries common to large cities. Sassen (1999) credits the expansion of producer services in global cities with the convergence of professional workers. Such scholarship tends to relegate the importance of destination in skilled migration decisions, the job opportunities available for foreign talent being somewhat generic to all global cities. Along with the opening up of China's national economy to foreign firms, the Shanghai metropolis has become a focal point for a converging flow of global commodities, capital and global talent. According to Taylor's (2006) investigation that compared the extent of global links in Hong Kong, Taipei, Beijing and Shanghai by measuring their connections with top international service firms, Shanghai emerges as a global city, while Taipei is more 'regionalist'.

However, some researchers have pointed out that skilled migration is city-sensitive. Florida (2005, 2012) has suggested that cities and urban areas will attract and retain a high proportion of the creative class by being diverse, tolerant, welcoming, liberal, cosmopolitan, bohemian, multicultural, significantly artistic and with substantial immigrant and gay and lesbian communities. These specific areas will then attract investment and companies, particularly high-tech industries. Thus, the importance of the 'three Ts' (talent, technology and tolerance) is highlighted. Florida has proposed that certain types of places attract specific kinds of workers and has listed several criteria that skilled workers or the creative class use to evaluate the quality of a given place: thick labour markets, lifestyle, social interaction and diversity.

The Emotional Understanding of Identity

In the process of migration, individuals leave their existing homes (conceptualised as houses, families or specific geographical locations) and then temporarily or permanently reside in another, less familiar place. There are a growing number of cross-border migration studies that discuss the emotions and feelings of individuals moving between places (Baldassar 2008; Ryan 2008). The literature on transnational migration (e.g. Schiller, Basch and Blanc 1995) has focused mostly on the physical and geographical mobility of migrants in different regions as well as their participation in local or transnational communities. In the process of defining their identity, individuals must look to which group or community they belong, which is often beyond their mere birthplace. Due to the development of network communications, the groups or communities that they belong to can be transnational and extraterritorial. All of this has profound consequences on senses of identity, which means that migration itself shapes new cultures and lifestyles and (trans)forms identities.

According to Yeoh and Willis, many Singaporeans working in the mainland strengthen their Singaporean identity as a means of distinguishing themselves from the Chinese. It was indicated that Chinese Singaporeans often feel disappointed with their actual experiences connecting with local people. One of their interviewees shared the following sentiment: 'The Singaporean Chinese is very different from the Chinese. We keep telling ourselves not to be deceived by skin colour' (Yeoh and Willis 2005: 275).

With regard to the identity (trans)formation of migrants, Lan and Wu (2011) advocated the use of a spectrum-oriented perspective in examining how migrants view ethnic or national differences between the 'self' and 'others'. In the authors' approach, one end of the spectrum involves assimilation, whereas the other end entails differentiation. Between these two poles is where mixed or mobile identity is negotiated to differentiate between the 'self' and 'others' in various degrees and ways.

Young Taiwanese in Shanghai: Research Methodology

From June 2016 to February 2017 I visited Shanghai for a total of nine months to carry out in-depth interviews and participant observation with a group of Taiwanese young people who had been living and working in Shanghai for at least six months. My interviews included questions relating to their initial aspirations for moving to Shanghai and the reasons behind their migration trajectories, their settlement and initial experiences at their destination, and what factors contributed to a decision regarding their next step.

I conducted twenty-eight semi-structured interviews with Taiwanese young people who had moved from Taiwan to pursue their dreams in Shanghai. The sample included fourteen males and fourteen females. Informants ranged between the ages of twenty-two and thirty at the time of their interview. Two of them were married and twenty-six were single. Informants had moved to Shanghai between 2000 and 2016, with 82% (twenty-three out of twenty-eight) having travelled in the previous five years (2012–17). Among the twenty-eight informants, only one-quarter (seven out of twenty-eight) had spent at least one year studying or working in another country before moving to Shanghai for work, such as the United States, Canada and the United Kingdom. A diversity of occupations was also represented, including engineer, medic, financial director, product manager, relationship manager, marketing director, research executive, journalist and scriptwriter. Most of them (twenty-one out of twenty-eight) had working experiences before moving to Shanghai, either as interns or in full formal employment. All of them had attained high levels of education, ten with master's degrees and eighteen with bachelor's degrees.

It is not enough to attempt to generate an accurate picture of Taiwanese young adults in Shanghai solely from published statistics. I decide to conduct in-depth interviews using a semi-structured questionnaire. Participant observation in social gatherings and public events in Shanghai was also carried out. Several Taiwanese young people living in Shanghai assisted as key informants, identifying additional informants through their networks. I do not intend to generalise about Taiwanese young people who are settled temporarily or permanently in Shanghai, but rather to acquire a nuanced understanding of the circumstances of individuals while presenting the complexities of their experiences in a global city.

Aspirations of Young Taiwanese to Work Overseas

Migrants' aspirations, as purposeful constructions of the future that evolve over time, are a meaningful, fascinating, but relatively neglected research subject (Boccagni 2017). Stalker (2001) explains that one of the motivations behind people's decision to migrate is the individual factor, which argues that an individual will choose the easiest path based on rational judgement. The other elements that influence motivation are structural in nature. The society in which an individual lives will affect his or her choices; a society's economy, culture and politics can be factors that influence individual decision-making and judgement. To transfer to another company is an important way for workers to raise their salaries, improve their job title, learn new skills and gain experience. According to my informants' narratives, individual and structural factors are the main issues that affect their decision-making process as to whether they should relocate to Shanghai or not. These include individual factors such as higher pay, more promotion opportunities and better job prospects, while relevant structural factors include a wider market, an international environment and political stability.

These Taiwanese young people have very practical considerations in mind. As Bunnell, Gillen and Ho (2017) highlight, securing better future career prospects can be a long-term goal, while the efforts and energies required for any strategic objective need to be practised gradually in actualised situations. Achieving higher salaries and accessing greater opportunities for promotion are the primary motivations for them to work in Shanghai. This aspiration is not a figment of the imagination, but instead reflects a need to place Taiwan in a global context. In recent years, the labour market in Taiwan has deteriorated. Workers are faced with low salaries with pay scales that do not increase in line with their work performance. For young people in Taiwan, how to achieve rapid and efficient accumulation of capital has become a primary concern. Taiwan is not an economy that needs to rely on the export of labour as a source of remittances under globalisation, yet tens of thousands of young people have moved to work in neighbouring global cities to access more economic benefits for themselves.

Individual Aspirations: Financial Incentives and Career Development

During the decision-making process, the first consideration for my informants was the prospective salary on offer in Shanghai. As mentioned previously, salary growth has been stagnating in Taiwan in recent years. Maintaining a decent quality of life when faced with soaring prices is challenging. Under such circumstances, it is often a financially prudent decision for young Taiwanese people to decide to seek work opportunities abroad. From the narratives of my informants, it seems that the present salaries in Taiwan do not meet the expectations of young people and thus Shanghai appears to be the correct choice:

> My current company in Shanghai offered me a monthly salary of 10,000 RMB, which is equivalent to nearly 50,000 NTD. They also provide me with four return flight tickets back to Taiwan every year. In comparison with a starting salary that can be expected by university graduates in Taiwan in recent years – an average of 27,000 NTD – the pay in Shanghai is double, which is very tempting for Taiwanese young people. (Informant #1, female, twenty-five years old, merchandiser)

Informant #5 is a marketing director in a multinational company in Shanghai. She holds an MBA degree and has held down a stable job in Taiwan. However, when she was given the opportunity to receive a promotion, she was required to relocate to Shanghai:

> I hoped to leave Taiwan and to look further afield to consider my options. I thought coming to mainland China was like moving to another place . . . the salary is relatively high, so this was a crucial point for me and then the company is willing to give me . . . [a] promotion. I came here to take up a more senior manager position, as such opportunities are relatively rare in Taiwan. (Informant #5, female, twenty-nine years old, product manager)

When I asked her to elaborate more on her aspirations to come to Shanghai and if there was any specific motivation, she mentioned:

I felt that if I had to leave my hometown, of course there must be some incentives. If I earned less and I worked at the same position, then of course I would rather not accept it. But . . . I thought that . . . I want to leave Taiwan to see different places, this is a big incentive. (Informant #5, female, twenty-nine years old, product manager)

It is important to bear in mind that while the initial Shanghai salary may be 1.2 to 1.5 times the equivalent Taiwanese wages, after deducting expenses for local accommodation, living and transportation costs, the relative salary paid in Taiwan is not all that different. However, if workers continuously improve their skills and gain enough experience, their potential for increased wages is significant:

While working in Shanghai, nobody cares about the closed-pay system. If you know that the salary of other colleagues is higher than yours, you can go directly to your boss to negotiate a higher salary. (Informant #27, male, aged twenty-four, relationship manager)

When you have the ability, your starting salary may be 6,000 RMB, but your salary is doubled for each role that you move to. Of course, I am talking about capable people. (Informant #19, male, aged twenty-seven, product manager)

In 2015, a report on comparison of high-level executives' salaries in the Asia-Pacific region pointed out that Taiwan's annual salary is only NTD 1.85 million. It is lower than annual salary NTD 2.5 million in Beijing and Shanghai. Taiwan's low wages and long working hours have indeed worsened the job market and have contributed to the increasing brain drain. Apart from the problem of stagnant wages in Taiwan, another reason to move is that young people who have just started their career believe the current employment environment in Taiwan is too comfortable and they want to find a more challenging place to work:

I have carefully thought about my career prospects. When I was working in Taiwan, I had a stable job and I was well-versed in the job. But our clients were all developed by my senior colleagues, the market was saturated, therefore it was hard for me to make any potential breakthrough. It is better to come to Shanghai to develop my new customers. Although the risk is relatively high, if I succeed, it becomes evidence of my particular strengths and achievements. (Informant #12, male, thirty years old, business development officer)

My informants' aspirations for migration to Shanghai stemmed largely from their negative experiences or negative expectations of employment in Taiwan. It clearly showed that these Taiwanese young people wanted to change what they considered to be an unsatisfactory situation in order to bring about more desirable career developments.

Structural Aspirations: Large-Scale and Challenging Markets

In addition to individual motivations, such as money and career development, there are other structural factors that attract young people to Shanghai, such as global markets and industrial development. During the 1990s, China's central government poured resources into improving the city's infrastructure. Since then, massive redevelopment of the central city has transformed Shanghai's urban landscape into a showcase for China's open policy, designed to attract foreign capital (Wu 2000). Active global networks helped to bring in new actors and new ideas, as noted by Sassen (1999), and such networks have profoundly changed Shanghai's urban and cultural landscape:

> You can see that stores and the shopping streets in Xintiandi and Wai Tan have a new look every few months. Not only are we as customers stimulated, but also managers and operators in Shanghai are more courageous in terms of trying new business models. Working life in Shanghai is busier and more compact than in Taipei. We don't often experience such challenges or sense of fulfilment in Taipei. (Informant #20, female, thirty years old, marketing director)

Compared to the market in Taiwan, many enterprises in Shanghai are more willing to try out new ideas and business strategies and have the financial resources to pursue them. My informants mentioned that the ideas that are too new and too experimental for Taiwanese customers are more likely to be accepted by their Chinese equivalents. To take internet business as an example, many Taiwanese companies are just beginning to think about the implementation strategies while companies in Shanghai have already carried out plans and thought about the next steps:

> In the process of talking with clients, I can also feel the differences between the two places in relation to ambition and management levels. Shanghai is indeed an environment that is more stimulating and has more opportunities and challenges if we consider work only. (Informant #7, female, twenty-eight years old, senior research executive)

One of my informants made an observation that seemed to echo Florida's (2012) theory that cities should focus on attracting the skilled migrants in order to see an increase in investments, the number of companies and commercial activities:

> You can always find seminars, lectures, art exhibitions, etc., in Shanghai and I attended these events as self-enriching and learning activities outside the workplace. No matter what field, there are always various kinds of small to large-scale sharing sessions, seminars or forums in Shanghai that can also be used as social networking occasions. It is easier and more frequent to see a 'big name' invited to these events in Shanghai than Taiwan. This kind of resource is relatively unobtainable for many friends who work in Taiwan while it is relatively easy to access when working in Shanghai. (Informant #15, male, twenty-seven years old, e-commerce marketing)

Among my informants, there are two kinds of negative and positive interpretations of the aspirations to leave Taiwan and work in Shanghai. On the negative side, the 'push force' of a poor domestic economy, low investment and low wages results in Taiwanese young people's aspirations to leave and seek opportunities elsewhere. However, on the positive side, the 'pull force' of a large number of employment opportunities and a high degree of international competitiveness within global cities attract Taiwanese young people to develop their future careers elsewhere. This situation impels Taiwanese young people to leave their homeland and go overseas to make a living and seek self-fulfilment.

Settlement and Employment Experiences

From Taiwan-Funded Companies to Foreign-Invested or Chinese-Owned Companies

In the past there was less information about how to find jobs in China, so Taiwanese working in China had usually been transferred there by their companies in Taiwan. Nowadays young Taiwanese can easily find information about job opportunities in China and they can also choose to work in foreign-invested or Chinese-owned companies. From information gained through my interviews, most informants who have studied abroad or in China will first choose foreign or Chinese-owned companies, while those who graduated in Taiwan will first look for Taiwanese companies to work for, but will also have foreign-funded or Chinese-owned companies in mind. This phenomenon reflects the gradual decline in evaluation that young people have of Taiwanese-owned companies:

When I started working in a Taiwan company based in Shanghai, the company did not sign a contract with me, nor did they tell you what your rights and obligations are. Everything was very vague. The foreign company which I am currently working for told me very explicitly about my annual salary, my insurance and what was included in the whole package they offered me. My salary in the foreign-funded company and the salary increase are definitely much higher. Taiwanese businessmen basically do not raise wages. Instead, they rely on fear that workers won't dare to give up a stable job. These are two very different attitudes toward employees. (Informant #3, male, twenty-nine years old, financial director)

In fact, Taiwanese companies are relatively unpopular in China because mainland Chinese people think Taiwanese bosses are stingy and how they treat employees is not good. So they are actually facing one problem . . . they are increasingly unable to recruit local people. I also want to transfer to a Chinese-owned or foreign company. Comparing with such Taiwan-owned enterprises, their annual salary increase is relatively high. (Informant #4, male, thirty years old, IT product manager)

Drawing upon my informants' narratives, it can be suggested that Taiwanese companies in China are running their businesses in the same way as they are run in Taiwan. Workers are not regarded as professionals and companies hope to reduce personnel costs by recruiting cheaper labour. There are few welfare considerations, no salary increases, contracts are vague and the space for career development is limited. Hence, Chinese-owned companies become more attractive to young people.

The Reconstruction of Identity in Shanghai

Because of long-term political tensions, there are many social barriers and differences between Taiwanese and Chinese people, and my informants all believe that national identity is an unavoidable issue. Once outside their country of origin, national identity is difficult to ignore (Colic-Peisker 2010). My informants talked about their sense of identity, how they saw themselves and presented themselves to others, and the group of people they felt they belonged to. The long-standing political conflict between China and Taiwan has complicated the national identity of Taiwanese working in Shanghai:

I think Shanghai people are very practical, they won't specifically fight you; however, people in northeastern China or Beijing are more critical, they would like to hear your ideas about Taiwanese independence, they will deliberately mention this matter. Shanghai people are more pragmatic and shrewder, they don't pay much attention to politics, they have seen a lot of the world . . . they have seen people from many countries . . . They are very smooth. They avoid talking about sensitive political issues. Some of my friends might have been asked about their opinions, but in my personal experience, I have never been asked. (Informant #5, female, twenty-nine years old, product manager)

The shared common language and Han ethnicity of the majority in Taiwan and Shanghai are beneficial, not only in terms of Taiwanese workers finding jobs more easily, but also for Taiwanese students to be able to successfully complete their education there:

In the past, Taiwanese professionals who needed international experience went to the United States as their first option, while some went to Hong Kong or Tokyo, which are the most important global cities in Asia. However, now Shanghai has many more opportunities. We do not experience language barriers here as we speak Mandarin. (Informant #19, male, twenty-seven years old, product manager)

Having a common language does not mean that the interpretation of every phrase is also the same. The autonomous development of Taiwan over half a century has resulted in a diverse range of common phrases and idioms. Generally speaking, phraseological expression on the mainland is much more direct and grounded than in Taiwan. Conversely, the most obvious feature of Taiwanese when they are speaking – apart from their upward tone and accent – is always talking more elaborately, from a Mainlander's perspective.

In general, cross-cultural issues often arise between people of different racial, ethnic or cultural backgrounds. Although Taiwan and China are both largely Chinese societies, cross-cultural issues are still perceived as prominent. There exist a number of subtle differences in cultural practices and characteristics because of these two societies' different social, economic and political developments. For example, Taiwanese young people in Shanghai experience a specific language issue: the Shanghai dialect, which challenges the assumption of a shared cultural identity across the Taiwan Strait:

Shanghai people are accustomed to using the Shanghai dialect, so it is difficult for nonlocal people to feel being integrated with local community. When there is a meeting in my company, if some local colleagues do not want foreign or nonlocal colleagues to hear what they were talking about, they will speak in Shanghai dialect. (Informant #5, female, twenty-nine years old, product manager)

In addition, traditional Chinese characters are preserved and used in Taiwan; however, simplified Chinese characters have become the contemporary standard in China and globally. Though the spoken language, Mandarin, is the same on both sides of the Strait, the differences in characters used is easily perceived when Taiwanese people first come to the mainland:

Maybe I have got used to it; I don't feel any incongruity between the simplified Chinese characters and the traditional ones at present. There are no difficulties for me to read and write the simplified Chinese characters. I think it is a natural feeling to use them because you are in this environment. (Informant #6, male, twenty-nine years old, scriptwriter)

While I am working here, I use the simplified Chinese characters rather than the traditional ones because I feel like using the simplified Chinese characters is the most 'correct' moral practice. On the other hand, it is also 'incorrect' morally for me to use the simplified Chinese characters. I realise that they are not mine. The simplified Chinese characters belong to them [the PRC]. In terms of pronunciations and language, the characters should be the traditional ones. I still used the traditional Chinese characters even though I can now read and recognise the simplified Chinese characters now. (Informant #20, female, thirty years old, marketing director)

One of the reasons why Taiwanese young people in Shanghai feel that they are 'outsiders' is because local people's habits and attitudes are different from those Taiwanese have been taught since childhood and sometimes they feel offended and even come into conflict with local people. As one informant expressed a related sentiment:

Sometimes I feel that I am different to the locals, especially when I take public transportation. There are always some people who try to cut the queue to buy a ticket. Even though you try to restrain them from cutting the queue, they will pretend to hear nothing. Some of them, surprisingly, argue back. It seems that as long as you speak louder than others you are correct, even though it is incorrect essentially. (Informant #5, female, twenty-nine years old, product manager)

Another informant also elaborated on a similar experience. Given the difference in etiquette and self-cultivation between himself and others, he felt that he was the opposite of the locals:

> You seldom see young passengers give their seats to their elders on public transportation here in Shanghai. Needless to say, expecting cars to give way to pedestrians courteously doesn't happen. As for 'thank you' or 'sorry', these are common words to use in everyday situations. However, here nobody, or I should say fewer people use these phrases. I always used to argue that Taiwan has the worst traffic in the world. Since I've been here, however, I now think that Taiwan is really advanced and awash with politeness. (Informant #13, male, thirty years old, relationship manager)

The prosperous outlook and seemingly endless business opportunities in Shanghai are cited as the most attractive aspects for informants working in the mainland. However, most of my informants also pointed out the different dispositions between cross-strait societies, distinctions that resulted in respective alienation. Their impression of Shanghai today is characterised more by frustration than excitement, more by disappointment than satisfaction. Politeness emerged as one of the critical values. Although the standard of living in Shanghai is no different from that in Taiwan, the sociocultural gap between Shanghai and Taiwan is still sizeable. It is also a crucial point of divergence and affects the tendency towards self-identity among Taiwanese young people in Shanghai.

Migration Dilemmas of Taiwanese in Shanghai

Migrants' aspirations are a purposeful construction of the future. Past studies have shown that migrant workers' current aspirations may be significantly different from the aspirations they held in the past before leaving their hometown. A gap is formed because of their limited scope to negotiate a way across local and transnational life (Boccagni 2017). For instance, most of my informants found it very demanding to always be on high alert regarding possible information censorship. In Shanghai it is still a risk to read news from any platform other than local publications. The cost is higher and there is also a political risk. An informant provided the following reflections:

> I had to adapt to the Chinese way of doing things from the top down, but it took a lot of adjustments. In Taiwan, most of the time, bottom-up views on public affairs are totally acceptable. (Informant #2, male, thirty years old, branch director)

This discrepancy between increased economic opportunities in the host society and better sociopolitical provisions in the home society means that many Taiwanese young people aspire to hold on to various life chances offered by either China or Taiwan. The following quote highlights this discrepancy very succinctly:

> I cannot imagine living in China for long, because it is so annoying being blocked from accessing outside information. (Informant #11, female, twenty-nine years old, journalist)

Most informants choose to simultaneously build and maintain a social life across the border because although they prefer making a living in China, they want to keep open the prospect of having a life in Taiwan. Most of them said they are unsure whether they will still be in China in five years' time. Such uncertainty is expressed in their ambivalent evaluations regarding their relations with China as a host society. This is less because of their employment and career prospects in China and more due to their negative evaluations about quality of life in terms of public provisions, such as public education, environmental standards, medical care and health insurance. The same negative evaluations about China are often shared by the younger generation, even though many of them have lived in China since childhood. Some planned to return to Taiwan for their university education, while others had decided to move to other developed countries. While an increasing number of Taiwanese young people now look for jobs in China, the return migration of sons and daughters of Taiwanese migrants is indeed a reverse trend. Every year, there are thousands of overseas Taiwanese applying for university admission in Taiwan. Although in the last decade there has been an increasing number of Taiwanese attending university in China (Lan and Wu 2011), many Taiwanese young people I interviewed consider Taiwan as providing better-quality higher education. Furthermore, most of my informants value the Taiwanese medical system's public provision and universal health coverage, and they spoke highly of the efficiency and professionalism of Taiwan's medical system:

> Shanghai is my home as I am familiar with Shanghai. Taiwan is also my home because I am Taiwanese. I would like to go back to Taiwan to retire, as the Medicare system is much better and I still have the family members there. (Informant #21, male, thirty years old, public relations director)

Most informants continue to maintain ties with the social welfare system in Taiwan and do not feel the need to be incorporated into China's social welfare system. In addition to their negative evaluations of public services in China, uncertain migration prospects also played a significant role in their relations with the host society. A majority of the informants had a very ambivalent attitude in terms of their long-term plans. However, most stated that they were almost certain to retire back home, not only because of personal connections and family ties, but also because they perceive Taiwan as allowing for a better quality of life as a whole.

Conclusion

The aspirations of Taiwanese young adults working in Shanghai often include personal aspirations such as financial incentives and career development opportunities, and are linked with structural realities of China's large and challenging markets. Resettlement, employment and lived experiences affect Taiwanese young people's reconstruction of identity in Shanghai. Their happiness, achievements and frustrations are evident through their interview narratives. These cross-strait migration experiences influence Taiwanese young people's future aspirations and migration strategies and it is evidenced that youth exodus has become a significant phenomenon of educated and skilled migration from Taiwan. Regardless of whether these Taiwanese young peoples' imagined and aspirational futures are realised, studying them is critical in understanding their changing life projects in both the host and home societies.

My study of Taiwanese young people in Shanghai helps to broaden the literature on youth migration. My informants are undoubtedly young and skilled, but do not earn salaries that would take them into the category of carefree elites. Despite their high levels of educational qualifications and professional credentials, these Taiwanese young people experienced a challenging job-seeking process in Shanghai and as such there is a degree of risk and uncertainty about their economic position. These Taiwanese young people do not form an ethnic minority group in Shanghai, but, even so, there are cultural variations that have an impact on their identity (trans)formation.

Some issues such as how and why migrants' aspirations change over time and how different types of aspirations affect their migration trajectories have brought rich insights into migration studies in urban contexts. In my understanding, aspirations are emotional representations of what the future might and should look like. Aspirations are based on both the current situation and past experience. Before moving to Shanghai, the way in which these Taiwanese young people imagine the place they are moving to may be based on talking to those who have been there before or by written accounts, so to explore the formation and transformations of these Taiwanese young people's aspirations and identities is of considerable importance. An examination of the narratives of Taiwanese young people in Shanghai can shed light on the subjective and emotional drivers of their life trajectories overseas, as well as the developing and changing external opportunity structures.

Chia-Yuan Huang is a postdoctoral scholar at the Research Center for Humanities and Social Sciences, Academia Sinica, Taipei, Taiwan. She received her Ph.D. from the Department of Geography at University College London. From 2017 to 2019, she worked as Project Officer for the SOAS Centre of Taiwan Studies. Her research interests include migration and transnationalism, as well as young adults, women and work in the global context of mobility. Several articles she has (co)authored have been published in journals such as the *China Review*, *Journal of Population Studies* and *Translocal Chinese: East Asian Perspectives*.

References

Baldassar, Loretta. 2008. 'Missing Kin and Longing to Be Together: Emotions and the Construction of Co-Presence in Transnational Relationships', *Journal of Intercultural Studies* 29: 247–66.

Beaverstock, Jonathan V., and Sarah Hall. 2012. 'Competing for Talent: Global Mobility, Immigration and the City of London's Labour Market', *Cambridge Journal of Regions Economy and Society* 5(2): 271–87.

Boccagni, Paolo. 2017. 'Aspirations and the Subjective Future of Migration: Comparing Views and Desires of the "Time Ahead" through the Narratives of Immigrant Domestic Workers', *Comparative Migration Studies* 5(4): 1–18.

Bunnell, Tim, Jamie Gillen and Elaine Lynn-Ee Ho. 2017. 'The Prospect of Elsewhere: Engaging the Future through Aspirations in Asia', *Annuals of the American Association of Geographers* 108(1): 35–51.

Chang, Meg. 2012. 'Taiwan Gears up to Tackle Brain Drain', *Taiwan Today*, 9 September.

Chen, Luo-Wei. 2011. 'Headhunting from Neighbouring Countries: Brain Drain Has Become National Security Issue', *United Daily News*, 18 April.

Chiang, Lan-Hung, Nora, and Chia-Yuan Huang. 2014. 'Young Global Talents on the Move: Taiwanese in Singapore and Hong Kong', *Journal of Population Studies* 49: 69–117.

Chiu, P.S., and Lillian Lin. 2015. 'Brain Drain: A Serious Problem in Taiwan: Poll', *Focus Taiwan*. Retrieved 19 March 2020 from http://focustaiwan.tw/news/aeco/201511200009.aspx.

Colic-Peisker, Val. 2010. 'Free Floating in the Cosmopolis? Exploring the Identity-Belonging of Transnational Knowledge Workers', *Global Networks* 10(4): 467–88.

Conradson, David, and Alan Latham. 2005. 'Friendship, Networks and Transnationality in a World City: Antipodean Transmigrants in London', *Journal of Ethnic and Migration Studies* 31(2): 287–305.

Directorate-General of Budget, Accounting and Statistics, Executive Yuan of Taiwan. 2017. *Statistics on the Number of Taiwanese Overseas Workers in 2015*. Taiwan.

Florida, Richard. 2005. *The Flight of the Creative Class: The New Global Competition for Talent*. New York: HarperCollins.

———. 2012. *The Rise of the Creative Class, Revisited*. New York: Basic Books.

Fränberg, Lotta. 2014. 'Temporary Transnational Youth Migration and Its Mobility Links', *Mobilities* 9(1): 146–64.

Hsiao, Hsin-Huang Michael, I-Chun Kung and Hong-Zen Wang. 2010. 'Taishang: A Different Kind of Ethnic Chinese Business in Southeast Asia', in Yin-Wah Chu (ed.), *Chinese Capitalisms: Historical Emergence and Political Implications*. Basingstoke: Palgrave Macmillan, pp. 156–75.

Hsing, You-Tien. 1996. 'Blood, Thicker than Water: Interpersonal Relations and Taiwanese Investment in Southern China', *Environment and Planning A* 28(12): 2241–61.

Huang, Chi-Yuan. 2013. 'If You Are Young and Talented, Don't Stay in Taipei', *Business Weekly*. Retrieved 20 March 2020 from https://www.businessweekly.com.tw/article .aspx?id=3222&type=Blog.

Keng, Shu, and Gunter Schubert. 2010. 'Agents of Taiwan-China Unification? The Political Roles of Taiwanese Business People in the Process of Cross-Strait Integration', *Asian Survey* 50(2): 287–310.

Kung, I-Chun. 2005. *Stepping out: The Social Formation of Taiwanese Business in Southeast Asia*. Taipei: Center for Asia-Pacific Area Studies, Academia Sinica.

Lan, Pei-Chia, and Yi-Fan Wu. 2011. 'Between "Homeland" and "Foreign Country": Liminal Identity and Boundary Work of Taiwanese Students in China', *Taiwanese Sociology* 22: 1–57.

Lin, Hsing-Fei, and Teng, Kai-Yuan. 2014. 'Taiwan's Youth Exodus: The New Migrant Workers', *Commonwealth Magazine* 541: 110–20.

Lin, Jang-Chun. 2010. 'If I Stay in Taiwan, I May Not Have a Job', *Global Views Monthly* 294: 362.

Lin, Ping. 2009. 'Do They Mix? The Residential Segregation of Taiwanese People in China', *Taiwan Political Science Review* 13(2): 57–111.

———. 2010. 'Home Alone, Taiwanese Single Women in Mainland China', *Journal of Population Studies* 41: 111–51.

———. 2011. 'Chinese Diaspora "at Home": Mainlander Taiwanese in Dongguan and Shanghai', *China Review* 11(2): 43–64.

Morgan Philips Executive Search. 2017. '2017 Morgan Philips Talent Report'. Retrieved 19 March 2020 from https://www.morganphilipsgreaterchina.com/TalentRep ort/2017/2017_Talent_Report_English_Version.pdf.

MRI China Group. 2013. '2013 MRIC Talent Report: Greater China Region and Singapore'.

Ong, Paul M., Lucie Cheng and Leslie Evans. 1992. 'Migration of Highly Educated Asians and Global Dynamics', *Asian and Pacific Migration Journal* 1(3): 543–67.

Ramzy, Austin. 2016. 'As Taiwan's Workers Flock to China, Concerns about Economy Grow', *New York Times*, 13 January. Retrieved 20 March 2020 from http://www.ny times.com/2016/01/14/world/asia/taiwan-elections-china.html.

Ryan, Louise. 2008. 'Navigating the Emotional Terrain of Families "Here" and "There": Women, Migration and the Management of Emotions', *Journal of Intercultural Studies* 29: 299–313.

Sassen, Saskia. 1999. 'Hong Kong–Shanghai: Networking as Global Cities', *2G: International Architecture Review* 10(2): 106–11.

Schiller, Nina Glick, Linda Basch and Cristina Szanton Blanc. 1995. 'From Immigrant to Transmigrant: Theorizing Transnational Migration', *Anthropological Quarterly* 68(1): 48–63.

Stalker, Peter. 2001. *The No-Nonsense Guide to International Migration*. Oxford: New Internationalist Publications.

Taylor, Peter J. 2006. 'Shanghai, Hong Kong, Taipei and Beijing within the World City Network: Positions, Trends and Prospects', GaWC Research Bulletin No. 204. Retrieved 20 March 2020 from http://www.lboro.ac.uk/gawc/rb/rb204.html.

Tsai, Ming-Chang, and Chin-Fen Chang. 2010. 'China-Bound for Jobs? The Influences of Social Connections and Ethnic Politics in Taiwan', *China Quarterly* 203: 639–55.

Tseng, Yen-Fen. 2011. 'Shanghai Rush: Skilled Migrants in a Fantasy City', *Journal of Ethnic and Migration Studies* 37(5): 765–84.

———. 2014. 'Bordering Careers on China: Skilled Migration from Taiwan to China', in Kuei-Fen Chiu, Dafydd Fell and Ping Lin (eds), *Migration to and from Taiwan*. London: Routledge, pp. 42–56.

Wu, Fulong. 2000. 'The Global and Local Dimensions of Place-Making: Remaking Shanghai as a World City', *Urban Studies* 37(8): 1359–77.

Yeoh, Brenda. S.A., and Willis, Katie. 2005. 'Singaporeans in China: Transnational Women Elites and the Negotiation of Gendered Identities', *Geoforum* 36: 211–22.

Yeoh, Brenda S.A., and Louisa-May Khoo. 1998. 'Home, Work and Community: Skilled International Migration and Expatriate Women in Singapore', *International Migration* 36(2): 159–86.

3

ASPIRING TO THE GOOD LIFE
South Korea's Spec-Generation

Carolin Landgraf

Sora[1] was already waiting for me in the coffee shop near the subway station on this Sunday morning. As I entered, she waved her hand to signal to me where she was sitting, as this was the first time we had met in person. We greeted each other, went to the counter to order two cups of coffee and sat down in a quiet corner away from the rather busy entrance. I told her that my research is about the life trajectories of young South Koreans and I asked her to tell me about her life. She started to speak about her educational path, her work experiences so far, and her partner and family. At the end of our three-hour interview, I asked her what she hoped for her future and she answered: 'There are two things: I want to be able to do my work until the end and I want to found a family with my partner and live together with him happily.' Sora was a 27-year-old South Korean woman working as a so-called contract worker in the field of marketing. She came to Seoul to study social science at one of the city's numerous universities and since then had lived and worked in the capital city by herself. In this chapter, I ask how young Seoulites construct their lives in the face of urban (un)certainties and (un)happiness. Based on ethnographic fieldwork I conducted from September 2012 to September 2013 in the Capital Region, I argue that young Seoulites aspire to live a valuable life where they can develop their potentials and deepen their social relations. I want to follow Sora's journey and describe how she formed her academic way, working career and relationships to arrive, on reflection, at these specific aspirations and complement her journey with narratives of Jin-kyong who was a young working woman of the same age but, different from Sora, spent her life solely in Seoul.

Endnotes for this chapter begin on page 68.

Anthropologists describe young South Koreans like Sora and Jin-kyong as being subjected to changing economic conditions. Their actions are defined as investments and their practices are reduced to self-management and self-discipline (Cho 2015; Song 2009), which they enact 'on their own' (Abelmann, Park and Kim 2013). In public discourses, the term Spec-Generation captures these practices. It refers to young South Koreans aged between twenty to thirty years old who engage in accumulating specifications – *Spec* – to maintain a middle-class lifestyle. However, my research findings indicate that this representation is too simplistic. Young Seoulites start to question the desirability of a middle-class lifestyle, but they must create a balance between their own aspirations towards a desirable life and the expectations of their parents, friends and society of what a good life should look like.

Edward Fischer (2014) writes that adequate material conditions, as well as health and beneficial social relationships, are essential criteria for a good life, while at the same time subjective perceptions such as feelings of fairness, the capacity to aspire, to see opportunities and being able to engage in larger projects constitute a life worth living. The 'good life' does not need to be something utopian, but can be imagined in rather mundane and practical ways, such as working in a job that is satisfying, marrying the partner one wants to spend one's life with and having a supportive working environment. Thus, the concept of a good life is always highly specific and notions of the good life are 'laden – replete with ideas about value, worth, virtue, what is good and bad, right and wrong' (Fischer 2014: 5). Different configurations of values make the good life a local specific one and the capacity to aspire a cultural and social capacity, as Arjun Appadurai argues (2004, 2013). I take ethics as a further analytical lens to elaborate on the different values that constitute the aspirations of my research participants, its relational references and spatial and temporal frames. Unlike a universal character attributed to terms such as 'ethic', 'moral' and 'virtue' in public discourses, I want to draw attention to my research participants' personalised thoughts, reflections, judgement and reasoning about what is good or better, bad or worse (Fischer 2014; Keane 2015). In their narratives, these young Seoulites presented me with descriptions of situations and experiences that made ethical questions explicit and that called for this 'ethical evaluation' (Keane 2015: 144; see also Lambek 2015). In building an analytical framework that combines the concept of aspirations with approaches to ethics, I aim to deepen the understanding of how young Seoulites negotiate between and balance different notions of the good life.

In the following discussion, I elaborate on my concepts and methods of analysis and follow Sora and Jin-kyong in their narratives about education, work and marriage, which were important themes of a middle-class lifestyle. I aim to show how they conceptualised the good life in relation to these middle-class standards, how they negotiated, moved between and balanced different, juxtaposing and contradictory values, and engaged in practices they considered as right or good to pursue a good life.

One Generation among Many

When I started my research project in April 2012, I was interested in South Korea's so-called '880,000 Won Generation', a term I encountered on a one-year Korean language course followed by three months of preliminary fieldwork in September 2011. Characterised as overeducated and underemployed, young people of this generation came to be named after the minimum wage of 880,000 Won that they had to work for. However, as I began my fieldwork in Seoul in September 2012, I was told that the so-called '880,000 Won Generation' had become outdated and young people aged twenty to thirty were now called 'Spec-Generation' in public discourses. *Spec* referred to the collection of qualifications, experiences and certificates that students needed to acquire in order to enhance their chances on the job market. I soon learned through intensive interviews that the term Spec was also applied to describe immaterial and material assets necessary for belonging to South Korea's middle classes: graduation from one of Seoul's top-tier universities, working as white-collar worker in the headquarters of a conglomerate in the capital city, marrying and founding a family, as well as the acquisition of material assets. Another term I heard during interviews was 'Give-up Generation' (*N- p'osedae*), where a number was added at the beginning to indicate how many qualities young people had to give up: *Sam- p'osedae* – people give up marriage, good work and a loan, *O-p'osedae* – people give up two more things, social relations in general and an apartment, and finally *Il- p'osedae* – people give up life itself. Here, the term 'Spec-Generation' connects with the term 'Give-up Generation'. Young people work hard to obtain the required standards for a middle-class lifestyle; however, in the end, they must give them up because they cannot reproduce them.

Throughout East and Southeast Asia, social discourses generalise and summarise young people and their life prospects in a similar vein. *Freeters* (composed of the English word 'free' and the German word 'arbeiter') presents a term to address young people in Japan, who are working in part-time jobs. However, the term is an ambiguous phrase as it positively addresses young people who act against Japan's work ethic, while it is also used in a negative sense to blame youth for their lack of willingness to work (Driscoll 2007). Similarly, the term 'Strawberry Generation', which is used to label young people in Taiwan, negatively refers to the supposed weaknesses of young people to sustain hardship in work and life (Le Peasant 2011).

I suggest that these discourses of and on behalf of youth raise issues relating to the reproduction and 'moral configuration' (Durham 2004: 590) of society.

Barbara Ehrenreich (1989) stresses that the 'fear of falling' presents a constant threat to those who identify as middle class because the young can only partly inherit the status, but must reproduce the necessary middle-class 'capital' all by themselves. However, with changing economic and social conditions, reproducing the middle-class status has become different for young people in East Asia compared to their parents' generation and they start to question the values of a middle-class lifestyle.

In this chapter, I want to highlight the complexity of young Seoulites' perspectives and practices in a value-oriented social matrix. Young people's activities and efforts are induced with and motivated by curiosity, but also disinterest, their practices inconsistent, full of passion, joy, yet also angst and suffering. Living a meaningful life means to 'realize the direction and value in what we do' (Lambek 2015: 8). Following Helena Wulff (1995) and Mary Bucholtz (2002), I suggest that a perspective that takes youth as social actors who have their own perspectives on a wide range of social themes, and give meaning to these themes rather than merely responding to social and cultural power relations, can paint a more differentiated picture of the life trajectories of young people. I chose Sora and Jin-kyong from among a group of twenty young people I interviewed to highlight yet another perspective: gender. Summarising young people as one generation neglects the different experiences my female and male research participants had. South Korea is said to be a patriarchal society and women are often portrayed as subjected to patriarchal practices. I chose to represent the thoughts, considerations and experiences of two working women in order to explore the idea that gender is a 'social construct' (Abelmann 2002: 26) that becomes important in some situations but not others. Sora and Jin-kyong had to negotiate between diverse values and demands, which shows that patriarchalism is sometimes too simplistic an explanation for their experiences (see Holliday and Elfving-Hwang 2012). I develop a theoretical framework that combines the concept of aspirations with reflections about ethics to provide a deeper insight into and a more nuanced approach to their social life.

I employ a broad definition of ethics as a 'manner of life' that refers to values and ends as important in themselves (Keane 2015:133). Thereby, I understand moral principles and codes as special elements of ethics that people can draw on because morality systems present historically grown and socially embedded rules and obligations. However, an ethical life cannot be reduced to these principles; rather, it encompasses the 'everyday, taken-for-granted activities and processes of self-formation' (Keane 2015: 135). Following Webb Keane (2015), I take ethics to centre around the question of how one should live. 'Should' encompasses both the sense people have towards themselves – the self-cultivation and self-formation they enact to flourish (in the sense of virtue ethics) – and the social obligations and duties they feel obliged to follow. At the same time, it draws attention to the importance of social relations because it is only in social relations with others that ethics becomes explicit (Keane 2015). Thus, I centre my perspective on the dimension of ethics as conscious awareness and reflection, my research participants' judgement, reasoning and self-understanding about the person they should be and the form that a good life should take.

Appadurai (1996, 2013) asks anthropologists to pay attention to the techniques through which locality is imagined, produced and maintained. Seoul represents the cultural and social, as well as the educational, political and economic centre of South Korea, and my research participants distinguished strongly between the provinces (*chibang*) and the capital city Seoul. However, what they referred to as provinces were often cities with nearly one million residents, thus stressing the imagined and real importance of the capital city, as Sora and her parents did.

From There to Here: Sora's and Jin-kyong's Journey

Education

Sora came from what she referred to as *chibang*. The most important aspiration for her parents was that she would enrol in a university in Seoul. 'They thought that it would be good for me to go to Seoul. Thus, to study became their top priority and I, too, revived my thoughts and put a lot of effort into my studies', she explained. During her three years of high school, she prepared diligently for the entrance examination day. South Korean students enter university through the College Scholastic Ability Test (CSAT) or *sunŭng*, which consists of a standardised test issued by the Korea Institute of Curriculum and Evaluation (KICE). Another way to attend university is through early admission (*sushi*), where specifications such as school reports, TOEFL scores and awards in physics or maths are considered. In either case, students face enormous pressure and all the effort Sora put into her studies was directed towards successfully completing this one test, because education is of one of the most important assets to reproduce the middle-class status. Anthropologist Nancy Abelmann stresses the importance of education in South Korea with an analogy: 'Perhaps the most sensitive of social registers in South Korea, education is shorthand, a Rorschach for, dare I say, almost everything else' (2003: 100).

First and foremost, education in South Korea is a family business, as a common saying illustrates: good education requires 'the "grandfather's financial power, the mother's informational power and the child's physical strength"' (Cho 2015: 454). In Sora's narrative, the anxiety and concerns of her parents towards her future became tangible. Although the province was a city with more than 600,000 residents, four universities and a fluent art and festival scene, remaining there would reduce her opportunities, while studying and living in the capital city would enhance them.

Sora did not negotiate with her parents about her educational future, but rather did her best to fulfil their aspirations – even made them into her own aspirations – and finally managed to enrol in a university in Seoul through *sunŭng*. However, upon coming to Seoul, she felt lost. 'I had no goal for my life other than to study. When I could manage to achieve this longed-for goal and entered a university in Seoul, I really wondered what I should do now', she told me and added 'you know when the grades match, you have to go to university, but I was not that good in studying. I felt a dilemma and it gave me a lot of stress'.

Sora's parents had fulfilled their responsibility and managed to send her to a university in Seoul. Sora, however, had to think anew about her future life path and how she could and should live. 'When I moved to Seoul I felt that I lacked any spirit of independence. I was blocked', she explained. 'Actually, the first year is when everybody is enjoying oneself, a time full of amusement. However, I had to adapt to my new surrounding and was not able to have fun', she emphasised, but added that 'it was a process to learn and develop a sense of independence [*char-ipshim*], the spirit of independence [*tongnipshim*], but then I enjoyed university very much'. She could develop new aspirations, as she remembered her interest in books and decided to work towards the vocational field of marketing. However, her results from the *sunŭng* were not sufficient and she had to take another major according to her grade. As she felt that she aspired to this kind of work but could not study it during her years at university, she set about collecting her Spec for this outside of the campus. 'It was not easy, but I did a lot of volunteer work in the arts centre near my flat during the semester break and could do a two-month course in book marketing and I worked at book festivals', she paused and added that 'I made the best of my situation and hoped that employers would appreciate the work experience and now I have a job that I like very much'.

When talking with me in retrospect about the decisions she made during her years at university, Sora felt that she had been given the room for her own imaginations and aspirations concerning a larger life project. However, it was a process and she encountered diverse difficulties and struggled while adjusting to a place where she could not rely on the guidance of her parents, aspiring to a job whose specification she could not collect through university courses, but had to make extra effort to acquire. 'Actually, the top goal in my life was to enrol in a university in Seoul, but as I could not see the bigger picture, I worried a lot about my career', she emphasised again. 'After all, if I would have thought about entering a conglomerate like everybody else, I would have had even more worries. But I liked my ways and this work, so I gave it a try and I arrived here with a stable and comfortable life.'

Sora reflected on the aspirations of her parents regarding her education and she evaluated how she established her life in the capital city. The good life her parents aspired for her, based on the ethical consideration that she should not fall behind other young people, presented her with the need to think anew about how she herself should live not only in new surroundings, but also regarding a larger life project. In the end, she developed a sense of independence through self-formation and created herself a good life in Seoul: in a situation where most graduates aspired to work in a big cooperation, she decided to follow her own aspirations against this middle-class standard.

Work

Sora decided on a vocational field not pursued by the majority. As she mentioned in the quotation given above, most students aspired to work in a conglomerate and graduating from university was what would enable them to do so. The South Korean economic landscape is characterised by a striking divide between large corporations and small and medium-sized companies. Developed during the time of industrialisation, conglomerates evolved into global players dominating the domestic market with their octopus-like diversification in branches unrelated to their core business (Kong 2000; Gray 2008). However, conglomerates present a desirable working place for young people for several reasons: the first and most important of these is job security in the form of full-time and regular employment. Furthermore, working in a conglomerate guarantees the accessibility of loans. Nevertheless, working in a conglomerate is also a pursuit for social success and status. Small and medium-sized companies, on the other hand, require labour-intensive work, are characterised by temporary work without benefits and have a lower level of social recognition.

Sora emphasised that marketing is a labour-intensive job. That is why many graduates do not want to do this kind of work. 'You know that students who studied at a university see it as an investment and thus, want to work in a conglomerate or, if they don't achieve it, want to work in a medium-sized company', she explained. 'Marketing, however, is a job that many graduates like my case avoid. So, I graduated easily and found a job without difficulties. I received a lot of confidence in and also acknowledgement for my skills.' In contrast to her fellow students and their aspirations, she decided to take a different possibility offered by the job market and was ultimately recognised, as she had hoped for during her years at university. She considered juxtaposing practices of how to engage in the next life stage and successfully accomplished her aspired aim.

However, Sora emphasised that her first job was very stressful. 'You know marketing is a job that you learn while doing. It is difficult when you have to do work that you do not know. Furthermore, I had to work a lot overtime. It is a work that has no end.' Her working hours were scheduled between 10 AM and 7 PM; however, especially when new books were about to be released, she had to work late into the night. Her health got worse, her parents and friends became worried, which placed even more stress on her, and the pay was low, so she decided to resign and rest for some time. Thus, she worked in her first company for no more than one year.

After some time, she found a new job where she was responsible for the online presence of a clinic. There, she received a higher salary and had regular working hours compared to her first job. 'At first, it really was a good job, but after time went by, I started to think. I began to ask myself why I do this kind of work. Am I doing it just because I have to work or simple because of the money? I really lacked confidence [*nŏmu chashini ŏmnŭn kŏeyo*]', she explained and added 'so, I decided to quit this well-paid job and go back to marketing and in looking back, I made the right decision; I am satisfied'. She emphasised that: 'If I would have been interested in the topic of the clinic, then I would have stayed, but I had no interest at all. I quit after one year and two months.'

Sora engaged in critical thoughts about her work. She reflected on and tried to balance the workload, the salary and her health in order to justify her decision to leave her first company, although it was the work she had aspired to. The second job she acquired presented her with a reversed imbalance. Rather than working in the vocational field she aspired to, she was doing a job that did not satisfy her interests. However, she received an adequate salary and worked an acceptable number of hours without overtime. She felt her confidence declining and she decided to resign. She thought again about the person she aspired to be and gave the following self-account: 'Rather than to chase money, I prefer to chase honour [*myŏngye*], so my situation is different.' A third job opportunity balanced and settled her own self-approach. A friend of hers had founded a new company and asked Sora to work for her: 'Now, I have no problems after all and I do my job well. The company is like a family for me.'

When I asked her about her hopes for the future, she considered her work in this company to be important in terms of her future life trajectory: 'The truth is that I developed greed [*yokshim*] for my work. It was different when I was younger, but as I grew older, I have these thoughts.' She smiled and added: 'I had times when I just wanted to quit my work, quickly marry, stay at home and do housework.' Nevertheless, the difficult times passed by and she found herself a stable life in her own way. Her self-worth and the feeling of dignity were important impulses to cultivate the person she aspired to be in relation to her work. 'The main issue for my self-confidence is that I work until the end. If I earn much money or less money, I have to do it until the end', she assured me and added 'it is important for my self-esteem [*chajon'gam*]'.

This process of self-formation becomes clearer in the narratives of yet another young working woman living in Seoul. Jin-kyong, a young woman also aged twenty-seven, was born in Seoul and studied, worked and lived there together with her family. She had finished law school and just started to work in a law firm when I met her for our interview in a coffee shop near her workplace.

Jin-kyong's father worked as a legal practitioner himself and advised his daughter to follow his path because he felt that as a woman, employment as a lawyer would give her advantages. 'Being a lawyer is a very specialised job, because you need not only to study law, but also the licence which allows you to work in this field', she explained. 'Thus, my father told me that it is a stable and secure work for a woman, as the status as working woman in the free economy is insecure and the environment more discriminating.' The discrimination of woman in companies starts with inappropriate questions about their marital status during job interviews, can extend to the exclusion of women from important work tasks and meetings, and is revealed in the glass ceiling women can face during promotion processes, especially when they are to start a family (see also Janelli and Yim 2002).

Jin-kyong decided to follow her father's advice. However, unlike Sora, Jin-kyong was accepted at university through *sushi* (early admission) and decided to study for her master's degree at a graduate school for law, where she studied hard in order to acquire good grades and not fall behind in the competition with her fellow students. 'However, I didn't know if the work was really something I wanted to do until I started to work', she said and smiled. 'Now, I am sure that the work matches my interest and personality.' After her graduation, she immediately found a job in a law firm. 'I assume that my relatively young age was the decisive factor for the head to choose me. Older women tend to get married and gave birth sooner. I guess it was my good grades and my relatively young age', she clarified. Although her father had emphasised that the discrimination against women would be less distinctive in the field of law, during job interviews women still faced unfair conditions.

Yet, Jin-kyong told me later about another factor that was probably key in influencing the trajectory of her career. 'I had many interests in women rights. You know that women who encountered violence are shocked and feel helpless', she said, and added that 'there are centres who counsel women with such experiences in Seoul and I started to volunteer in this field.' 'Before I was allowed to speak with and counsel these women, I had to participate in and successful conclude a 72-hour preparatory course.' She finished that course and worked as a volunteer in diverse places that dedicated and focused their work on the counselling of crime victims. 'Looked at in retrospect, I think that this work was also a reason why I registered in law school and got my job quickly . . . It is also my character.' She reflected that besides her father's advice and objective factors like her grade and age, it was also her character that influenced her career process. 'I am still a newcomer, so I don't know much, but the work is more interesting than I thought.' She smiled and added, 'I feel that people think that the work as a lawyer requires many hours of overtime work and has inhuman working conditions. Further, they think lawyers just see the money. I thought the same to be honest.' However, after she started to work, her perspective changed. 'My colleagues are really nice, they have a good character. They even work without money for clients who cannot afford a counselling', she stated, voicing her respect and emphasising the good character of her coworkers. They made the atmosphere she worked in warm and comfortable, and encouraged her to think about her future: 'When I entered the company, I began to think a lot about what kind of lawyer I want to become and my colleges motivate me, strengthen me in my thoughts.' When we spoke about her hopes concerning her future, she specified these reflections. 'I want to become a lawyer with an area of expertise [chŏnmunbunyaga innŭn pyŏnhosa]. At the moment, I am very interested in women's and worker's rights, but I think it might change when I am really into work', she paused and mused 'I think also about doing my PhD or going abroad to study, but I have not yet decided.'

Jin-kyong discovered that her character matched the profession she had chosen and she aspired to become a skilful lawyer in order to counsel her clients in the best way possible. As in the case of Sora, professionalism meant not necessarily earning much money, but practice, experience and further education – that is, a continuous self-formation. Jin-kyong took her coworkers as guiding examples who encouraged her to think about her future and made her reflect about how a good lawyer should work. The interest that led her to volunteer in counselling centres for women who had experienced violence and injustice continued to hold her attention and ran like a thread through her narratives about her anticipated field of expertise.

Sora and Jin-kyong, each in their own way, formed their selves in accordance with ethical considerations about how they should live. Both reflected on and judged what kind of working women they wanted to become, and held on to values such as respect and care, dignity and motivation not as means to an end, but as an end in themselves. Both found a workplace where they could live in accordance with these values and further engage in their aspirations to become skilled professionals.

Both Sora and Jin-kyong wanted to expand the good life they experienced in their workplace to their lives outside work, and they thought and reflected about their future married lives. Yet, marriage was a dimension where ethical questions became explicit not only in processes of self-formation, but also in processes of negotiation with their parents. Both of them had to find a balance between different aspirations.

Marriage

'Although I am in a marriageable age, I am not yet married. You know, I have just started to work in the law firm and I want to call myself a real lawyer. Thus, I have to work for another two to three years', Jin-kyong explained. 'My parents press me to marry, but I have just started to earn my own money!' I have shown above that she felt her work experience was not yet sufficient to counsel, advice and guide her clients in a manner she perceived as appropriate. A marriage would put yet more constraints and demands on her, preventing her from concentrating on her professional aspirations. In addition, it was the first time that she had earnt her own salary. Enjoying and savouring this moment of independence was very important for her.

The anxious feeling about a marriage also resulted from Jin-kyong's parents being unsatisfied with her partner. As he was still a student, they suggested that she should find a partner already in work so that he could meet the gendered expectations as a provider husband. However, she was very firm in her decision. 'I really have no intention to separate from my boyfriend', she told me. 'Although I fight with my parents, they cannot object to the marriage in the end. It is my marriage and I choose the person I will live with.' She emphasised that her partner was really important to her because he understood her profession. 'My boyfriend understands the speciality of my job as lawyer and he says that he will help me a lot with the housework when we are married.' Jin-kyong and her partner aimed at dissolving the gender roles of provider husband and housewife that conformed to the standards of a middle-class household. Jin-kyong aspired to have both a professional career and a family, and she was very confident about her future with her partner: 'When both of us are working and earning money, then we have to distribute the housework fairly; that has to match I think. I think this way and my boyfriend thinks this way. That is why our married life will go well.'

Although her parents valued a partner with an income, Jin-kyong considered it more important to have a husband who would support her, help her and understand her in her aspirations to become a skilful lawyer. Ethics became explicit as the values her parents saw as important started to conflict with those meaningful for her, and she needed to judge and balance between these different values.

A marriage functions as an important rite of passage that encompasses, first, a change of status to adulthood, second, the possibility for social mobility and, third, a character change (Kendall 1996). Sora emphasised the importance of this life stage in referring to a gate that, once walked through, would make her life more stable, and she wanted to get married rather quickly: 'I don't have the imagination of marrying in any magnificent way, just marry. We have been meeting for three years now, so can't we just introduce each other to our parents and then give one's faith and then just live together?' She paused and added: 'that is what I am thinking. If it is too fast or too slow, if we could just live together that would be great. I hate it when we have to depart in the evening'. She emphasised her wish to live together with her partner: 'I can lead a stable life when we marry, more than I do now. When I come home, there is nobody. If there would be somebody who would care about me and I could care about him. When we would marry, then we would be two and after coming home from work there is somebody.'

Sora aspired to this worldly change in their relationship as she believed it would enhance the quality of their life. However, Sora's parents were against a quick marriage. 'My parents think that I should marry late. They wish that I work a little longer to secure my place in the company and then marry', she said. Later in the interview, she mused that her parents' refusal to accept a marriage might also have to do with her partner's age, as he was several years younger than she was. Further, her partner did not have a white-collar job, which presented an additional problem for her parents. A white-collar worker was the type of person her parents wished her to marry. She herself wanted to live together with this man and imagined starting a family with him, but she accepted her parents' tendency for the time being. The conflicting values nevertheless made her feel uncomfortable; she felt an ethical dilemma in balancing her aspirations with those of her parents, just like Jin-kyong did.

Another aspect in relation to which Sora needed to balance different aspirations was the organisation and arrangements of a wedding ceremony. A proper wedding ceremony was an important middle-class status symbol, yet the social expectations with regard to the form and content of a wedding ceremony often exceeded the financial abilities of the couple.

Arirang TV/ Radio, a South Korean broadcaster designed for an international audience, looked into the financial costs of wedding ceremonies and presented a survey conducted by the Korea Consumer Agency (Park 2013). According to this survey, a bride and groom must pay almost $50,000 each for a wedding. These costs included the wedding location and decorations, the presents and the honeymoon. In times of neolocal residence, these costs increased considerably when renting or buying an apartment. The survey stated that 85% of its participants found the costs for the ceremony far too extravagant, yet decided to submit due to social pressure. Sora clarified the complex situation: 'You know, the focus of a wedding ceremony is not so much the couple, but the family, the parents. The wedding has to be adjusted to their wishes, but I want the wedding according to my partner's and my ideas. I want it simple, but memorable . . . Rather than a hectic wedding hall, I prefer a nice restaurant or a location outside, in the open air. Rather than a borrowed wedding dress, I would like to wear a vintage dress or something handmade.' Concerning their home after marriage, she was quite pragmatic: 'I don't want to purchase the standard house and household appliances for newlyweds; I want to reuse our own things we already have.'

Sora was also very clear about her anticipated life after marriage: 'I want to lead a married life where both rely on each other, understand and respect each other. Even though you lead a married life, you have to grow and secure politeness [yeŭi] and manners [maenŏ].' She paused and added: 'When you marry, you unite each other's life into one and that does not go without creaks. You have to constantly put effort in your married life.'

Sora based her idea of a good married life on an ethical manner of living where both partners needed to enact a continuous process of self-formation. She aspired to a married life based on thoughtfulness and attentiveness from each towards their partner; two lives that would converge into one happily lived.

Conclusion

In this chapter I have followed the narratives of my research participants Sora and Jin-kyong, two young women living and working in contemporary Seoul, to illustrate the diverse aspirations towards a life well lived that members of the Spec-Generation have.

Asking how they constructed their lives in the capital city, I argued that they aspire to lead a 'good life', that is, a life where they can develop their potential and deepen their social relations. I combined the concept of aspiration with the analytical lens of ethics to approach these young women's narratives about the themes of education, work and marriage. These themes are significant issues in a middle-class lifestyle. Being educated at one of Seoul's top-tier universities, working in a conglomerate, getting married and acquiring specific material assets characterise the middle-class status in South Korea. Following Barbara Ehrenreich (1989), I have also stressed that the position of the middle classes is vulnerable because young people must reproduce all the necessary capital by themselves. The term 'Spec-Generation' exemplifies the anxiety that young people in South Korea are no longer able to reproduce this status and the good life associated with it. However, I have suggested that what is referred to as Spec in South Korea are not only qualifications collected or specifications that define a certain middle-class lifestyle, but rather indicate aspirations – both social and personal – based on values that developed over South Korea's complex history. Young Seoulites think about, reflect upon and judge these values, and form their aspirations of a good life in accordance with the meaning they attribute to their practices and, in a broader sense, to the world in which they live.

Aspirations are future-oriented, combining the past and the present in the form of wants, projects and goals to help people find their positions in unknown circumstances. Aspirations form in the 'thick of social life' (Appadurai 2004, 2013) and they are saturated with values and ideals held publicly and shared. Sora and Jin-kyong's accounts illustrate the processes of negotiation and balancing between the values that form middle-class notions about a good life and how the past and present merge to form the future. In their aspirations towards becoming skilled working women and towards their married life, they drew on values of the past – working hard and diligently, and respecting and caring for their partner (see Abelmann 2003;

Janelli and Yim 2002). These values did not constrain them in their own aspirations towards a valuable life, but instead made possible their goals and projects.

While these values show a continuity with the past, a discontinuity became apparent at the same time. Sora and Jin-kyong decided on working paths that were not pursued by most young people, aspired to differences in the form and content of a wedding ceremony, and had contrasting expectations of their partners. When values differed, they needed to engage in processes of negotiation and balancing, which shows the complexity of their practices and thoughts. Situated between care and considerations, their aspirations towards a good life are neither solely about self-interest nor duty; rather, these aspirations are informed by ethical reflections centring on the question of how one should live, revealing the significance of the social relations they grew up in and encounter in their lives, and illustrating the different relational references of aspirations.

Jin-kyong developed her aspirations towards her work by reflecting on her wider social surroundings. She wanted to become a skilled lawyer in order to be able to offer her knowledge to her clients and help them solve their problems. Sora developed her aspiration of becoming a skilled working woman by reflecting on the value of her work. She centred her aspirations around her developing self-respect and self-esteem. Both Jin-kyong and Sora formed their selves in alignment with these reflections and judgements, and built their aspirations into larger ethical ideas about the form and content a good life should have.

Furthermore, Sora's and Jin-kyong's aspirations are also urban aspirations. Appadurai (1996, 2013) stresses that people constantly imagine, produce and maintain locality. The city is a unique location people aim to maintain; yet, it consists of diverse – and often juxtaposing – aspirations and practices of people who are themselves situated in different structures and power relations. Seoul is not only the capital city, but also the economic, political, social and educational centre of South Korea. The importance of Seoul as an educational centre became especially visible in the aspirations of Sora's parents in sending their child to a university in Seoul, and Jin-kyong's education as lawyer further highlights the sophisticated educational infrastructure of the capital city. In addition, their aspirations towards their occupations were also partly made possible through the aspirations to maintain Seoul as an economic centre. For example, Seoul was announced as a UNESCO creative city in 2010 and the so-called cultural industry was envisioned as a new growth engine to advance the metropolis. Although social scientists view such developments critically (e.g., see Oakes and Wang 2016), literature was defined as a central element in these processes offering opportunities for working woman such as Sora.

The personal aspirations of Sora and Jin-kyong developed within a framework of middle-class conceptions of a good life and in an urban context with a dense infrastructure of experts, networks and politics. This chapter is one example of the more general argument made by Westendorp, Remmert and Finis (see their chapters in this volume) that aspirations form part of a framework that emerges in and out of cultural contexts, enabling people to construct a meaningful life. However, the form and content of a meaningful life is pervaded with ethical questions (Fischer 2014). Considering ethical thoughts and reflections about how one should live and how a good life should be constituted contributes to an understanding of how people form their aspirations, how they relate their aspirations to their social matrices and how they develop them in different spatial-time horizons.

Carolin Landgraf is a Ph.D. student, researcher and lecturer currently associated with the Institute of Social and Cultural Anthropology and the Ethnographic Collection, Georg-August-Universität Goettingen, Germany. She has a special interest in economic anthropology and her regional focus is on South Korea. She teaches bachelor's and master's courses, such as economic anthropology, anthropology of youth and ethnographies of East Asia.

Note

1, Pseudonyms have been used for the research participants mentioned in this chapter out of respect for their privacy.

References

Abelmann, Nancy. 2002. 'Women, Mobility and Desire: Narrating Class and Gender in South Korea', in Laurel Kendall (ed.), *Under Construction: The Gendering of Modernity, Class and Consumption in the Republic of Korea*. Honolulu: University of Hawaii Press, pp. 25–53.

———. 2003. *The Melodrama of Mobility: Women, Talk and Class in Contemporary South Korea*. Honolulu: University of Hawaii Press.

Abelmann, Nancy, So Jin Park and Hyunhee Kim. 2013. 'On Their Own: Becoming Cosmopolitan Subjects beyond College in South Korea', in Ann Anagnost, Andrea Arai and Hai Ren (eds), *Global Futures in East Asia: Youth, Nation and the New Economy in Uncertain Times*. Stanford: Stanford University Press, pp. 100–26.

Appadurai, Arjun. 1996. *Modernity at Large: Cultural Dimensions of Globalization*. Minneapolis: University of Minnesota Press.

———. 2004. 'The Capacity to Aspire: Culture and the Terms of Recognition', in Vijayendra Rao and Michael Walton (eds), *Culture and Public Action*. Stanford: Stanford University Press, pp. 59–84.

———. 2013. *The Future as Cultural Fact: Essays on the Global Condition*. London: Verso.

Bucholtz, Mary. 2002. 'Youth and Cultural Practice', *Annual Review of Anthropology* 31: 525–52.

Ehrenreich, Barbara. 1989. *Fear of Falling: The Inner Life of the Middle Class*. New York: Pantheon Books.

Cho, Hae-joang. 2015. 'The Spec Generation Who Can't Say "No": Overeducated and Underemployed Youth in Contemporary South Korea', *Positions: Asia Critique* 23(3): 437–62.

Driscoll, Mark. 2007. 'Debt and Denunciation in Post-Bubble Japan: On the Two Freeters', *Cultural Critique* 65: 164–87.

Durham, Deborah. 2004. 'Disappearing Youth: Youth as a Social Shifter in Botswana', *American Ethnologist* 31(4): 589–605.

Fischer, Edward F. 2014. *The Good Life: Aspirations, Dignity and the Anthropology of Wellbeing*. Stanford: Stanford University Press.

Gray, Kevin. 2008. *Korean Workers and Neoliberal Globalization*. London: Routledge.

Holliday, Ruth, and Joanna Elfving-Hwang. 2012. 'Gender, Globalization and Aesthetic Surgery in South Korea', *Body & Society* 18(2): 58–81.

Janelli, Roger L., and Dawnhee Yim. 2002. 'Gender Construction in the Offices of a South Korean Conglomerate', in Laurel Kendall (ed.), *Under Construction: The Gendering of Modernity, Class and Consumption in the Republic of Korea*. Honolulu: University of Hawaii Press, pp. 115–40.

Keane, Webb. 2015. 'Varieties of Ethical Stances', in Michael Lambek, Veena Das, Didier Fassin and Webb Keane (eds), *Four Lectures on Ethics: Anthropological Perspectives*. Chicago: Hau Books, pp. 127–73.

Kendall, Laurel. 1996. *Getting Married in Korea: Of Gender, Morality and Modernity*. London: University of Chicago Press.

———. 2002. *Under Construction: The Gendering of Modernity, Class and Consumption in the Republic of Korea*. Honolulu: University of Hawai'i Press.

Kong, Tat Yan. 2000. *The Politics of Economic Reform in South Korea: A Fragile Miracle*. London: Routledge.

Lambek, Michael. 2010. 'Introduction', in Michael Lambek (ed.), *Ordinary Ethics: Anthropology, Language and Action*. New York: Fordham University Press, pp. 1–38.

———. 2015. 'Living as if It Matters', in Michael Lambek, Veena Das, Didier Fassin and Webb Keane (eds), *Four Lectures on Ethics: Anthropological Perspectives*. Chicago: Hau Books, pp. 5–52.

Le Peasant, Tanguy. 2011. 'Generational Change and Ethnicity among 1980s-Born Taiwanese', *Journal of Current Chinese Affairs* 40(1): 133–57.

Oakes, Tim, and June Wang. 2016. 'Introduction', in June Wang, Tim Oakes and Yang (eds), *Making Cultural Cities in Asia: Mobility, Assemblage and the Politics of Aspirational Urbanism*. London: Routledge, pp. 1–13.

Park, Jiwon. "Average Korean Wedding Costs nearly $50,000 per Person." *Arirang*. October 23, 2013. http://www.arirang.co.kr/News/News_View.asp?nseq=152471.

Schwenkel, Christina, and Ann Marie Leshkowich. 2012. 'Guest Editors' Introduction: How Is Neoliberalism Good to Think in Vietnam? How Is Vietnam Good to Think Neoliberalism?', *Positions: Asia Critique* 20(2): 377–401.

Song, Jesook. 2009. *South Koreans in the Debt Crisis: The Creation of a Neoliberal Welfare Society*. Durham, NC: Duke University Press.

Wulff, Helena. 1995. 'Introduction: Introducing Youth Culture in Its Own Right: The State of The Art and New Possibilities', in Vered Amit-Talai and Helena Wulff (eds), *Youth Cultures: A Cross-cultural Perspective*. London: Routledge, pp. 1–18.

4

NAVIGATING TOWARDS A 'GOOD FUTURE'

The Significance of Appearance in the Aspirations of Middle-Class Girls in Dhaka

Suborna Camellia

We are now living in a time when our career starts as soon as we are in high school. In addition to do well in our studies, we have to look for opportunities to build networks and skills. For girls, looks play a big role in there. I was part of a selection committee for a youth network. Whenever we used to recruit girl volunteers for our events, looks was the primary criterion. Girls who did not look presentable to us were out during the preliminary selection process.

—Sameera, a seventeen-year-old high school girl, Dhaka

These observations were made by Sameera[1] while I was interviewing her as part of my research, which I conducted among fifteen to nineteen-year-old middle-class girls in Dhaka, the capital of Bangladesh and one of the fastest-growing megacities of Asia. She indicated that appearance has become a central concern for Bangladeshi urban middle-class girls in the context of their aspirations of building a successful career. Sameera came straight from her school for our interview, which took place at a restaurant near her school. I had been expecting to see her in school uniform, but she was wearing a nice maroon tunic over a pair of skinny denim blue jeans. As I looked into her eyes, I saw a trace of eyeliner too. I told her that she looked pretty and she replied with a smile: 'I have been to my friend's place from school who lives right next door. I had to change my uniform

---

Endnotes for this chapter begin on page 88.

and to quickly freshen up. We are meeting for the first time and I didn't want to look exhausted to you. First impression is important, right?' This was pretty much a common experience for me throughout my interviews with the girls. They usually came well dressed, sometimes wearing makeup too. Like Sameera, other participants also mentioned that they wanted to look good in front of me because they saw participating in the interview as part of their networking process. Girls expressed their future plans of going to Western countries for their higher education and thought I could help them in terms of information and advice.

Throughout my conversation with Sameera and other girls, it became very clear that appearance is a central concern in Dhaka middle-class girls' lives against the backdrop of what they consider their 'good future', which they define as having a successful career and becoming an economically independent woman. They are well aware of the high level of competition in the existing labour market and of the gendered expectations that girls have to look good in order to beat the competition. The girls' desire to look good was clearly evident in our conversations. Even a girl who was known as the prettiest girl in her school told me that she wanted to look prettier. Girls who thought they were not pretty and felt shame about their looks said they always try to look 'better' by wearing clothes or makeup that help them to look slimmer, taller, fairer and smart. Others confided that they are sometimes on a strict diet or go to the gym to lose a few pounds. Only a few girls challenged the idea that girls have to look pretty in order to succeed in their career.

Bangladesh is one of the South Asian countries that has experienced significant changes over the last two decades due to rapid urbanisation and economic growth. On 26 March 2018, the United Nations declared that Bangladesh had met the criteria for graduation from the category of LDC (least developed country) to that of a developing country. The middle class is booming in Bangladesh and a significant proportion of them are now affluent and transnationally mobile and are contributing to the global consumer market (Sabur 2010; Karim 2012; Sadique 2013; Khan 2017). A greater number of women now have mobility outside of the home and access to public domains through education and paid employment. While premarital sex remains taboo, there has been a noteworthy shift in marriage norms among the middle class from arranged marriage to love marriage and from early marriage to delayed marriage. Parents only approve of romantic relationships that lead to marriage and do not breach the social code of premarital sex. While girls are still expected to get married, they are no longer expected to get married early; instead, they are also expected to complete their higher education and contribute to the economy. Girls have been steadily attaining better academic results than boys in Secondary School Certificate (SSC) and Higher Secondary Certificate (HSC) exams over the past few years (Islam 2016). How this larger sociocultural shift shapes girls' aspirations to look good and how they experience and deal with at times conflicting and changing demands while navigating towards their future has not yet been explored.

The research questions this chapter seeks to address are as follows: in which ways do girls use looks to negotiate a 'good future' in their specific urbanising, middle-class and gendered environment? What choices do they make and which strategies do they apply and why? Drawing on findings from an ethnographic study, this chapter shows how girls often make careful choices about taking pathways that lead to their envisioned 'good future' and avoid pathways that contradict their dreams. In the process of their navigation, it can be argued that they are reproducing certain ideas of patriarchy by reinforcing the norm that girls have to look a certain way. However, I challenge this view, because it overlooks their everyday struggles of negotiating shame in a very gendered world and does not acknowledge their critical consciousness or political awareness. If I analyse it using an emic perspective, it shows that girls use the aspiration to look attractive as a tool that Appadurai (2013) has called 'navigational capacity', in order to avoid shame and align their choices or strategies towards their broader aspirations of securing a 'good future'.

This chapter contributes to the emerging South Asian feminist scholarship on 'New Womenhood' that defines 'New Women' of South Asia as middle-class, highly educated women who are constantly negotiating and challenging the boundaries of tradition and modernity, culture and religion, local and global and discourses on gender and sexuality (Azim 2010; Hussein 2018). This new strand sees 'New Women' as active agents of their lives, in contrast to how the earlier scholarship viewed South Asian women as trapped between 'tradition' and 'modernity' and as objects upon which traditional rules were inscribed (Talukdar and Linders 2013). The 'New Women' are not a homogeneous category, as they are constantly being constructed at the intersection of gender, class and culture (Hussein 2018). I see these girls as active agents as well as participants in this construction of new womanhood. What I would like to add to this scholarship, based on the findings presented in this chapter, is that the aspiration for good looks is an integral part of this new womanhood for this new generation of middle-class girls in Dhaka. I will also show that these girls do not see themselves as mere victims of body shaming, but as active navigators of shame towards their envisioned 'good future'.

This chapter takes inspiration from Appadurai's concepts of 'aspiration' (2013) and the 'capacity to aspire' (2004). Appadurai argues that one's capacity to aspire depends on one's access to power and resources, which are defined by one's class position in society. Therefore, people from a higher social class have a greater capacity to aspire and thicker navigational maps. In addition to the participants' socioeconomic positioning, this chapter will take into account their gendered position as being 'girls' in a highly patriarchal society, which puts girls at greater risk of encountering shame for transcending social norms regarding sexuality. This chapter will investigate the significance 'looks' have in relation to girls' aspirations for a good future and what kinds of maps they consider and which resources or strategies they use to navigate towards that good future. A key idea of Appadurai's thesis is that aspirations are formed in a continuous process of interaction and negotiation between individuals and their society, which is shaped by larger political or economic factors such as globalisation and urbanisation. Following his lead, I will carefully analyse concrete steps that girls undertake in their everyday lives and will explore which aspects of their social lives shape their individual narratives of choices and decision-making, focusing on class and gender.

The findings presented in this chapter were collected over the period of a year between 2016 and 2017 from thirty-two girls aged between fifteen and nineteen living in Dhaka. Initially, a few participants were recruited from my personal network as well as from online youth networks. The rest were recruited using snowball sampling from various Bangla schools[2] that were known as schools for middle-class children, located in different middle-class neighbourhoods of the city. Anthropological methods, such as in-depth interviews, focus groups and small talk (Driessen and Jansen 2013), were used to ensure an informal atmosphere and to encourage an open conversation. Parental permission was sought prior to interviewing participants who were younger than eighteen years old.

All the participants identified themselves as belonging to the middle class. They generally understood schools, neighbourhoods and lifestyles as the key markers of middle-classness. They defined their middle-class position in opposition to both the 'poor', who live in slums and lack access to basic amenities, and the 'rich', who they saw as those who live in upscale neighbourhoods, study in expensive English schools, wear expensive clothes, own the latest model iPhone or iPad, eat out with friends in high-end restaurants on a regular basis and even spend holidays in Western countries with their parents at least once a year. In response to my questions about what it feels like 'being a middle-class girl', participants commonly referred to their future aspirations of becoming an independent woman, and the privileges and pain they share for being in the 'middle' between the rich and the poor. According to them, they live a better life than the poor; however, they encounter greater pressure than girls from poor or rich backgrounds in relation to upholding their sexual reputation. They thought girls from poor and rich backgrounds have more room to manoeuvre the societal shame about sexuality than they did. 'A poor girl can relocate to another slum or a rich girl to abroad and start a new life there if her sexual reputation is jeopardised', explained one participant during a focus group. Participants pointed out that in Dhaka, the middle class group together in relatively smaller bounded communities in order to cope with the insecurities of city life. Most of their parents are first-generation migrants to the city and therefore have had to work hard to gain a foothold on the social ladder and build their lives together. As will be shown in the rest of this chapter, while girls have relatively greater opportunities to negotiate, they also have to remain cautious not to jeopardise their sexual reputation, which they see as one of the core elements of middle-class girlhood.

The following section is divided into three parts. The first part lays out a brief overview of findings on how girls define 'good future' and the second part summarises girls' responses on the role of physical appearance in their understanding of 'good future'. In the last part, I will present narratives of three girls as examples to show how girls navigate through existing options and choices using physical appearance in relation to their aspirations toward this 'good future'.

Defining 'Good Future'

In response to what girls aspire to as a 'good future', my respondents commonly contrasted their mothers' lives with what they had in mind for themselves. In many cases, they were critical about how their mothers were treated by their fathers and other family members, and shared that they envision a life for themselves that is better than what their mothers experienced:

> The way my father and his relatives treat my mother, seems that she is their slave. If she had a job and earning, they could not treat her like that. (Simi, sixteen years old, in-depth interview)

Simi's father has joint ownership of several cloth stores with his brothers and they all live as a big family unit with fourteen members. Simi was not happy with how her father and other family members treat her mother. Since her mother is a housewife, in addition to taking care of the elderly family members, she has to cook meals for everyone in the family. Simi mentioned that because her mother does not work outside and bring in money, she has to do an unfair share of chores and is denied a respected position in the family. Instead of appreciating the hard work her mother does from dawn to dusk, her father and other family members often criticise her mother for not doing the chores properly. According to Simi, if her mother was a working woman like her two aunts, then things would be different.

During a focus group, I asked participants whether any of them ever considered being a stay-at-home housewife in the future. It took less than a moment for them all to answer 'No' together in a loud and clear voice, while vigorously shaking their heads. Faiza then explained why not:

> We live in a strange society. All the praises go to fathers and blames to mothers. If we achieve good grades father will take all the pride and say 'after all she is my child' and if we fail he will yell at his wife 'do you eat

grass all day at home? Can't you look after what your daughter is doing?' (Faiza, seventeen years old, focus group discussion)

Faiza mentioned – and others agreed – that they want to live a life with dignity and respect (*shonman*) in the future, for which they think economic independence is the only means. They consider Bangladesh as a patriarchal society where women are not given respect and instead have to earn it. Some participants used the word 'purushtontro' (the Bangla word for 'patriarchy') and said that they learnt the word from newspaper articles and TV talk shows.

While speaking with girls who were critical about how their mothers were being treated at home, I tried to understand their perception of marriage in relation to their envisioned 'good future'. Everyone said they wanted to get married and thought good marriage to be an integral part of a good future. Here is an excerpt from my conversation with Neela:

I do think marriage is a beautiful thing and it's a way to build your own family. No one wants to live alone . . . You are married, aren't you? And I guess your marriage is not that bad, otherwise you two wouldn't be together now. See, marriage is not the problem, [the] problem is how husbands and in-laws treat women and it's changing now. You are an independent woman and you are in a happier marriage and if you were not happy, you could have left anytime! (Neela, eighteen years old, small talk)

This quote was drawn from our casual conversation, which took place during a hangout in a rickshaw. Neela was sharing her feelings towards her parents' separation. She shared the above thoughts when I asked her about her opinion on marriage. Despite the fact that she witnessed her mother experiencing mistreatment by her father and other relatives, she did not think marriage was a bad thing. She and other girls did not challenge the notion of marriage, but they clearly challenged the unequal power relations between a husband and a wife. They saw self-reliance through economic independence as the only solution to achieve an equal status quo and a respectful, dignified married life. Participants also mentioned the English word 'companionship' as an important element of happy marriage:

Most of our mothers are housewives and all they can talk about is household affairs [*ghor-shongshar*] and TV serials. If the husband is a scientist, what is he going to talk about with such a wife? Companionship is only possible in equal relationships. (Rupa, seventeen years old, focus group discussion)

Rupa thought that companionship can only exist when both partners are economically and intellectually equal. All seven girls who participated in this particular group discussion agreed that for better communication in marriage, it is important for wives to work outside the home in order to gain a better knowledge of the outside world, which is important for intellectual development.

While talking about their thoughts of a 'good future', some connected the idea of individual wellbeing with notions of the nation's progress. They said that they want to see Bangladesh as a violence-free country where everyone enjoys equal rights (*shoman odhikar*). They thought that in order to turn Bangladesh into such a country, girls collectively need to push boundaries further with their academic and extracurricular success. Participants felt that girls are already making a good progress towards this goal:

> We have already come quite far from our mother's generation. We do not have to face boy child/girl child discrimination within our home anymore. We enjoy the same opportunities our brothers do in terms of education or extracurricular activities. Now our job should be to equip ourselves using these opportunities to make a better world outside home. For that, we have to prove we are no less than boys . . . and we have been beating boys in HSC and SSC exams over the last few years already. (Rohini, seventeen years old, in-depth interview)

Rohini's statement shows how she takes the task upon herself to contribute to a better future for girls in Bangladesh more broadly. She believes that equal opportunities at home have enabled girls to establish an equal, respectable position both at home and outside, and emphasises that all girls should work together towards this.

Linking Physical Appearance with 'Good Future'

> In today's world, competition is so high! One will always remain behind if she does not get noticed . . . and for that, looks is very important. If she looks good, everyone will immediately notice her. If she doesn't, she has to work really hard. (Shutopa, sixteen years old, focus group discussion)

As noted at the start of this chapter, participants made it clear that they are well aware of the high level of competition and the gendered expectation that girls have to look good in order to survive the competition. It has become very important for girls to be visible in the public arena in order to build a network that they see as a pathway to obtaining a successful career. Girls use Facebook for this purpose:

> Women are judged by their looks first, then by their qualities [*Aage dorshondhari por-e goon bichari*]. When I first opened my Facebook account,

I used a beautiful photo of a flower as my profile photo. No one sent me a friend request. Beauty has many benefits, you will get many friends, many likes on your photos if you look pretty. You have more support if you post something online. (Sreya, fifteen years old, in-depth interview)

This fifteen-year-old girl recounted that she had opened her Facebook account when she was twelve years old. She felt uncomfortable and insecure in terms of showing her face to strangers, which is why she chose a photo of a flower as her profile photo. She waited for three weeks, but there were no likes or comments on her photo. Then she took a selfie of just her eyes and set it as her profile photo and this got a few likes. After a month or so, she replaced her profile photo again with one of her full face, which received over a hundred likes. She negotiated her discomfort and fear with her desire to receive likes. Except for two of the girls, all my respondents had Facebook accounts and I was connected with all of them. After talking with the girl quoted above, I checked other participants' Facebook profile photos and found an intriguing pattern. Only a few had used photos of their face as their first profile photo. The rest used photos of landscapes, flowers, birds or leaves and after two to three weeks, they had changed it to either a group photo with friends or family members, or to a selfie that only disclosed partial features of their faces. These later photos received a few more likes than the previous ones. Within a month or two, they replaced these photos with new ones where their faces were clearly visible. These photos received significantly more likes than the previous photos. This shows how girls use their looks to create visibility and claim public space, which is certainly a new phenomenon for the young women of Bangladesh, where traditionally women are discouraged from showing off their looks or socialising with strangers. All the research participants had their own mobile phones with access to the internet. Except for two, all had personal Facebook accounts on which they spent three to four hours every day.

In focus groups and in-depth interviews, girls shared that they post their photos on Facebook not only to build networks, but also to attract boys. Although they do not envision getting married early, they are aware that good looks are beneficial not only for building a successful career, but also for ensuring a good marriage:

For guys, looks are important too, but it's not mandatory for them to look good in order to find a good-looking woman. Do you think anyone will like a female version of Himu? We all have to be like Rupa. (Rima, sixteen years old, in-depth interview)

Here the girl referred to Himu, a popular fictional character in his late twenties created by the Bangladeshi novelist Humayun Ahmed. The character does not care about his looks at all. He does not comb his hair or shave and walks barefoot on the streets[3] of Dhaka. Despite his careless, unorthodox look, girls find Himu very attractive and fall for him easily. With this example, the participant tried to explain the significance of good looks for girls in the marriage market and hinted at the existing gender discrimination against women in society. Men like Himu do not need to be good-looking to attract beautiful women like Rupa. The following section describes how girls use their desire to look good or attractive as their navigational capacity to steer towards their perceived 'good future'.

Navigation towards a 'Good Future'

In this section I will introduce three girls: Dahlia, Ramisha and Lamiya. All of them were born and brought up in Dhaka. I have chosen to present their narratives because they are good examples of the diverse concerns and experiences of girls in relation to their appearance and the desire for a 'good future'. Furthermore, these three stories allow me to provide an in-depth analysis of the different ways in which girls construct 'attractiveness' in their construction of a good future, as well to probe contradictions and ambiguities in their stories about their capacities to aspire to that future. I will begin by recounting each of their stories, followed by an analysis of the key implications in a discussion section.

Dahlia: 'Sexy' and 'Appealing'

To me, beautiful means sexy. There are plenty of girls who have good features, but not necessarily boys will find them all sexy. For example, you know the Bollywood actress Deepika, right? She has a perfect body, perfect face and everything, but still I find Anushka Sharma [another Bollywood actress] prettier, because she is sexy. The way she talks and moves, her body language, her smile, expressions, eyes all are so appealing and so full of life! She is just my dream girl! I wish I could be like her! (Dahlia, seventeen years old, in-depth interview)

Dahlia aspires to achieve a 'sexy' look. To her, Bollywood actress Anushka Sharma is an ideal 'sexy' woman. Anushka is more attractive to her than fellow actress Deepika because she thinks Anushka's body embraces certain behavioural attributes that make her seem more 'appealing' and 'sexy'. Dahlia's understanding of these behaviours as 'appealing' and 'sexy' were shaped in her social interaction with boys. She said that boys often call her 'sexy' and tell her that they find her 'chanchalta' (by this she meant being chatty and behaving silly) to be sexy because it enhances her 'appeal' and 'youthfulness'. Dahlia said that she loves to receive such compliments from boys. She acknowledges that she is not tall and fair-skinned like Anushka, but that she has other qualities: she is thin, has a pretty face and is youthful (*chanchal*).

Dahlia mentioned that her aspirations in relation to her looks have changed over time. She remembers being not very conscious about her looks until the day her ex-boyfriend told her that she was 'too short', 'too dark' and not 'sexy enough' for him. It made her feel 'very low' about her appearance and motivated her to try out different looks and to post selfies on Facebook wearing makeup, red lipstick, trendy haircuts and fashionable and revealing outfits (sleeveless, low-cut tops) with high heels to see whether boys would find her appealing or not. She said that receiving comments like 'you look hot' or 'sexy' has felt rewarding for her ever since, as it boosts her confidence about herself. At the same time, she says that while posting selfies on Facebook, she has to remain careful not to wear clothes that are too revealing in order to avoid being called a 'slut'. She now regularly visits a beauty parlour at least once a month for facials and to get her hair, eyebrows, hands and feet done.

According to Dahlia, having a 'sexy' body is beneficial in order to find a good match, which is important in terms of ensuring a 'good future'. She finds exams boring and hard, and wishes she could quit school and get married. However, she knows that this is not possible because being a housewife is no longer considered a respectable option for young women these days and her parents would be very unhappy if she quit her education:

> Nowadays we have to find our own husband. So you have to have some sort of qualities to attract good guys. I am not a very bright student, although my grades are not that bad, but I am not that super-bright . . . for me, it's easier to use what I have, which is my look. (Dahlia, seventeen years old, in-depth interview)

In this statement Dahlia indicated that arranged marriages are no longer a norm among the middle class. She feels there are two ways of attracting potential grooms: through attaining academic success or through being beautiful. Being the only daughter of a doctor father, she said that she feels guilty for not being good enough to get into a medical school. She mentioned that she has a plan in mind to compensate for this and to make her parents happy in the future by finding a husband who is a doctor. According to her, doctor-grooms are in high demand among middle-class women in Bangladesh and therefore she has to prepare herself well to win that competition by finishing her education and nurturing her 'sexy' look.

Ramisha: 'Confident' and 'Change Maker'

> I want to look intelligent because I find intelligent girls the most beautiful. The confidence they have on their faces, in their gestures and postures, makes them even more beautiful than someone who is physically prettier.

My favourite woman is Joyeeta, the main character of the novel *Gorbhodharini*.[4] She looks so sharp and intelligent, she does not look 'meyeli' [feminine], does not wear any makeup at all . . . rather, she dresses like boys, hangs out with boys, scores top grades in her class. She is fearless, rebellious and dreams to be a change-maker of the society. I want to be someone like her. (Ramisha, sixteen years old, in-depth interview)

Drawing on the example of Joyeeta, a young woman in her early twenties who did not believe in gender binaries and proved in the novel that a young woman can be as robust and resilient as a man, Ramisha mentioned that she wants to look 'confident' and 'intelligent'. She thinks an intelligent and confident look is essential to succeed in a career and be a 'change-maker' in society. She feels that the position of women needs to be changed and believes that girls have the capacity to do so with their academic and extracurricular success.

Ramisha thinks her aspiration of attaining an intelligent, confident look came from witnessing her mother suffering from emotional and social pain due to her unhappy married life. Seeing her mother, she realises that being beautiful did not help her to find happiness. Against the backdrop of high divorce rates and marital violence, she thinks it is time that girls shift their goals from 'being beautiful' to being 'independent' and 'successful' through pursuing education and other skills development activities. She thinks that there has been a significant transition from the past and that girls nowadays have far more opportunities to consider themselves as 'equal' to boys, to compete with them and to surpass them:

Girls who wear a lot of makeup lack confidence . . . and wait for Prince Charming to come and rescue them from their cage. I find these girls absolutely empty-headed, pea-brained. Why would you need a prince to rescue you and restore your confidence when you can do it yourself? We are not living in the eighteenth century anymore. Neither do we live in cages anymore. We are allowed to step out and educate ourselves. I think these girls are actually the lazy ones. It's a lot easier to put on makeup and attract boys than to compete with them and achieve equal success in education or in extracurricular activities. (Ramisha, sixteen years old, in-depth interview)

Ramisha stated that she recognises marriage as an important marker for securing a 'good future' and that wearing makeup and looking feminine are important in order to attract a suitable husband. However, she thinks she is too young to worry about this now and does not see any point in investing time and energy in being physically beautiful at this moment. As such, she has made a strategic choice to invest in developing her intelligence because, to her, the job market is highly competitive and she feels she does not have much time to waste. The only spare time she gets after finishing all her homework and other extracurricular educational activities, such as participating in quiz competitions or science festivals, she spends working for an organisation to earn some extra pocket money.

In response to my question about whether she does anything to look 'confident', Ramisha replied that she avoids wearing makeup and tries to keep a neat and natural look to give others the impression that she is confident about her features. She stated that her friends often call her 'pichchi'[5] (kiddo), which she thinks is a big obstacle to her attaining a 'confident' image among her peers. She follows certain strategies so that she looks a little older than her actual age, such as keeping her hair long or occasionally posting selfies or photos of herself wearing a *saree* (traditional clothing usually worn by adult women). While she wants to look older, she mentioned that at the same time, she does not want to look too old like a *khalamma* (aunt). Her fear of looking like a *khalamma* comes from her high-prescription eyeglasses and she takes them off when taking selfies or photos or while attending special events such as wedding parties, even though she hardly can see without them.

Ramisha also said that in order to look 'intelligent', she keeps herself well informed about current affairs and shows others her awareness by initiating or actively taking part in conversations about these issues. She spoke of how she also exhibits her interests through participating in academic and extracurricular activities and competitions. In addition, she joins protests and speaks up about social issues, for instance, regarding violence against girls and women. She mentioned that photos showing her participating in various protest demonstrations have been in the newspapers a couple of times already.

Lamiya: The 'Cool' Girl

Lamiya, a sixteen-year-old high school girl, did not explicitly talk about her aspirations in relation to physical appearance. She thought she did not have the 'privileges' of aspiring to obtain certain looks, but rather that her vulnerabilities led her to embrace a rebellious 'cool-girl' image; someone who smokes cigarettes in public, wears boys' clothing and mingles with boys. She said that she smokes not because she likes the taste of it, but because holding a cigarette gives her a great sense of power, which she thinks has helped her to fight the trauma that she experienced two years earlier. She said that back then, she used to be a 'very girly' person and was considered one of the 'hottest' girls in her class (she later explained that by 'hot', she meant having a pretty face and good body, slim but with curves). Her image completely changed from the moment her best friend made public a sexual Facebook conversation between Lamiya and her boyfriend, which had included a semi-nude photo of her:

People just could not take 'too much hotness' of me [she said, trying to sound cynical] . . . Since that very moment, from a 'hot girl' I became a 'slut'. Everyone started calling me 'khawa' [leftover food, already eaten by someone else]. Our seniors [girls] began pointing their fingers at me, 'look at her boobs and bum. She looks like a *khalamma* [older women like aunts]. Must be doing this [referred to sexual intercourse] for ages!' I stopped eating because I wanted to become thin, so thin that my boobs and bum cannot be seen and had to go to hospital twice because I became so weak. (Lamiya, sixteen years old, in-depth interview)

Lamiya mentioned that she suffered tremendous anxiety thinking of what would happen if her parents found out that she had been sexually active. She attempted to commit suicide several times. She thinks that being part of a combined family unit heightened her anxiety since all her extended family members from her father's side lived under the same roof and so it would have been too shameful for her and her parents if anyone found out. She said that she had stopped going to school for almost two months and that her parents were OK with this since she was unwell and as the doctor had suggested a break from school to get some rest. During this period, she thought she would never be able to face going back to school and started finding alternative ways to get out of this situation and keep pursuing her future goal of being independent. She looked for an organisation that could teach her other skills so that she could still secure a job in future. She contacted an organisation through the internet and through them was introduced to a group of young photographers, boys and girls between eighteen and twenty years old, who all belonged to affluent, well-to-do families. All of them went to English middle schools and some of them were from very influential families (social and political elites). They lent her a camera and she began to join different photography projects with them, which she found helped her to improve her mental state considerably. After two months, she started going to school again, although not on a very regular basis. She was spending most of her time with the photographers. She began copying other girls in the group and started wearing jeans and t-shirts instead of a *kameez*,[6] smoking cigarettes and using *galis* (slang or rude terms) that are usually only used by men and boys in Bangladeshi middle-class society. Together they organised a couple of street photo exhibitions, which received coverage in newspapers and on television. After six months, she was in regular attendance at school again. By that time, she was already famous and had obtained multiple awards as a young photographer. She still maintains her friendship with this new group of friends because it gives her social protection. No one dares to say anything bad to her at school anymore because they know she is now very well connected with an elite group or because she has upper-class friends:

That's how I got my reputation back. I had to change my look, I am well accepted in my school again, but they see me in a very different way now! I went back to my school, made a handful of good friends who really think I am 'cool' . . . Somehow I now became one of the 'coolest', 'free-spirited' girls to them. (Lamiya, sixteen years old, in-depth interview)

Lamiya thought that none of this would have been possible if her parents had found out about the Facebook conversation between her and her boyfriend. Lamiya and her parents live quite far from her school and therefore they do not get to socialise with other parents or students. She considered herself lucky for that. When I asked her whether she smokes in front of her parents, her response was:

Are you crazy! They will kick me out of home. I don't do it in front of my family or teachers. In front of them, I am a very pleasant, normal, *bhodro meye* [modest girl], but as you see now I am a *beyadob* [arrogant, boastful], *oogro* [antisocial], *obhodro meye* [immodest] to all of them [indicating other people around us in the restaurant]. (Lamiya, sixteen years old, in-depth interview)

Lamiya mentioned that she might change her physical appearance in the future after she gets into a university. She said that she might go back to a 'normal girl' image, the one she used to have before, being 'girly' and 'hot'. She expressed her desire of having a 'normal life' in university and that she thought this 'cool' image, particularly smoking cigarettes and wearing jeans, might pose a problem for her, given her social and economic background and coming from a middle-class family. By 'normal life', she meant a life that will make her family proud, one with a decent career and a good husband.

Discussion

New Girlhood

The findings presented in this chapter reiterate what Chowdhury (2018) has pointed out about the Bangladeshi new womanhood. She suggested that contemporary constructions of the Bangladeshi *new woman* are shaped by discourses of development and modernisation processes that rely on the logic of neocolonial capitalism, such as the notion of women's empowerment through education and entry into the labour market. However, what I would like to add based on my closer analysis of the findings presented in the previous section is that it is a two-way process. Girls are shaping these discourses too. Inclusion of certain phrases often used by nongovernmental organisations (NGOs), such as *shoman odhikar* (equal rights), *purushtontro* (patriarchy), 'career', 'economic freedom' or 'change maker' do show the influence of development discourses in their everyday conversations. They did not understand these concepts as empty concepts; instead, they located them in their real lives, reflected on them and co-constructed their meanings. Their understanding of unequal rights or patriarchy are shaped by witnessing their mothers living a dependent, vulnerable life within marriage and their own experience of encountering societal gendered expectations. I want to argue that they are embracing social changes because they want those transformations to come and hence are actively shaping them by participating in that process.

My research findings demonstrate a remarkable consensus in terms of how all these girls share their broader goal of living a violence-free, dignified life and how they were consistent on this point throughout our conversations. The findings presented above show that the girls notably have critical capacities and political consciousness in relation to issues on gender, patriarchy and rights. They skilfully unpacked the power relations using their observations about their everyday social encounters. The final subsection shows how girls make strategic choices to get what they think will lead them towards their desired 'good future'.

Navigational Strategies: Reconstructing the Boundaries of Feminine Respectability

The findings indicate that in the face of these emerging ideas of womanhood, girls constantly encounter societal expectations that are contradictory. They are expected to find their own marital partner while remaining a virgin until they are married. On the one hand, girls are expected to attain an 'equal' status, while on the other hand, they are expected to follow the imposed norms of virginity and sexual modesty. Parents want them to remain sexually innocent, yet among their peers, 'sexy', 'hot' looks are desirable as these help to draw people's attention – something girls consider crucial in their competitive world. However, 'too much' hotness or sexiness can jeopardise a girl's reputation among her peers. Girls' aspirations are shaped within these very contradictory notions of feminine respectabilities. As will be discussed below, they have to carefully navigate through their available options and reconcile all these clashing ideas.

In the narratives of three girls, we see them making strategic choices in order to steer towards their aspirations. Dahlia's choices to invest in her beauty – that is, going to beauty parlours and wearing makeup – come from her desire to find a good husband in the future. She chooses to stick to her 'sexy', 'appealing' looks as she fears that she might not have a great, successful career ahead of her. She reflects on her capacity and makes these strategic choices in the hope that her looks will help her secure a good marriage. Dahlia actively seeks out opportunities to exhibit her 'appeal' to others, particularly to boys, and she remains careful of avoiding cultural repercussions of being 'too sexy'. She uses Facebook and posts her photos in order to uphold her 'sexy' image, but she remains cautious of not looking 'too sexy' or 'slutty' by avoiding wearing clothes that are too revealing.

Unlike Dahlia, Ramisha dissociates 'ideal beauty', although temporarily, from the social norms of looking pretty and feminine. She is aware that the job market is highly competitive and that she needs to use all her time and energy effectively to achieve her aspiration of becoming an independent, successful woman. She is also aware of gender inequalities and issues such as violence against girls and women in society, seeing academic and career success as instrumental in achieving equality and a violence-free life. Her strong belief that she has the capacity to reach her aspiration is the main driving force that keeps her going, which emerges from her access to education, extracurricular activities and mobility outside her home. She sees these opportunities as resources and tries to make the most of them by scoring top grades in exams, participating in various academic, social and political activities, and claiming her place in public spaces through joining protests and being part of the news. She decides to invest in attaining a 'confident' look because she thinks that at her age she should now focus on building her career. She sees the social transformation of early marriage into delayed marriage as another opportunity that gives her leeway to set aside the thought of gaining a feminine, beautiful body for now and invest all her time and energy in building her future career.

Lamiya's responses reflect her overarching aspiration of securing a respectable position in society. She juggles between different 'ideal bodies', depending on the context. For instance, when she is at home, she becomes a 'normal', 'modest' girl, and when she is with her peers or in public places, she becomes the 'cool' girl. Unlike Ramisha, she did not draw hierarchies between different bodies; instead, she constructed and embraced multiple bodies in order to conform to social norms and fight the stigma she experienced and to restore her respectable position in society. This latter aspiration led her to go out and seek alternative strategies and techniques in order to get her out of a difficult situation. She created a completely new social network, one that was stronger than the previous one since members of this new network belong to the 'elite' section of society. Using her membership of this network, she created a new 'cool' appearance, participated in and won photography contests, and made news headlines, thus successfully restoring her to a respected position in her own previous middle-class network.

All three narratives clearly show that these girls are not merely passive recipients of the societal prescriptions about feminine respectability; rather, they are active agents in the construction of these. Both Dahlia and Lamiya have experimented with their bodily presentations after their bodies became objectified by boyfriends and peers respectively. They have found their ways out of shame by reinventing and reconstructing their looks, transforming them from 'simple' to 'sexy' or from 'hot' to 'cool'. This also shows that they saw 'attractiveness' as temporal notions that are subject to change based on how they experience them socially and emotionally.

All these findings demonstrate that adolescent girls' navigational capacity is very much linked to their location in the social hierarchy, which shapes their access to resources such as beauty parlours, education or photography clubs. Dahlia's ability to go to a beauty parlour to change her look and her access to Facebook to post selfies of her new 'trendy' look helped her to overcome her feeling of shame. Similarly, Lamiya's access to the photography club is very much linked with her access to the upper-class group, through which she could overcome her earlier trauma and remove the stigma associated with this. I argue that capacity to aspire is embedded in one's class position. This supports Appadurai's (2004) claim that better-off people have 'thicker' and clearer maps, with more options and more certain routes that help them to better navigate towards their desired goals. All three girls have a relatively clear idea about their aspiration. They have made careful choices of strategies and were able to implement them. However, findings caution that this may not always be the case and the following section will explain the reasons why this is so.

Navigational Challenges: Risks of Losing One's Reputation, and Fierce Competition over Limited Resources

Although these girls demonstrated clear ideas about their aspirations and their abilities in terms of making strategic choices to negotiate boundaries of feminine respectability, based on the findings presented here, I argue that it posed certain challenges for them too. All three narratives reveal that whatever choices these girls make must be made within certain boundaries – boundaries that are gendered. Girls can express and practise their individuality, but only within the boundaries of what is deemed to be socially acceptable. Girls position their bodies between certain categories that are socially defined, such as 'sexy' and 'too sexy', between 'pichchi' (kiddo) and 'khalamma' (aunt), 'cool' and 'oogro' (antisocial). Ramisha mentioned that while Joyeeta's gender-neutral look is what she perceives as an ideal beauty and what she dreams to practise, in reality she has to curb her desire more towards what is accepted in broader society. This is reflected in her choices of posting photos on Facebook to replace her image of 'pichchi', while simultaneously being cautious of not looking too old like a 'khalamma'.

These findings suggest that the boundaries between these categories are thin and therefore can easily be transgressed. On the one hand, this offers opportunities to reach their aspirations of being attractive and deal with shame and, on the other hand, it poses great risks for girls to lose their reputation and be considered a 'slut' within moments. Lamiya's story is an example of this. Her experience of crossing the boundary between 'hot' and 'too hot' caused her tremendous anxiety and social exclusion. She survived and could fight her stigma successfully because fortunately her parents did not know about the Facebook message that had exposed her to ridicule. If they had found out, she probably never would have been allowed to step outside her home without being escorted by her parents and would not have joined the photography group that has proven so influential and life transforming for her. Middle-class society in Dhaka is a relatively conservative and bounded, closed space and therefore the fear of shame is higher. A few studies that have conceptualised girls beyond the 'victim' category suggest that girls in Dhaka slums have relatively higher capacities to avoid shame about premarital sex. An ethnography conducted among 153 young women in Dhaka slums found that an unmarried girl can get pregnant without losing face and can get the man to marry her with support from her neighbours and community leaders if her socioeconomic status is higher than that of the man. The study also shows that many girls elope and get married without their parents' approval (Rashid 2006). Another study found that since slums provide anonymity to women, it is easier for them to hide their past marital history and to relocate and remarry without facing stigma (Jesmin and Salway 2000). These findings can help us to understand the vulnerabilities that middle-class girls experience. Although they have better access to material resources than those who belong to a lower socioeconomic group, middle-class girls might also suffer from a higher level of stigma.

There is another set of challenges I see in the narratives presented here, which results from the very notion of the 'New Womanhood'. While this idea does sound liberating, it can also be experienced as a restrictive phenomenon in real life. These three girls seem to have relatively increasing levels of control over their lives, but they use this control to scrutinise and regulate their bodies in order to attain standards of modern, independent, successful womanhood. Their aspirations of seeking respect through becoming one of these Bangladeshi New Women is not easy to attain, considering the growing competition over scarce resources and the social pressure to reach it.

Conclusion

This chapter sheds lights on the links between young women and Bangladesh's sociocultural transformation, and shows that aspirations for good looks constitute an important element of the construction of a 'new girlhood' among Bangladeshi middle-class girls. Girls use their looks and set them to work as a navigational capacity to deal with shame and stigma, and attempt to sail towards what they perceive as a 'good future'. This chapter has unpacked the ambiguities of middle-class feminine respectability and the thin line between respect and shame that girls must carefully navigate. While middle-class girls have the capacities to draw specific maps in their mind of where to go or how to get there and can make strategic choices using the resources and skills available to them, they have more to lose if they transgress that line. This chapter highlights the unique vulnerabilities that Dhaka middle-class girls experience in the face of urbanisation and a fast-changing sociotechnological realm. It argues that belonging to a higher socioeconomic group does not necessarily mean a girl will have higher capacities to implement her navigational plans. The capacities are determined by a combination of one's class position, gender, age, sexual norms, the sociocultural significance of marriage, as well as modernised discourses of women's empowerment.

Suborna Camellia is a cultural anthropologist by training and a researcher at BRAC James P. Grant School of Public Health, BRAC University, Bangladesh. She has a long track record in conducting ethnographic research on sexuality, sexual and reproductive health, and gender-based violence in the context of Bangladesh. Her areas of interest include innovative qualitative research methods, the urban middle class and youth. She is also a doctoral researcher at Radboud Gender & Diversity Studies, Radboud University, the Netherlands.

Notes

1. Pseudonyms have been used for the research participants mentioned in this chapter out of respect for their privacy.
2. Bangla schools follow the national curriculum and use the local Bangla language as the instruction medium, whereas English schools mostly follow the British Cambridge curriculum and teach in English.
3. Walking barefoot on the street in Bangladesh is considered inappropriate for middle- and upper-class people. Only extremely poor people who cannot afford buying shoes walk barefoot.
4. A Bangla novel written by Samaresh Majumdar, a popular Indian Kolkata-based writer. It is a story of a powerful friendship between four youngsters who dream of changing society into an equal society free of gender and class discrimination.
5. In my conversations with Ramisha and other girls, it was clear that they perceive words such as *khalamma* or *picchi* as derogatory terms. When someone is called *picchi*, this refers to an underdeveloped body, considered too thin and without curves. On the other hand, *khalamma* implies a girl whose body is thought to look too old and to be in bad shape (as though she already is married with children).
6. A long tunic worn by girls/women in South Asia, typically with a *salwar* (loose pants) and *orna* (long scarf).

References

Appadurai, Arjun. 2004. 'The Capacity to Aspire: Culture and the Terms of Recognition', in Vijayendra Rao and Michael Walton (eds), *Culture and Public Action*. Stanford: Stanford University Press, pp. 59–84.
——. 2013. *The Future as Cultural Fact: Essays on the Global Condition*. London: Verso.

Azim, Firdous. 2002. 'Women and Freedom', *Inter-Asia Cultural Studies* 3(3): 395–405.

——. 2007. 'Women and Religion in Bangladesh: New Paths. Open Democracy', *open-Democracy*. Retrieved April 2020 from https://www.opendemocracy.net/en/wom en_and_religion_in_bangladesh_new_paths/

Azim, F. (2010) 'The New 21st Century Women', in Azim, F. and Sultan, M. (eds.) *Mapping Women's Empowerment: Experiences from Bangladesh, India and Pakistan.* Dhaka: BDI and UPL, pp. 261–278.

Chowdhury, Elora H. 2018. 'Made in Bangladesh: The Romance of the New Woman', in Nazia Hussein (ed.), *Rethinking New Womanhood.* London: Palgrave Macmillan, pp. 1–22.

Driessen, Henk, and Willy Jansen. 2013. 'The Hard Work of Small Talk in Ethnographic Fieldwork', *Journal of Anthropological Research* 69(2): 249–63.

Glaser, Barney G., and Anselm L. Strauss. 1967. *The Discovery of Grounded Theory.* Chicago: Aldine.

Hussein, Nazia. 2018. 'Introduction', in Nazia Hussein (ed.), *Rethinking New Womanhood.* London: Palgrave Macmillan, pp. 1–22.

Islam, Shahidul. 2016. 'Girls Outperform Boys in GPA-5, Pass Rate in PEC, JSC Examinations', *bdnews24.com*, 30 December. Retrieved 20 March 2020 from https://bdnews24.com/bangladesh/2016/12/30/girls-outperform-boys-in-gpa-5-pass-rate-in-pec-jsc-examinations.

Jesmin, Sonia, and Sarah Salway. 2000. 'Policy Arena. Marital among the Urban Poor of Dhaka: Instability and Uncertainty', *Journal of International Development* 12: 698–705.

Karim, Shuchi. 2012. 'Living Sexualities: Negotiating Heteronormativity in Middle-Class Bangladesh', Ph.D. dissertation. The Hague: International Institute of Social Studies of Erasmus University (ISS).

——. 2018. 'Heterosexual Profession, Lesbian Practices: How Sex Workers' Sexuality Right Positions through Intersection of Sexuality, Gender and Class within the Hierarchy of LGBT Activism in Bangladesh', in Nazia Hussein (ed.), *Rethinking New Womanhood.* London: Palgrave Macmillan, pp. 189–210.

Khan, Shahiduzzaman. 2017. 'Burgeoning Growth of the Middle Class', *Financial Express*, 22 November. Retrieved 20 March 2020 from https://thefinancialexpress .com.bd/views/burgeoning-growth-of-the-middle-class-1511362584.

Rashid, Sabina Faiz. 2006. 'Small Powers, Little Choice: Contextualising Reproductive and Sexual Rights in Slums in Bangladesh', *IDS Bulletin* 37(5): 69–76.

Sabur, Seuty. 2010. 'Mobility through Affinal Relations: Bangladeshi "Middle-Class", Transnational Immigrants and Networking', Ph.D. dissertation. Singapore: National University of Singapore.

Sadique, Mahfuz. 2013. 'Uniqlo Looks to Cash in on Bangladesh's Middle-Class', *BBC News*, 12 July. Retrieved 20 March 2020 from http://www.bbc.co.uk/news/ business-23222484.

Stavropoulou, Maria, Rachel Marcus, Emma Rezel, Nandini Gupta-Archer and Caroline Noland. 2017. *Adolescent Girls' Capabilities in Bangladesh: The State of the Evidence.* London: Sage.

Talukdar, Jaita, and Annulla Linders. 2013. 'Gender, Class Aspirations and Emerging Fields of Body Work in Urban India', *Qualitative Sociology* 36(1): 101–23.

5

SEARCHING FOR A FULFILLING LIFE

Temporary Migration to Dublin amongst Young Japanese Women

Ayako Suzuki

It's not because I wasn't content with my life or that I felt uncomfortable living in Japan . . . I needed to leave Japan because I had done everything I had wanted to try there . . . I wanted to try something different in my life.
—Ayaka, twenty-seven years old, working holiday maker

On a sunny October afternoon, Ayaka[1] and I sat in a café in Dublin. Ayaka was a 27-year-old working holiday maker who had been living in the city for seven months at that time. Looking back on when Ayaka had left for Dublin, she explained to me that her reason for coming to Dublin was more of an attempt to seek various life opportunities than career or economic advancement. She was one of the Japanese women whom I met during my fieldwork in Dublin. Just as she desired to make a change in her life, the women with whom I spent time expressed their longing for life-changing experiences and self-development abroad. Ayaka's above statement epitomises their pervasive sense of the uncertainty of life and their resistance to leading an expected life course, as well as their eagerness to pursue self-interest. These attitudes were translated into the practices of going abroad to leading a fulfilling life. Yet, what is 'a fulfilling life'?

The term *ikigai*, literally meaning 'a life worth living', denotes one's personal sense of satisfaction and an evaluation of life courses (Kanda 2011: 114–16). The discourse of *ikigai* started to surface in the late 1960s (Kanda 2011: 111–12).

Endnotes for this chapter begin on page 105.

From the 1980s, it began to take on a greater significance, particularly in the lives of Japanese youth (Kato 2010: 49). In accordance with Japan's postwar economic development, a shift has been detected in the ways that Japanese people seek life orientation and their *ikigai*. Japan's economic affluence has not only made the pursuit of people's own lifestyles and *ikigai* possible beyond work and family, but may also be seen as having imposed upon individuals a task of seeking self-realisation. Today, how does the pursuit of self-realisation intersect with migration practices? While unpacking a growing trend of temporary migration amongst Japanese young adults, this chapter reveals ways in which they navigated their personal desires and the middle-class discourses of femininity. This examination of their narratives argues for the significance that aspirations played in their migration processes.

The ideals of social roles and middle-class life pathways of Japanese women have been constructed and forged through Japanese political and historical trajectories. The primary social roles of Japanese women and their personal satisfaction have been thought to be embedded within the realm of *uchi* – home/inside. Rooted in Confucianism and the elite samurai-class during the Tokugawa Shogunate (1603–1868), an *ie* (family) system, promulgated under the Meiji Civil Code in 1898, defined the values of a patriarchal familial structure, thereby identifying women's social positions primarily in domestic roles (Ronald and Alexy 2011: 1). From the late 1890s, the expected contribution of women to the *ie* developed together with the ideology of a 'good wife, wise mother' (Lowy 2007: 4). The 'good wife, wife mother' ideology was the ideal of Japanese women's education in prewar Japan. This ideology recognised women's responsibilities for the *ie* and by extension to the nation-state in order to strengthen the military nation (Senno 1998: 687). Gendered roles delineated through Japan's modernisation and industrialisation processes have become consolidated in the course of Japan's postwar social and economic transformations.

The idea of women's domesticity being fundamental to their gender identity is reflected in the emergence of the term '*sengyō shufu*' (full-time housewife). Through the postwar industrialisation process, a gendered division in social roles has been articulated, designating men as the 'salaryman' (salaried male workers), being the breadwinner of the households, and women as the *sengyō shufu*, with the responsibility for household chores and childrearing (Dasgupta 2010: 192; Hidaka 2010: 2–3). Although women's participation in the workforce increased throughout the immediate postwar period, women were mainly to be found in the temporary workforce, as it was assumed that the working life of women would be interrupted by marriage and childrearing and in becoming a *sengyō shufu* (Roberts 1994; Ueno 1987).

It was during the 1970s that a life as the *sengyō shufu* came to represent the middle-class ideal of womanhood as a result of the government incentives to consolidate the institutions of family and company (Aronsson 2015: 39). Therefore, a clear gender division of labour, together with women's limited white-collar career prospects, served as the background to the formation of the ideals of middle-class women's life course. Moreover, in accordance with Japan's economic growth, the idea of Japanese society as '*ichioku sōchūryū*', literally meaning 'one million mass middle-class', had become prevalent since the late 1960s (Clammer 2001: 118). The construction of the *sengyō shufu* lifestyle model and the idea of a class-free society therefore informs the achievement of a common sense of nationhood and mainstream consciousness, leading to the ideals of stability regarding life courses and gendered roles.

However, in recent years, the mainstream life course underpinned by these gendered ideals has been resisted by Japanese youth. The internationalisation that Japan started to experience in the 1980s has served to expedite women's increased participation in the workforce and educational opportunities. For many women, this has contributed towards a self-oriented and career-seeking lifestyle, as well as comparatively later marriage (Kelsky 2001: 2–3). These resulting changes in lifestyle demonstrate a shifting focus from women engaging in roles associated with the conceptual *uchi* domain to acquiring roles beyond it.

Young people have also become responsive to diversified lifestyle choices. The more individualised and flexible lifestyles that they have come to embrace are significantly attributed to the prolonged economic recession following the 1990s collapse of the economic bubble. Changes in employment structures have resulted in an increase in the number of youth falling outside of regular employment. This has brought about a growing ambiguity in relation to their job prospects and future outlook (Cassegård 2014; Genda 2005; Matsumiya 2006). In a time when one's life trajectory and identification have become increasingly deregulated and privatised, it is individuals who are imbued with responsibilities for managing the risks and opportunities of life, as well as achieving an appropriate lifestyle (Bauman 2000: 32; Giddens 1991: 78). It is within this context that individuals seek an *ikigai*. For instance, the rhetoric of *ikigai* is heavily employed in Japanese retirement migration, which is seen as a way of achieving a desirable and meaningful lifestyle (Ono 2014: 16). Seeking the fulfilment of the self has become an individual quest.

The propensity of people to shape their own life paths and identities is also informed by the phenomenon of lifestyle migration. The conceptual framework of lifestyle migration proposed by Benson and O'Reilly (2009: 609) encompasses a set of migration practices among the affluent middle classes who are driven to move in an effort to pursue a better quality of life in a society other than their own. Lifestyle migration approaches migration discourses in a way that transcends the classical notions of migration and other forms of mobility, particularly of tourism, and reconsiders class-based analyses of migration. This individual quest for an improved quality of life, stretched across the international arena, is fundamentally driven not by the search for economic benefits, but for self-development and self-exploration. Discourses of the pursuit of self-interest, freedom and self-searching entailed in lifestyle migration reveal affluent individuals' migration practices. Such an ongoing quest for self-fulfilment is equated with what Giddens terms 'the reflexive project of the self', reflecting one's ongoing processes of 'becoming' (Giddens 1991: 75; see also Bauman 1997: 25).

With this in mind, the type of migration that contemporary Japanese youth practise has increasingly become associated with the search for a sense of individuality, self-fulfilment and a rewarding life elsewhere. Their journeys involving a process of self-remaking might well allow them to redefine their life orientation and may lead them to a lifestyle that is more personally appropriate. However, what is it that influences their decision to migrate and how does aspiration play out in their migration experiences? This chapter examines the intimate intersection of aspirations involved in the initial stage of migration practices amongst middle-class Japanese women. Research into how migration is undertaken by middle-class people with the privilege of being able to move and who are at an age during which adult roles may be attained and stabilised provides an insight into the role that aspiration plays in this growing trend of lifestyle migration.

Japanese Contemporary Migration

Previous studies on the outflows of Japanese youth in the context of postwar Japan have been predominantly analysed in terms of students, in particular single women from urban upper-middle-class backgrounds who aim at enhancing their cultural capital through Western higher education (Andressen and Kumagai 1996; Habu 2000; Ichimoto 2004; Matsui 1995). Simultaneously, studies recognise that these women's underlying motives for educational opportunities are closely intertwined with the desire to be freed from the gendered expectations placed on Japanese women. It is often the case that student mobility is utilised by those who experienced gender constraints.

Correspondingly, the phenomenon of youth travelling overseas outside of student mobility has become prominent. As represented by working holiday makers, those who travel through avenues other than degree programmes are not always engaged in employment or education in the destination society. Work by Fujita (2009) and Kawashima (2012) relates such mobile youths' migration experiences that might lead to a better way of life abroad. Labelled as 'spiritual migrants' by Sato (1993), 'cultural migrants' by Fujita (2009) or 'lifestyle migrants' by Nagatomo (2015) and Benson and O'Reilly (2009), there has been a tendency amongst youth to search for independent lives beyond material and financial affluence and in a society other their own. The underlying implications of youth travelling in the form of nonuniversity students and as working holiday makers can therefore be seen to inform an important intersection of migration and the desire for freedom and self-fulfilment.

Imaginations of Lifestyle and Migration Destination

The desire for freedom from what a person feels to be a constraint and the wish to live abroad is intimately correlated with cultural imaginings of particular places as offering a better lifestyle (Benson and Osbaldiston 2014: 3). Individuals' aspirations for a better lifestyle work elsewhere in conjunction with a critical reflection on their current lifestyles and social norms (Griffiths and Maile 2014: 147–48; Kurotani 2007: 22–23).

Common to such individuals' decision-making about migration is the assumption that migration is a practical solution to their sense of predicament and a means of obtaining an appropriate work-life balance (Benson and Osbaldiston 2014: 3). Narratives of lifestyle migration encompass a broad scope of motives and destinations. These include aspiring to a life in a rural idyll or small town (Benson 2011, 2014; Hoey 2005; Vannini and Taggart 2014) or to a bohemian lifestyle (Korpela 2009, 2014), escaping from an urbanised capitalist society (Oliver and O'Reilly 2010) or desiring to experience cultural richness in major global cities such as Berlin (Griffiths and Maile 2014). In this regard, particular destinations embed a desire for what the individual thinks of as an authentic and better way of life (Benson and Osbaldiston 2014: 9). Conventionally, migration trajectories are predominantly shaped through ancestral and cultural links between the societies of origin and destination (Wilson, Fisher and Moore 2010) or through kinship and/or friendship networks (Limpangog 2013; White 2010). However, the mobility paths that my informants undertook in their journeys to Dublin underline the significance of the roles that imaginings of a particular place and lifestyle play.

In recent years, an increase has been noted in the transient global flows of Japanese youth. In particular, the working-holiday scheme that has now grown to apply to twenty-six countries and regions is undertaken as a popular means of youth migration; this is due to it having fewer restrictions on employment and study than student visas (Japan Association for Working Holiday Makers n.d.). The working-holiday scheme with Ireland that started in 2007 has proved conducive to a steady stream of youth travelling to Ireland. This is reflected in the increase in the number of young Japanese travelling to Ireland, rising from 165 in 2010 to 248 in 2013 (Ministry of Foreign Affairs of Japan n.d.).

Having said that, socioeconomic relations between Japan and Ireland have not had a great influence on either society. Although postwar Japanese migration has been predominantly characterised as Western-bound, the 2017 statistics show that Ireland ranks eleventh among European countries and thirty-sixth among foreign countries as a place of destination, with 2,316 Japanese nationals residing in the country (Ministry of Foreign Affairs of Japan 2018). In comparison to other English-speaking counties such as the United States, Canada, Australia and the United Kingdom, Ireland is seen as a less popular educational and working-holiday destination. Unlike global cities like London, where lifestyle migrants are able to benefit from abundant economic opportunities (Conradson and Latham 2005), Ireland is not regarded as an attractive destination for career opportunities or permanent settlement. Also, as cultural contact with Ireland is critically scarce, Ireland inevitably falls into the overarching cultural construction of 'the West'.

Cultural imaginations play an important part in facilitating the migration processes of individuals seeking a better and freer lifestyle. Scholars (Appadurai 1996, 2001; Fujita 2009; Nagatomo 2015; Salazar 2014) recognise the mass media as a medium through which socially circulated imaginaries of a particular destination may be constructed. Appadurai's (1996) concept of mediascapes points to the roles that the mass media play in creating imaginations that influence the individual's social life; through such imaginings, certain visions of self and lifestyle are socially constructed and desired. Similarly, de L'Estoile (2014: S64) argues that expectations are not merely reflective of personal desires, but are shaped within life conditions and by the expectations of others. Aspirations that mediate socially formed expectations and imaginations are therefore an important element in understanding migration processes. Simultaneously, aspirations for a particular lifestyle, I argue, inevitably involve the processes of transforming the self. As Boccagni (2017) claims, the orientation of the future that is articulated in aspirations equates to remaking the self. This process of transforming the self is reliant on discarding existing roles and gaining new ones.

In the construction of the shared imaginations of cultures, a perception of the West as culturally superior has continued to inform Japan's long-term engagement with the West throughout its modernisation processes. A migration trajectory to a city in a Western country embeds such a desire for Western lifestyles. This prevalent view of Western countries has often become a rationale for Japanese youths' decision to travel to Western destinations such as London and New York (Fujita 2009), as well as Canada (Kato 2010) and Australia (Andressen and Kumagai 1996; Sato 2001). With this in mind, Ireland – as part of the West – is imagined as offering positive characteristics necessary for self-advancement. Thus, despite being a relatively minor migration destination for the Japanese, Ireland is situated as a social space through which an individual may access a Western modernity and thereby accumulate cultural capital.

This chapter draws on data collected from fieldwork carried out in 2010–11. In order to access potential informants, I identified as a social space a 'Japan-Ireland Social Group' where mobile young Japanese gathered to socialise. I frequented these weekly gatherings and through them, I developed my research. My empirical data was primarily gathered through participant observation and semi-structured interviews with twenty-seven women. My informants were single women aged between twenty-five and forty who had travelled to Dublin on temporary visas; they consisted of work permit holders, working holiday makers, language students and university or college students. Apart from three informants, they were all from middle-class families. The Japanese middle class is by no means a homogeneous group. While class is defined in relation to socioeconomic status on the basis of income, occupation and cultural capital, the enlarged middle strata is partly underpinned by a subjective ascription of class (Kanbayashi 2013). Therefore, class identification does not merely signify individuals' actual socio-economic status, but also a particular consciousness that reflects one's sense of belonging in society (Olwig 2007: 88–90). Therefore, their self-identification as having a middle-class status that also reflects homogenising lifestyles and an equal sense of place in Japanese society needs to be taken into account. Their educational levels were relatively homogeneous: apart from four informants who had entered the workforce following the completion of high school and two after vocational college, my informants had received or were in the process of receiving higher education. The majority of them (twenty people) had been engaged in white-collar jobs and therefore had financial security prior to their relocation to Dublin.

In the following sections, with an emphasis on the initial stage of their migration experiences, I will introduce two representative narratives of Japanese women: Ayaka and Aoi. Whilst my informants cited varying rationales for their travel to Dublin, my ethnographic data elicits two major tendencies regarding their motivation: there were those who had travelled out of a growing sense of frustration about gendered expectations of Japanese women and a resistance to pursuing an expected life course; and there were those who had moved with a tangible objective of career aspiration. These rationales were intricately intertwined with each other. The migration trajectories of Ayaka and Aoi juxtapose the aspirations of other women who had a desire for self-growth and freedom, even if temporarily. By ethnographically exploring the narratives of these two women, I will discuss the ways in which gendered and familial expectations and their personal aspirations mediated migration processes.

Ayaka: Eager for New Challenges

Ayaka, the informant who I introduced at the outset of this chapter, was from a middle-class family and had grown up in the Tokyo metropolitan area. Because her father lived separately from her family following the relocation of his job,

Ayaka formed very strong bonds with her mother. Having seen her mother, a *sengyō shufu* who committed herself to her family in order to raise her children, this naturally developed into Ayaka's own idealised image of womanhood. Yet even while holding hopes of marrying and being like her mother at some stage in life, Ayaka simultaneously desired to be independent: 'If I hadn't been strong enough to yearn for independence, I would already have been married in Japan.' She articulated the idea that marriage would provide not only financial and emotional security but also a women's sense of belonging in society.

Ayaka's job at the airline company and previous career in the service sector required English language skills. Although she felt comfortable using English in the workplace, the sense of accomplishment that she attained through work had facilitated her desire to further improve her English abilities and to realise her dream of living abroad. Ayaka's cross-cultural contact began with an experience of her family hosting an Irish student. Ever since then, she developed an interest going abroad and learning English. Seeing her peers getting married, she had decided to take on new challenges in Dublin. Her wish to carve out an independent and more fulfilling life had also been emotionally supported by her mother, who had wanted her to become an international person.

In Dublin, Ayaka was working as an au pair. In exchange for her work she obtained first-hand life experiences in an English-speaking country, a small salary and free accommodation. Caring for children was irrelevant to her previous career; nonetheless, Ayaka seemed content with what she had been experiencing in Dublin: 'I don't mind looking after children. I love children and the kids I'm taking care of are very adorable. Experience is what counts. I wanted to try anything new.'

Aoi: For a Change of Profession

Aoi, another of my informants, was a 36-year-old student from Osaka. She paid her first visit to Ireland in 2001 with an Irish friend. A life-changing experience happened to her in a village there. She recalled:

> All my life I lived in an urban setting, in my home as well as in Tokyo to work for seven years. I had never lived in the country before. So I was very frustrated by the rural environment of Tipperary in the beginning . . . There was electricity in the home [her friend's house] but no electric cooker. Burning turf and placing a cast iron plate in the fireplace, they cooked all of their meals over two hours. The open fire provided all of their home's energy needs. On top of that, food waste was used as a fodder for cattle. They lived a self-sufficient life.

Intrigued by this eye-opening experience of rural life, Aoi had visited Ireland over the following seven years and started to develop an emotional affinity with Irish culture. Simultaneously, it had made her question the work-oriented lifestyle she had been accustomed to. She explained:

> I started to feel differently about what I was doing with my life in Japan. My work always kept me very busy; usually, it required me to stay as late as 10 pm or 11 pm in the office, sometimes to sleep overnight during a hectic job. I worked as a systems engineer for eight years, but I wasn't confident that I could continue that lifestyle for another twenty years. I wanted a job that would allow me to face human beings, not a computer screen.

A feeling of job insecurity, combined with the Irish experiences that she had encountered, gradually developed into Aoi's aspiration to find an alternative life for herself in Dublin. This involved a career shift to becoming a qualified tour coordinator. For Aoi, it was not only a rural idyll that represented a Western quality of life, but also a freer exchange of views she had found there that she embraced. When asked how she felt living in Dublin, she responded:

> Living in Ireland helps me feel less pressure from society than in Japan, in the sense that people here are open to differing views. So it feels like Ireland offers a place for free expression . . . I was always told that I was not Japanese enough [*nihonjinppokunai*] while living in Japan. People said as much, perhaps because I was always outspoken and made myself clear so that they thought of me as a self-assertive person. But Japanese people living here don't fear expressing their own opinions. I find this level of communication very comfortable.

However, Aoi's experience in Dublin had not always gone smoothly. She did not hide her conflicting feelings about the gap between her expected lifestyle in Dublin and the realities of her own life. Due to the cancellation of a business course she had wanted to attend and the bankruptcy of another business school in which she had enrolled, she could not study as she had wished to. Instead, she sought a means to survive in Dublin to give herself more time. Luckily, she succeeded in finding full-time employment just at the point at which she had almost resigned herself to returning to Osaka. However, she had to capitalise on her engineering skills. Simultaneously, she admitted to missing her mother, stating: 'I feel very conflicted because I won't be able to meet my *okan* [mum] for a little while more.' Also, her life in Dublin was akin to her busy life in Japan. Aoi saw Dublin as not 'authentically Irish' in the sense that it was a consumer society, which was not to her liking. Being trapped between her ideal and the reality, she juggled her studies and jobs in order to try and achieve her career goals before her visa expired.

Motivations for Leaving Japan

Career Aspiration and a Resistance to Expected Life Courses

Apart from university students, all of my informants had at least a few years of working experience prior to their relocation to Dublin. Thus, they had financial independence and resources that enabled them to make a new start there. The desire of my informants to travel to Dublin significantly intersected with various sorts of constraints that they had felt in Japan and the desire to overcome an impasse in their lives. Previous studies relate the outflows of the Japanese to various impetuses, such as the desire for cultural opportunities (Fujita 2009), for a career change and English-language acquisition (Kato 2010) and for a more desirable lifestyle (Nagatomo 2015). More importantly, however, these studies acknowledge the underlying aspiration for self-transformation in a foreign country. In line with these works, my informants' decisions to leave Japan had been made with a view to establishing a new and fulfilling lifestyle abroad. My empirical data recognise that, as we saw with Ayaka's and Aoi's narratives, their desire to travel to Dublin was in part motivated by anticipation of a career change. This attitude is also reflected in Otone's narratives. Otone, the oldest informant aged forty, was studying in order to realise her dream of becoming a professional holistic therapist. Ever since she had paid her first visit to Ireland in 2003 to attend an English language school, she periodically had come back to Ireland. She had drifted from job to job. Whilst none of the jobs that she had held required any English skills, she had developed a vague desire to live abroad, learn English and have vocational skills. Eventually, she realised her dream. Thus, the desire for a career shift was evidently a factor in their motivations to leave Japan. They resorted to temporary migration when faced with the sense of stagnation arising from their career prospects.

Simultaneously, there was a tendency that my informants' migration was a form of resistance against leading an expected life course framed by career stability. As exemplified by Ayaka's resistance to the secure and normative life path that her peers had taken, many of my informants had interrupted their careers, some quite promising, in order to travel to Dublin. Common amongst these informants was the fact that they embraced a high level of flexibility in their working life. Instead of valuing a stable life and seeking career advancement in Japan, they sought new life opportunities in Dublin. In these instances, their migration experiences were fraught with uncertainties without a clear picture of how a life in Dublin would alter their life paths. Nevertheless, with an emphasis on the importance of owning their own lives, they left the mainstream career treadmill.

Gendered Expectations

Another tendency relating to my informants' motivations to travel to Dublin was closely linked to issues of marriage. As we saw in Ayaka's narratives, marital status was identified as a primary source of women's identity and sense of belonging in Japanese society. The ideals of womanhood shaped around 'marriage and child-bearing' (Goldstein-Gidoni 2012: 205) were evidently embodied by my informants. Indeed, there is an indication that women's international travel and the sense of failing to meet the dominant ideals of womanhood – i.e. as unmarried, divorcees or widows – are likely to act on each other (Thang, Sone and Toyota 2012: 250). Hiromi's example was a case in point. Hiromi, a 37-year-old single woman, noted:

> By my late twenties, I found myself to be the only singleton left in my group of friends. Everybody was married and I had no one to hang out with because they were so occupied with family affairs. So I was left with no choice but to go somewhere on my own during the holidays. I started travelling abroad alone and the more I went overseas, the more I wanted to stay there.

With the difficulty in identifying a sense of belonging with her work or society where her singlehood served to develop a sense of being a misfit, Hiromi had embarked on a journey to Dublin on a working-holiday visa. Similarly, Megumi at the age of thirty-four, had arrived at Dublin via the United Kingdom to volunteer in providing care for the disabled. Feeling overwhelmed during her messy divorce, she had started to yearn for a new start somewhere else. Going overseas and volunteering was her long-held interest. The divorce processes had affected her whole family. However, they had been supportive of her decision to make a new start elsewhere.

The family is considered to be an important social establishment through which to enact an individual's life orientation. Nevertheless, the decision of my informants to travel to Dublin underlined their desire to extricate themselves from the roles associated with the family and the ideals of womanhood. Embodying the idea that a women's sense of belonging essentially lay in the stability of the roles associated with marriage, single women like my informants felt isolated in Japanese society. Their escaping to what they imagined to be a better lifestyle illuminated their pressure to conform to the pervasive expectations around marriage. From this example, it could be argued that the escapism entailed in the practice of migration constitutes an important part of the narratives of aspirations. For my informants who embodied the idea of *sengyō shufu* as the middle-class ideal of womanhood, imagining a different lifestyle through the act of migration was understood as a form of deviance. While seeing themselves as deviating from the middle-class ideal life course, they pursued a more fulfilling life abroad. A noteworthy fact is that while they struggled to navigate through career, gendered ideals and their personal desires, this process did not essentially involve negotiations with their family members; their decision-making was entirely a voluntary choice. The women I interviewed were financially independent and self-reliant. Although in most cases their decisions were supported by their families, the ways in which they attempted to pursue their own way of life beyond social relationships in Japan represented the kind of privatised and individualised life choices Japanese youth embrace today.

Why Ireland?

There were cases in which my informants chose Ireland, as with Ayaka and Aoi, as the result of their previous cultural contacts with Ireland or interests in music, Irish literature, dance or the arts. In such cases, the women's interests in Ireland stemmed from their education, hobbies, friends and/or first-hand experiences with Irish people. However, it was often the case that these women started off their lives in Dublin with little knowledge of the destination society and without any prior contacts. My informants referred to a diverse array of incentives that Ireland could offer. For Kaori, another working holiday maker, Ireland seemed to be an affordable place in which to live and its rich nature was appealing. Mai, a university student stressed that she and her parents shared the idea of a perceived lack of safety in the United States, which made it an unattractive place in which to live and that Europe was their preferred destination for cultural advancement and respect for tradition. What was also prominent amongst the narratives recounted by my informants was that many of them, particularly the working holiday makers, had chosen Ireland as an alternative destination because of a failure to obtain a UK visa. Moreover, the smaller number of Japanese residents in Ireland was greatly appreciated and seen as being beneficial to English-language acquisition.

Whilst my informants offered a diverse range of reasons for choosing Ireland, the fact that the country is recognised as being located in Western Europe was a common frame of reference in their decision-making. Ireland was largely subsumed into the overarching cultural construction of 'the West'. In fact, it was common for my informants to have had various cross-cultural experiences prior to their move to Dublin, ranging from short-term study abroad to previous working holidays to travelling overseas. Their previous cultural access was predominantly limited to regions in North America and Oceania. Therefore, Europe, let alone Ireland, was a new social context for many of them. In this context, the informants' aspiration towards Europe was cited with reference to cultural diversity, tradition and even the physical characteristics of Westerners themselves. In line with the Japanese public perception of Europe that is closely associated with tradition (White 1992; Fujita 2009) and of the West in general as models of a superior social state (Morris-Suzuki 1998), an assumption was made that Western cities, particularly in Europe, would accommodate cultural diversity. Making contact with Westerners in cosmopolitan environments was therefore seen by my informants as being of great benefit in their accumulation of cultural capital. Their embedded ambiguous images of the West and Ireland deriving from TV programmes, brochures, advertisements and even advice from study-abroad agencies turned into positive imaginings, leading to an image of Ireland as a 'good country', to quote Kaori. Ireland thus became a site of the informants' migration desires. Simultaneously, Ireland – and by extension the West – was imagined as offering a freer lifestyle without being bound by the straitjacket of Japanese normative societal and gender expectations (Kelsky 2001; Habu 2000; White 2003). My informants yearned to carve out a freer and more fulfilling life in Dublin by discarding their existing roles.

A New Life in Dublin

Since reality and ideal are not the same, their first-hand life experiences in Ireland often resulted in demythicising their embedded positive images of Ireland and desired lifestyles. Despite this, they attempted to make the most of their stay. This was particularly because the timeframe was imposed by visa requirements. These women's desire for freedom and self-transformation was directly tied to the proliferation of cultural capital. In their postmigration phase, these women actively engaged in a wide range of new activities, such as learning English, gaining work experience, making foreign friends, travelling around Europe and gaining knowledge of Western mannerisms, which were perceived as contributing to their accumulation of cultural capital.

One such activity was gaining new roles through employment. Because they travelled with the adequate financial resources that they had accumulated in Japan, these women did not find themselves needing to find employment immediately in Dublin. Nevertheless, the majority of them strove to find employment in the hope of improving their English and expanding their social networks beyond Japanese ones. Although eighteen women managed to obtain part-time jobs in most cases, the jobs that they held were in the service sectors – typically jobs at Japanese restaurants and shops, Irish pubs and hostels. Low-skilled jobs in which the women engaged were not perceived as beneficial to career advancement, but rather were undertaken out of a desire to try out new experiences for the broader purpose of 'searching for a fulfilling life abroad', as seen in Ayaka's case. In fact, apart from two of the women who expressed their desire for a change of profession, career advancement through migration was not a major motive for my informants. This tendency distinctively contrasts with migration decisions centred on career development and upward mobility, as revealed in previous studies on Japanese migrants (Kelsky 2001, 2008; Mizukami 2007). Although this propensity was intertwined with the migration processes of several informants to some degree, the desire to improve their career prospects was essentially absent in the narratives of my informants.

Moreover, learning English was crucial to transforming themselves into an international person. Whilst English proficiency has been recognised as a requisite factor for women's upward mobility (Kelsky 2001: 101), all my informants shared the idea that improving their English might not directly open up their career opportunities, but would definitely be a way of gaining a broader perspective and connecting with the outside world of *uchi*. All the activities that they had not had the opportunity to undertake while in Japan were regarded as an important part of a Western-quality lifestyle and thereby as adding to their cultural capital. Simultaneously, it is important to stress that there was a pervasive expectation that they would not be able to capitalise on their Irish experiences in terms of their improved social status or an immediate financial return. It was clear that the cultural capital that they attempted to accumulate was not intended to be transferrable to other forms of capital. Increased financial capital or social status did not necessarily fit their definition of self-fulfilment. For them, their quest for a new way of life in Dublin per se represented a process of finding an *ikigai*. In this understanding, their self-development was achieved only in the fleeting freedom of living in a foreign country. What they aspired to have, in this sense, was a temporal attempt of self-transformation that was a separation from the realities of Japan.

Conclusion

Aspirations involve a future-oriented activity. As Strathern (2005: 51) acknowledges, 'people's actions are all the time informed by possible words which are not yet realized' and imagining the future in the present serves to facilitate practices. In the case of my informants, aspirations shaped through expectations and cultural imaginations facilitated moves of migration. Certainly, while the capacity to aspire, as discussed in the Introduction in this volume, is not exclusive to a particular social class, the capacity to realise these aspirations is subject to 'access to economic resources and powers of symbolic legitimation, neither of which are distributed equitably' (Smith 2006: 54). Within structures mediating individuals' personal aspirations, my informants' quest for self-realisation was made through their privileged access to various forms of capital. In view of this, class privilege entailed in lifestyle migration per se represents that aspirations are structural. Simultaneously, however, aspirations are individual, acting on agency.

The narratives of the women with whom I spoke articulated various constraints from which they wished to free themselves; the decisions to travel to Dublin were intricately linked to constraints created around work and marriage in Japan. The notion of leading a seemingly secure yet regular life course was challenged by them. Moreover, social pressures to conform to the expected roles pertaining to marriage also shaped their decision to migrate. In line with previous studies on Japanese women's migration that address the interrelationship between migration and social expectations about women's domesticity (Andressen and Kumagai 1996; Habu 2000; Kato 2010; Matsui 1995; Mizukami 2007; Nagatomo 2015), my data support the claim that women's constraints were primarily entangled with fulfilling the roles in the *uchi* (home/inside) sphere. It was clear that my informants had bought into the middle-class ideal of a woman's lifestyle as an important point of reference for designing their lives. Their inability to meet or resistance to meeting the expectations imposed by various social establishments turned into a drive to break free from the status quo. In this respect, migration was exercised in a way that allowed them to achieve self-realisation.

A yearning for freedom was evidently a central theme to their migration narratives, as addressed in the body of lifestyle migration scholarship (Griffiths and Maile 2014; Korpela 2014). The desire to be freed from social expectations and an expected life course was achieved by these women placing themselves outside the web of social relationships that existed in Japan. However, this form of freedom is essentially fraught with uncertainties and risks. Indeed, migration does not always lead to upward mobility, but inherently involves the risk of downward mobility and losing social security (Korpela 2014: 40). In contrast to those who value social capital as a way to cope with uncertainties and risks (de L'Estoile 2014), my informants instead attempted to shake off their existing roles and social relationships, and prioritised freedom and challenges. Their flexible lifestyle choices, as represented by their career interruptions, inevitably added to the uncertainties of their future outlook. In this understanding, the imaginings of a particular self and lifestyle in the West did not always lead to positive transformations in life. Their narratives of the desire for self-transformation encapsulated in escapism indicate that there is a need to consider not only the positive but also the resulting negative dimensions of analysis in the notion of aspirations.

Ayako Suzuki is a part-time lecturer at Chuo University in Tokyo, Japan. She is the author of 'Young Japanese Men's Transnational Mobility: A Case Study in

Dublin', *Asian Anthropology* (2015). Her fields of interest include lifestyle migration, youth migration, mobility, identity, gender and nationalism.

Note

1. Pseudonyms have been used for the research participants mentioned in this chapter out of respect for their privacy.

References

Andressen, Curtis A., and Keichi Kumagai. 1996. *Escape from Affluence: Japanese Students in Australia*. Brisbane: Griffith University.

Appadurai, Arjun. 1996. *Modernity at Large: Cultural Dimensions of Globalization*. Minneapolis: University of Minnesota Press.

——. 2001. 'Grassroots Globalization and the Research Imagination', in Arjun Appadurai (ed.), *Globalization*. Durham, NC: Duke University Press, pp. 1–21.

Aronsson, Anne S. 2015. *Career Women in Contemporary Japan*. London: Routledge.

Bauman, Zygmunt. 1997. *Postmodernity and Its Discontents*. Cambridge: Polity Press.

——. 2000. *Liquid Modernity*. Cambridge: Polity Press.

Benson, Michaela. 2011. *The British in Rural France: Lifestyle Migration and the Ongoing Quest for a Better Way of Life*. Manchester: Manchester University Press.

——. 2014. 'Negotiating Privilege in and through Lifestyle Migration', in Michaela Benson and Nick Osbaldiston (eds), *Understanding Lifestyle Migration: Theoretical Approaches to Migration and the Quest for a Better Way of Life*. Basingstoke: Palgrave Macmillan, pp. 47–68.

Benson, Michaela, and Karen O'Reilly. 2009. 'Migration and the Search for a Better Way of Life: A Critical Exploration of Lifestyle Migration', *Sociological Review* 57(4): 608–25. doi:10.1111/j.1467-954X.2009.01864.x.

Benson, Michaela, and Nick Osbaldiston. 2014. 'New Horizons in Lifestyle Migration Research: Theorising Movement, Settlement and the Search for a Better Way of Life', in Michaela Benson and Nick Osbaldiston (eds), *Understanding Lifestyle Migration: Theoretical Approaches to Migration and the Quest for a Better Way of Life*. Basingstoke: Palgrave Macmillan, pp. 1–23.

Boccagni, Paolo. 2017. 'Aspirations and the Subjective Future of Migration: Comparing Views and Desires of the "Time Ahead" through the Narratives of Immigrant Domestic Workers', *Comparative Migration Studies* 5(1): 1–18. https://doi.org/10.1186/s40878-016-0047-6.

Cassegård, Carl. 2014. *Youth Movements, Trauma and Alternative Space in Contemporary Japan*. Leiden: Brill.

Clammer, John R. 2001. *Japan and Its Others: Globalization, Difference and the Critique of Modernity*. Melbourne: Trans Pacific Press.

Conradson, David, and Alan Latham. 2005. 'Friendship, Networks and Transnationality in a World City: Antipodean Transmigrants in London', *Journal of Ethnic and Migration Studies* 31(2): 287–305. doi:10.1080/1369183042000339936.

Dasgupta, Romit. 2010. 'Performing Masculinities?: The "Salaryman" at Work and Play', *Japanese Studies* 20(2): 189–200. https://doi.org/10.1080/713683779.

De L'Estoile, Benoit. 2014. 'Money Is Good, But a Friend Is Better', *Current Anthropology* 55(S9): S62–S73. https://doi.org/10.1086/676068.

Fujita, Yuiko. 2009. *Cultural Migrants from Japan: Youth, Media and Migration in New York and London*. Lanham, MD: Lexington Books.

Genda, Yuji. 2005. *A Nagging Sense of Job Insecurity: The New Reality Facing Japanese Youth*. Tokyo: International House of Japan.

Giddens, Anthony. 1991. *Modernity and Self-Identity: Self and Society in the Late Modern Age*. Cambridge: Polity Press.

Goldstein-Gidoni, Ofra. 2012. *Housewives of Japan: An Ethnography of Real Lives and Consumerized Domesticity*. New York: Palgrave Macmillan.

Griffiths, David, and Stella Maile. 2014. 'Britons in Berlin: Imagined Cityscapes, Affective Encounters and the Cultivation of the Self', in Michaela Benson and Nick Osbaldiston (eds), *Understanding Lifestyle Migration: Theoretical Approaches to Migration and the Quest for a Better Way of Life*. Basingstoke: Palgrave Macmillan, pp. 139–59.

Habu, Toshie. 2000. 'The Irony of Globalisation: The Experience of Japanese Women in British Higher Education', *Higher Education* 39: 43–66. doi:10.1023/A:1003807009463.

Hidaka, Tomoko. 2010. *Salaryman Masculinity: The Continuity of and Change in the Hegemonic Masculinity in Japan across Three Generations*. Leiden: Brill.

Hoey, Brian A. 2005. 'From Pi to Pie: Moral Narratives of Noneconomic Migration and Starting over in the Postindustrial Midwest', *Journal of Contemporary Ethnography* 34(5): 586–624. doi:10.1177/0891241605279016.

Ichimoto, Takae. 2004. 'Ambivalent "Selves" in Transition: A Case Study of Japanese Women Studying in Australian Universities', *Journal of Intercultural Studies* 25(3): 247–69. doi:10.1080/0725686042000315759.

Japan Association for Working Holiday Makers. n.d. 'System of Working Holiday', Retrieved 20 March 2020 from https://www.jawhm.or.jp/system.html.

Kanda, Nobuhiko. 2011. 'Concept of "Ikigai" (1): Interpreting Thinking Regarding "Ikigai" from the Meiji Period to End of World War II', *Living Science Institute Bukyo University* 33: 111–22.

Kanbayashi, Hiroshi. 2013. 'Yoku wakaranaikara 'chū nanoka: Kizoku kaisō handan no shukanteki seikakuseki no kentō' ('Self-Rated Accuracy of Status Identification: A Preliminary Study'), *Faculty of Liberal Arts Review, Tohoku Gakuin University* 164: 1–20.

Kato, Etsuko. 2010. 'True Self, True Work: Gendered Searching for Self and Work among Japanese Migrants in Vancouver, Canada', *Japanese Review of Cultural Anthropology* 11: 47–66. https://doi.org/10.14890/jrca.11.0_47.

Kawashima, Kumiko. 2012. 'Becoming Asian in Australia: Migration and a Shift in Gender Relations among Young Japanese', *Intersections: Gender and Sexuality in Asia and the Pacific* 31: 1–10.

Kelsky, Karen. 2001. *Women on the Verge: Japanese Women, Western Dreams*. Durham, NC: Duke University Press.

———. 2008. 'Gender, Modernity and Eroticized Internationalism in Japan', in David B. Willis and Stephen Murphy-Shigematu (eds), *Transcultural Japan: At the Borderlands of Race, Gender and Identity*. London: Routledge, pp. 86–109.

Korpela, Mari. 2009. 'When a Trip to Adulthood Become a Lifestyle: Western Lifestyle Migrants in Varanasi, India', in Michaela Benson and Karen O'Reilly (eds), *Lifestyle Migration: Expectations, Aspirations and Experiences*. Farnham: Ashgate, pp. 15–30.

———. 2014. 'Lifestyle of Freedom? Individualism and Lifestyle Migration', in Michaela Benson and Nick Osbaldiston (eds), *Understanding Lifestyle Migration: Theoretical Approaches to Migration and the Quest for a Better Way of Life*. Basingstoke: Palgrave Macmillan, pp. 27–46.

Kurotani, Sawa. 2007. 'Middle-Class Japanese Housewives and the Experience of Transnational Mobility', in Vered Amit (ed), *Going First Class?: New Approaches to Privileged Travel and Movement*. New York: Berghahn Books, pp. 15–32.

Limpangog, Cirila P. 2013. 'Migration as a Strategy for Maintaining a Middle-Class Identity: The Case of Professional Filipino Women in Melbourne', *ASEAS* 6: 307–29. http://dx.doi.org/10.4232/10.ASEAS-6.2-5.

Lowy, Dina. 2007. *The Japanese 'New Woman': Images of Gender and Modernity*. New Brunswick, NJ: Rutgers University Press.

Matsui, Machiko. 1995. 'Gender Role Perceptions of Japanese and Chinese Female Students in American Universities', *Comparative Education Review* 39(3): 356–78. https://doi.org/10.1086/447327.

Matsumiya, Kenichi. 2006. *Furītā Hyōryū: Nihon no Wakamono no Gonin ni Hitori ga Furītā dato Iwareteiru* (*Drifting Freeter: One out of Every Five Japanese Youth is a Freeter*). Tokyo: Junpōsha.

Ministry of Foreign Affairs of Japan. 2018. 'Annual Report of Statistics on Japanese Nationals Overseas'. Retrieved 20 March 2020 from https://www.mofa.go.jp/mofaj/files/000368753.pdf.

———. n.d. 'Basic Information about Ireland'. Retrieved 20 March 2020 from http://www.mofa.go.jp/mofaj/area/ireland/data.html#section5.

Mizukami, Tetsuo. 2007. *The Sojourner Community: Japanese Migration and Residency in Australia*. Leiden: Brill.

Morris-Suzuki, Tessa. 1998. *Re-inventing Japan: Time, Space, Nation, Japan in the Modern World*. Armonk: M.E. Sharpe.

Nagatomo, Jun. 2015. *Migration as Transnational Leisure: The Japanese Lifestyle Migrants in Australia*. Leiden: Brill.

Oliver, Caroline, and Karen O'Reilly. 2010. 'A Bourdieusian Analysis of Class and Migration: Habitus and the Indivisualising Process', *Sociology* 44(1): 49–66. doi:10.1177/0038038509351627.

Olwig, K.F. 2007. 'Privileged Travelers? Migration Narratives in Families of Middle-Class Caribbean Background', in Vered Amit (ed.), *Going First Class?: New Approaches to Privileged Travel and Movement*. Oxford: Berghahn Books, pp. 87–102.

Ono, Mayumi. 2014. 'Commoditization of Lifestyle Migration: Japanese Retirees in Malaysia', *Mobilities* 10(4): 609–27. https://doi.org/10.1080/17450101.2014.913868.

Roberts, Glenda S. 1994. *Staying on the Line: Blue-Collar Women in Contemporary Japan*. Honolulu: University of Hawaii Press.

Ronald, Richard, and Alison Alexy. 2011. 'Continuity and Change in Japanese Homes and Families', in Ronald Richard and Alison Alexy (eds), *Home and Family in Japan: Continuity and Transformation*. London: Routledge, pp. 1–24.

Salazar, Noel B. 2014. 'Migrating Imaginaries of a Better Life . . . Until Paradise Finds You', in Michaela Benson and Nick Osbaldiston (eds), *Understanding Lifestyle Migration: Theoretical Approaches to Migration and the Quest for a Better Way of Life*. Basingstoke: Palgrave Macmillan, pp. 119–38.

Sato, Machiko. 1993. *Shin Kaigai Teiju Jidai – Australia no Nihonjin* (*The New Era of Migration – The Japanese in Australia*). Tokyo: Shinchosha.

———. 2001. *Farewell to Nippon: Japanese Lifestyle Migrants in Australia*. Melbourne: Trans Pacific Press.

Senno, Yoichi. 1998. *Ryosai Kenbo, Sekai Daihyakka Jiten 29*. Tokyo: Heibonsha.

Smith, Andrew. 2006. '"If I Have No Money for Travel, I Have No Need": Migration and Imagination', *European Journal of Cultural Studies* 9: 47–62.

Strathern, Marilyn. 2005. *Kinship, Law and the Unexpected: Relatives are Always a Surprise*. Cambridge: Cambridge University Press.

Thang, Leng L., Sachiko Sone and Mika Toyota. 2012. 'Freedom Found? The Later-Life Transnational Migration of Japanese Women to Western Australia and Thailand', *Asian and Pacific Migration Journal* 21(2): 239–62. doi:10.1177/011719681202100206.

Ueno, Chizuko. 'The Position of Japanese Women Reconsidered', *Current Anthropology* 28(S4): S75–S87. https://doi.org/10.1086/203592.

Vannini, Philip, and Jonathan Taggart. 2014. 'No Man Can Be an Island: Lifestyle Migration, Stillness and the NEW Quietism', in Michaela Benson and Nick Osbaldiston (eds), *Understanding Lifestyle Migration: Theoretical Approaches to Migration and the Quest for a Better Way of Life*. Basingstoke: Palgrave Macmillan, pp. 188–208.

White, Anne. 2010. 'Young People and Migration from Contemporary Poland', *Journal of Youth Studies* 13(5): 565–80. doi:10.1080/13676261.2010.487520.

White, Merry E. 1992. *The Japanese Overseas: Can They Go Home Again?* Princeton: Princeton University Press.

White, Paul. 2003. 'The Japanese in London: From Transience to Settlement?', in Roger Goodman, Ceri Peach, Ayumi Takenaka and Paul White (eds), *Global Japan: The Experience of Japan's New Immigrant and Overseas Communities*. London: RoutledgeCurzon, pp. 79–97

Wilson, Jude, David Fisher and Kevin Moore. 2010. 'The OE Goes "Home": Cultural Aspects of a Working Holiday Experience', *Tourist Studies* 9(1): 3–21. doi:10.1177/1468797609360590.

6

The Imaginations of Talking Back

Exploring Identities among the Indian Youth in Urban, Middle-Class Malaysia

Sally Anne Param

Ammresh[1] is a seventeen-year-old collegiate and the middle child of three siblings. Living and studying in Kuala Lumpur, Malaysia, he talks about some aspects of his life that reveal normative patterns of an Indian middle-class household:

> Dad wanted me to become a doctor if I go into the sciences, or a lawyer, if I go into the humanities. He says those are the only two options of career I should choose from. I mean, I like biology as a subject, but I can't see myself doing medicine at all. Mom said I should at least do a Bachelor of Science and I know she is trying to work out a middle path. I think I want to do zoology instead. My siblings are also unsure of what they want to do. They have to figure it out, I guess . . . As for places of employment, I want to work overseas. Both my parents studied locally, but I have cousins studying or working in Australia, Canada and Europe and I would like to conclude that my future, too, lies further than Malaysia.

Ammresh's parents are apprehensive. When they were students, they did not have much choice and had to settle for the few degrees available at local universities. They made it in life from the limited career options they had. They had come from a diasporic background and maintaining middle-classness as a way of life was important to them. This class position would secure not only their lives, but also the future of their children.

Endnotes for this chapter begin on page 126.

This opening vignette explains a common stance of Indian middle-class parents in Malaysia. The preoccupation with their children's education and 'safer' options of undergraduate study is to ensure that, although being a minority community, their children's future employment could still be secured in Malaysia. However, this quote also exposes the dilemma that many young Indians face. Ammresh wants to pursue study and work in Australia. He wouldn't mind considering a transnational consultancy that still had dealings with Malaysia, but going abroad and venturing into new possibilities is his key aspiration. This is the divergence that shapes the identity of many urban Malaysian Indian adolescents today. This chapter explores how adolescents of Indian descent in urban Malaysia contemplate and negotiate who they are and how they want to progress. By examining their responses to the concept of aspirations, what is shown is their attempt to navigate cultural and familial norms and their own expectations about their personal futures.

As a precursor to the discussion in this chapter, two broad frameworks of definition need to be addressed: one relates to being young and the other refers to being Asian. Ever since age-based studies began to increase in academic narratives (Qvortrup 2005), defining the age range of 'youth' or the 'young' has become necessary. The youth in my research are all of school age, between the ages of twelve and nineteen. I will not be using the distinction of 'children' for those under the age of eighteen in this age group (cf. UNCRC 1989), but rather will use the terms 'adolescent', 'young person' and 'youth' interchangeably in referring to the age range of my respondents. Secondary schooling in Malaysia begins at thirteen and ends at nineteen. I have included twelve year olds in my study as some young people had not officially turned thirteen when the research was carried out. In the words of the social geographer Peter Hopkins, this cohort of young people is 'located uncomfortably between – yet simultaneously overlapping – childhood and adulthood' (2010: 3).

When 'Asian' youth are studied, a broader understanding of their identity is needed. While it would be inaccurate to use sweeping generalisations on an entire age cohort for the entire continent of Asia, there have been studies that refer to certain traits as 'Asian'. Tsuya and Bumpass (2004) mention how a young person is expected to observe obedience to elders and conformity to cultural norms, defining such practices as part of the traditional Asian context (Tsuya and Bumpass 2004). Other studies also refer to the expectations placed on young individuals and how filial compliance has been accepted as normative 'Asian' culture. Whether among the Chinese in Hong Kong (Chen and Wong 2014), the Indians in India (Kumar 1995) or the Malays from Singapore (Mohd Ali 2013), the show of respect by younger generations towards their elders is evidenced as a sustained practice. This background is important to establish before the identity of urban youth is explored further and helps explain the tensions often felt by present-day young people as they attempt to create an identity that goes beyond mere respect for elders' wishes. In the past, this strain was evident even in 'First World' nations of the West, where young people were deemed as not having an identity until they became adults (Beazley et al. 2009; Burman 1994). Research shows that only in the late twentieth century did individuality, agency and identity emerge as normative concepts in Europe that adolescents and children could own (Corsaro 2011; Qvortrup 2005). The concept and practice of young people having their own identity and the ability to exercise agency is thus relatively new in Asia and, more especially in relation to this study, Southeast Asia.

This chapter looks at the aspirations of urban Indian youth in Malaysia and how particular contexts and processes shape their identities. They come from the historical background of being a diasporic minority and these intersections of age, ethnicity and place have affected their aspirations and the formation of their identity. Beginning with an attempt to illumine the overlapping complexities of these individuals' historical and national background, I will then contextualise their quotidian lived reality within the spaces of home and school. Through their casual views on career choices and leisure patterns, I aim to discuss to what extent intergenerational tensions exist between adolescents and parents, and how the youth navigate these tensions. The social processes they undergo are complicated by urbanisation and globalisation, and outcomes of normative compliance over many generations are now replaced by new and varying aspirations within these young individuals.

As this discussion shows, this shift towards accepting adolescents' partic-ipation in society is still fairly new in this region. Two factors influencing this phenomenon are urbanisation and globalisation. As Malaysia modernised into the twenty-first century, families began to break away from being kin-based units and become more nuclear. Living in households near workplaces or schools became the practical solution for urban residents (Param 2016). In smaller house-holds, young people's individuality began to be appreciated (Tien and Sim 2010). Together with urbanisation, the effects of globalisation also impact how young people see themselves. Even as the transmission of images, signs, texts and media is simplified via globalisation, 'the relations between young people, place and identity' take on new levels of meaning and interpretation (Hopkins 2010: 173). This elucidates how Asian youth are able to enjoy processes of self-expression that have been more strongly associated as Western practices in the past. As glo-balisation opens the door for Western attributes and characteristics to be felt in non-Western locations, young people in Asia are now able to validate their age-based identity much more than the past. Using this argument, it is evident that the social spaces that Malaysian youth of Indian descent enjoy are globalised values that have been absorbed into local contexts of self-expression. These youth have been shaped and influenced by what Appadurai (1996) calls *scapes*: *ideoscapes* that refer to different ideas and *mediascapes* that refer to different mediums, both operating globally. It is within this localised setting that has been flavoured with 'global cultural flows' (Appadurai 1996: 33) that the query into youth aspirations can begin.

Since the adolescents of this study come from a middle-class context where the schooling experience takes centre stage, their aspirations are streamlined into what they want to venture into for their career pathway and also if they have hobbies or interests they would like to pursue. Why education and leisure are selected as the two sites for the study of their aspirations will be explained as the sections unfold. The responses of these urban Indians will explain their localised search for youth identity and it is hoped that this can contribute to the gap in Southeast Asian youth-centred narratives.

Diasporic Tractions

Malaysia is a multicultural nation, made up of three main ethnic groups among many others. The dominant ethnic group are the Malays, with the other two main groups being diasporic communities that originated from India and China.

The Indian population came to Malaya (as it was then called) in the late nineteenth century as a diaspora from India. Since the British were the colonial power of both countries, it was easy to navigate the flow of required labourers from one colony to another. However, the migratory process was not homogeneous for the Indian population. The majority of Indian immigrants were brought in as labourers for the rubber estates, as the rubber industry was targeted by the British as one of their main income revenues in Malaya (Sandhu 2006). Apart from the labourers, a smaller amount of English-educated Indians were also arriving from the professional and commercial lines (Sandhu 2006: 154). This latter group was needed to fill vacancies in the rapidly expanding government services. Eventually the wives and children of these male migrants also came, and this is how the local Indian middle-class population grew.

After gaining independence in 1957, Malaya, now called Malaysia, was free from colonial power and the Indians made attempts to fit into their new homeland as a diasporic community. However, the processes were rife with contradictory distinctions. In India, the subethnic communities were strongly divided by intra-ethnic lines and these ethnolinguistic subdivisions continued on Malaysian soil. Malaysian historians called this a 'polyglot' group, conveniently covered under the label 'Indian' (Appadurai and Dass 2008). If intra-ethnic categories were not divisive enough, class differences made matters worse. As the majority of these diasporic Indians were labourers of the working class, their concerns were largely different from their counterpart community in the higher economic bracket. The working-class Indian community faced marginalisation in their plight to overcome poverty, lack of educational opportunities and lack of jobs (Sandhu 2006). Issues important to working-class Indians, such as overcoming social ills and increasing development plans, were more prominently featured in media spaces (Appadurai and Dass 2008; Muzaffar 2006). However, the middle class were hardly featured in public narratives. They qualified for white-collar jobs that were considered 'secure' (as they were mostly government jobs) and this structural advantage denoted their only visibility. The fragmentation of the middle-class collectivity was further exacerbated in the drawing up of national policies and the creating of public narratives, as the government naturally prioritised the majority poor over the minority well-to-do. These contexts meant that middle-class Indians did not have a recognised space to call their own, resulting in a symbolic disadvantage in multicultural Malaysia (Daniels 2005).

Complicating this situation, the British encouraged the migration of another diasporic community to develop the tin mining industry in Malaya – the Chinese from mainland China. Comparing them to the Indian population, historians termed this group 'the more stabilised . . . population' (Sendut 1976: 77). In terms of social cohesion, the Chinese fared much better than the Indians, as the former 'were much more homogenous culturally' (Muzaffar 2006: 215). The Chinese dominated economic activities and evidenced fiscal strength as a community, despite being a minority. They easily gained public space in media narratives due to their collective migrant identity and, despite their minority status, they could hold 'a larger percentage of the higher echelon and better-paying jobs' (Lim 1971: 62).

The discussion of the racial composition of early Malaysia is not complete without a mention of the dominant group, the Malays. The Malays are the native population, forming the majority of the nation. Official statistics under British colonial rule clearly dichotomised racial groups into 'Malays and non-Malays' (Puthucheary 2006: 353). In the local literature, they are called the *bumiputera* ('prince of the soil' in literal translation). Being the indigenous majority and the main racial group, the Malays are awarded rights and government-initiated financial assistance in ownership of land, housing, education and higher-ranking occupations. National narratives support their cultural dominance and their 'position as the privileged natives' (Daniels 2005: 40). These factors further entrench the position of invisibility of middle-class Indians. They are eclipsed by the social ills of their working-class cohorts (in terms of visibility in media texts), the economic strength of the other main migrant community and the dominant space occupied by the native Malays in society. In the words of a local scholar, this sociocultural context explains the 'marginalisation of sorts of the Indian middle-class' (Muzaffar 2006: 226).

Living in urban cities of Malaysia, this community favoured government (state-owned or led) jobs, as these were seen as secure and stable (Daniels 2005;

Muzaffar 2006). Middle-class jobs helped them to simultaneously create, maintain and protect their class-based identity. The security of these measures shed light on their intention to ensure the same for their children. This was observed by earlier commentators, who referred to urban Indians as citizens who saw English education as necessary for their children in order 'to equip them for senior positions in the government' (Puthucheary 2006: 358). Recent literature on middle-class Indians tells the same story of how the middle class remain a minority within their own ethnic group as they strive for their own concerns and aspirations (Jayasooria and Nathan 2016).

These intergenerational sensitivities are what middle-class Malaysian Indian youth have inherited in their search for an identity. They are overshadowed by the internalisation of contradictory notions of being part of the middle class and yet a minority. Should they carry the existing impasses their parents experienced and continue to experience? Or can ideas of the future be free and separate from those of the past? The rest of this chapter will discuss the young people's aspirations and their processes of identity formation.

Evolving Youth Identity: A Conceptual Overview

Prior to the discussion of these youth's identity, or what can be called their 'individualizing tendencies of modern life' (Taylor and Spencer 2004: 31), an overview of the concepts used and referred to is outlined first. This can then shed light and add depth to the discussion at hand.

Aspirations

Arjun Appadurai (2004) referred to how aspirations can mean a person's wish for 'commodities' like work and leisure. This chapter will examine aspirations for both (future) work and leisure in the lives of middle-class Indian youth in Malaysia. The socioeconomic position of these youth is the perfect backdrop as to why career-related achievements are probably a natural goal of their aspirations. Yet, it cannot be claimed that work-related concerns are the only aspirations these youth have; latent or concealed aspirations can also exist. This is why leisure is also taken into consideration as part of these individuals' aspirations. These adolescents' everyday experience consists of going to school and returning home, and having this cycle repeated five times a week. The only other tangible engagement for the remainder of their time is probably leisure-based, especially over the weekend. This justifies the scope of aspirations that this chapter will examine. The trajectory of a future career path entails the possibility of leisure pursuits and both can be meaningfully intertwined in the lives of the youth.

Kinscripts

Stack and Burton have defined *kinscripts* as families having 'their own agendas, their own interpretation of cultural norms and their own histories' (1994: 34). In their study of family units in marginalised or minority communities, they found that personal family scripts were the norms that shaped their lived realities. These scripts were then passed down as normative patterns that would govern the lives of other or new family members. Kinscripts is thus the coined terminology of 'kin' and 'script' that depict the 'intergenerational transmission' of family norms (1994: 34). The social categorisation of middle-classness is an example of kinscripts and it is an important factor that can reinforce a group's collective identity. This concept will be referred to in the discussion of the potential opposition between parental and adolescent values.

Scapes

Situated in the contextual setting of both urban and global, the lives of these youth are shaped by the globalisation of culture. Appadurai (1996) suggests five dimensions of global cultural flows (called *scapes*) that shape and influence how people experience their everyday lives. Only two of the dimensions will be referred to for the purposes of this chapter. *Mediascape* refers to how forms of media are increasingly made available and *ideoscapes* refers to different ideologies operating globally. Both of these global scapes affect the youth of this study interchangeably.

The Research Design

Fifteen school and college-age Indian youth are the subjects of this project. They are aged between twelve to nineteen and belong to nuclear households in which their parents are dual-income breadwinners. All the youth live in urban districts within Kuala Lumpur, the economic core and capital of Malaysia. The research framework is qualitative in nature and capturing the voices of the youth is key. It is also important to move away from positing the youth as victims, as some age-based studies tend to do, due to their nonadult status. Sensitivity to the voices of the adolescents enables them to be recognised as active social creators of meaning (Beazley et al. 2009). The semi-structured interview is the main tool used, where predetermined and open-ended questions were combined. This tool allows an openness to changes in the sequence and form of questions, depending on the nature of responses (Kvale 1996). The semi-structured interview can be seen as one of the best methods that supports the unfolding of stories through 'the unguarded practice of conversation' (Spivak 1988: 66). The other tool used is the 'daily clock' time use diagram. The 24-hour time diary data enables the researcher to see what is done at what time and how much time is used for which activity per day (Robinson and Harms 2015). During the interview process, the researcher and the participant filled in the diagram together. On the researcher's part, the qualitative framework is maintained through the indirect practice of observation and reflexivity. Through the practice of reflexivity, silences, omissions and withdrawal from the participants' point of view are found to be equally informative (Donner 2008). These other pieces of information are recorded privately and analysed together with the data from the interviews. The mothers of these young people are also interviewed, and the stories of their and their husbands' childhoods also provide valuable comparative information. Informed consent was obtained through signatures on documents prior to the research process and careful transcriptions of the interviews were made after the interviews were completed.

Posited in Transition

Living in the capital city of Kuala Lumpur and its surrounding vicinity, processes of contestation and identification take place more prominently than in small towns or rural areas, due to young people grappling with both the connections and disjunctures found in big city life (Burchardt and Becci 2013). The youth in this research come from middle-class households, situated within neighbourhoods that are safe and where schools are established institutions. As middle-class Indian youth take education very seriously – as do Malay and Chinese youth – an 'ideology of middle-classness' can thus be constructed from this environment (Donner 2008: 126). Access to better education becomes the cultural capital these middle-class youth have over their counterparts, who come from households with less economic capital (Bourdieu 1993).

This explains why the young people of this research are also engaged with private after-school tuitions, which aim to facilitate their study skills further (Nair 2012).[2] As if school and after-school tuition are not time-consuming enough, many young people are also compelled to pursue school-initiated extracurricular activities (Yeoh and Huang 2010). As a result, the average urban student spends more than two-thirds of their waking time in school, as proven further by the diary data research tool. In this context, we see that for these urban Indian youth, school becomes a middle-class institution within which negotiations and contestations are made (Donner 2008).

The adolescents in this research come from nuclear families that are close-knit, where overall children value their parents and where the adults take their parental roles seriously. Discussion with the mothers of these youth reveal how engaged they are in their children's education and how this 'key project of mothering practices' (Yeoh and Huang 2010: 32) is now the major preoccupation in urban households.

School and home, and the social networks within these two sites, form the context that these adolescents experience as their lived reality. My questioning asked about their aspirations for future career choices and their leisure preferences, and the rest of this chapter discusses their reflections.

Responses from some of the young people reveal that following in the same occupation as one of their parents is equated with becoming successful in life. The parents of these young people were socialised into choosing career paths that their parents approved of, and the case is similar with the present generation.

Twelve-year-old Jshan and thirteen-year-old Binash come from homes where life at home runs like clockwork. There is a time schedule for everything – school, sports, washing-up, dinner, TV and bed. Jshan said: 'I think I want to be an accountant, as I like maths and numbers, but I also would like to work in the bank, like my mother.' Jshan comes from a family where his mother is a successful bank manager. Though young, he sees that this tight schedule allows him to maximise all his time slots and it is drawn up by his successful mother. The role of the maternal parent is similar in the home of Binash, where he is the eldest of three children. As the eldest child, it has been instilled in him that his choices will affect those of his younger siblings. Binash wanted to prove to his mother that he intended to be successful. In a separate question, he said that pleasing his mother was the most important aspect in his life, although he also wants to emulate his father:

> My mother pushes me to study and do my homework, she is always checking on me. She says I must be a good example and cannot play too much. But when I grow up, I want to be a neurosurgeon, like my father.

I could see that Binash wanted to please both parents, but his desire to be a neurosurgeon was due to the medical profession being highly respected in the Indian community. Binash naturally equated this career choice with being successful.

Twelve-year-old Shireeni also has a strict mother like Jshan and Binash. Like Binash's mother, Shireeni's mother finds her child too playful and in need of a more serious attitude in relation to schoolwork. Shireeni talked about her career choice:

> At first I wanted to be a doctor, because I know that it is an important job. Many people can be helped and when I was younger, I liked to play 'doctor-and-nurse'. But now I think I want to be a news reporter. To be a news reporter is my father's choice, because he says I can be part of many events and I can go all over the world.

Shireeni's responses highlight the thought process that if a parent's choice of occupation for the child is referred to, then the career option is a good one. Gravitating towards a parent's choice of career is also echoed by sixteen-year-old Akash:

> I wanted so much to be a pilot. So when I started having eyesight prob-
> lems, I had to wear glasses and my dreams had to change . . . Maybe I will
> do aircraft engineering . . . but my father wants me to do medicine. So I
> think it's between engineering or medicine.

Akash is the middle child out of three boys at home and he is his mother's blue-eyed boy. The fact that both his brothers are not interested in pursuing jobs that are lucrative or esteemed in their community probably moved him to favour a career choice suggested by his parents.

The mother of sixteen-year-old Jonathan claimed that she followed what her parents wanted of her in terms of her career choice, and this 'good' intention is passed down to her children. In his interview, Jonathan said:

> Mmm, I am not so sure what I want to be. I don't really like my subjects
> at school and I prefer the sports part. I like playing basketball. But I think
> I want to be an engineer like my father, as mom says I should consider this
> I need to brush up on my science subjects.

What becomes evident is that these young people are greatly influenced by social relations within the home. Although career choices should be part of the decision-making processes associated with school or individual preferences, what is observed is that this very important choice has to be deemed 'successful'. This is done by constantly referring to a career in which one of the parents is engaged or by agreeing to pursue a future pathway that has been suggested by one of the parents. Through either of these equations, these young people see themselves as associating with success. Their aim to emulate their parents seems to indicate that a 'family agenda' is at work, where parents' position in society and the suggestions they offer are powerful and synonymous with cultural norms that are practised in this community. This comes back to how urban middle-class Indian households make it a point to practise kinscripts in order to maintain continuities, especially in light of socioeconomic or cultural nuances that may lead to disequilibrium on the national front. Career choices 'like my mother' or 'like my father' also speak of these young people wanting to affirm the cultural capital of the good education invested in them by their parents. These youth perpetuate the patterns their parents underwent when they were adolescents in the previous generation. They are unconsciously sustaining intergenerational patterns of shared values (Stack and Burton 1994). The Bourdieusian idea of cultural capital as 'a product of history' seems fitting here (Bourdieu 1993: 34).

Going back to the classification of 'Asian youth' discussed at the beginning of the chapter, conformity to existing mores as a sign of filial piety is seen as a normative practice. The closeness of family bonds is commonly based on spending time together and 'face-to-face contact' (Davies 2012: 8). While these measures seem to be valid approaches in assessing kinship ties in other societies, perhaps the ability to measure an 'intergenerational transmission of family norms' is a much more powerful tool in the community of this research (Stack and Burton 1994: 34). By aspiring to emulate an intergenerational career choice, could it be that these middle-class Indian youth reflect their closest relationships? Other parts of the youth's conversations with the researcher evidence their strong affinity towards pleasing their parents. In this respect, the aspirations of these youth and their processes of selfhood are thus embedded within familial values of obedience and conformity. Their ideas of and for the future seem to be as strong as those of the past.

Despite the strong echoing of generational traits demonstrated by some of the young Indians, there are responses by other Indian adolescents that display variances in their worldviews. In their answers to career-based aspirations, there are those who want something different from the paths taken by their parents.

Sixteen-year-old Lavinya's parents were both consultants in various fields. Although she had initially intended to follow suit, she changed her mind:

I thought of [being a consultant] when I was growing up. But halfway through my studies, I decided that that wasn't me. So going into accountancy is my ambition now. I want to be a management accountant.

Some of the youth talked about how the love of sports seemed to be an initial starting point in their future aspirations, but how these preferences got shifted. Sixteen-year-old Kiren talked about his aspirations:

I wanted to be a professional tennis player when I was younger. I was good at the game and I was beating my older opponents easily. Then as I grew older, I was playing a lot of computer games and so I wanted to be a software or graphic designer. But now I am seriously preparing for my future and I think I want to be a pilot.

Fourteen-year-old Jonah had also wanted to be a professional sportsman:

As I was growing up, I loved football and wanted to play football as a career. But now I wonder whether I would be good enough? So many good players remain only within the country and don't qualify to play for Europe. So I think I now want to be involved in what I think I can do best – business management.

Although not based on a love of sports, other youth talked about how they out-grew earlier ambitions. Sixteen-year-old Kylie was one of these:

> I wanted to specialise in early childhood education. I enjoy being with children. But then I started thinking about what I am good at. Writing comes very easily to me in school and I find I like to express myself through diaries. So I thought 'why not consider a job that has writing in it?' I think I would like to try my hand at mass communication.

Unlike the earlier group of adolescents, these young people reveal that they intend to pursue alternate career paths that seem preferable to them. Yet, it must also be mentioned that in the separate interviews with the mothers of these adolescents, they claimed that they wanted their children to follow their own personal notions for their future occupation rather than necessarily following in their parents' footsteps. The mothers spoke about how they and their husbands were willing to support their children even if the venture was new, as they had the finances to do so. For example, Jonah's mother was a Chief Operating Officer (CEO) in a government office, but she clarified that her son's future path would be his own. This element appears to transgress what is commonly seen as the normative practice of urban middle-class Indian households.

This batch of Indian young people seem to have different social relations compared to their parents. They have attempted to talk back to existing norms and are interested in moderating the influence of kinscripts on their lives. These nuances can be termed minor, as these responses are backed by parents who support their children's capacity to aspire. This by itself speaks volumes because much research in this part of the world still seems to showcase a direct link between filial piety, obedience and conformity of the younger generation. In fact, in one local study, Malaysian children were shown to have good psychosocial adjustment when they exercised conformity to parental wishes (Ismail, Tan and Ibrahim 2009). In another study, Malaysian adolescents' filial behaviour is lauded as even surpassing traditionally stipulated regulations for elder care (Tien, Alagappar and David 2011). Placed within a literature review that tends to highlight adolescent conformity, some adolescents in this study go against such trends. They are a figurative contrast that dare to challenge existing dominant social constructs of 'middle-class Indian youth' in Malaysia.

The role of urban education seems to be a double-edged entity between the constructs of middle-class Indian youth and their parents in Malaysia. This is because the parents represented in this study had previously exercised conformity to their own parents' educational aims for them and their choices resulted in a market position that is 'positively privileged' (Swingewood 2000: 105). While some of the adolescents continue to perpetuate this pattern of conformity, others have chosen to exercise agency and seek a different path. Intuitively, globalisation plays a part in this milieu. Through mediascapes and ideoscapes, the infiltration of images and ideas that promote new definitions of selfhood are now accessible by adolescents. Desiring a collective identity is not necessary today and aspirations can be as individualised as possible. Some of these urban Indian youth have benefited from contemporary sensibilities to construct aspirations that do not necessarily need to show a connection to their parents' choices in order to be termed successful. This new phenomenon shows a slight yet significant shift in the historical trajectory of kinscript practice in the lives of these urban youth.

Apart from the aspirations towards career options, the adolescents' opinions on leisure were also taken into consideration in exploring facets of their identity. As mentioned in the introductory section of this chapter, these adolescents' lives are lived out in two clear-cut spheres: the public domain of school and the private domain of home. Being part of urbanising Asia, education takes on such a monumental role in their lifeworld. The diary data tool also clearly demarcates how much of these young people's waking hours are taken up by school, homework and tuition. While not indicating that noneducation-related aspirations cannot be formulated during the youth's engagement with schooling activities, a time-use analysis does indicate that diary activities relate strongly to insights and meanings gained from those activities (Robinson and Harms 2015). This implies that there is minimal time left in the day for noneducational ideas or realities for these young people. It is thus important to consider whether there is *any* place for leisure, as a commodity, to shape the lives of these young people (Appadurai 2004). Youth aspirations that are separate from educational and career priorities can shed light on what they really have in their hearts.

Twelve-year-old Kumar gave a simple and yet honest response when asked about his aspirations regarding leisure: 'Leisure? No, I don't have time for that. Every day I have school and then there is homework to do and tuition to attend.' When asked about her leisure time, twelve-year-old Shireeni went into a brief account of a typical day for her:

> I get up at 6.15 AM, to get ready for school. After school, I eat lunch at the canteen and then a driver sends me for tuition classes. When I get home, it is already past 4 PM and I am tired. Sometimes I just chuck my [school] bag away and go to sleep . . . sometimes I don't even change out of my school uniform . . . I really like to watch TV. Our TV is upstairs and I love to sit and watch *Astro* programmes. That is the only time I have to relax. But when I suddenly hear my mother coming home [from work], I switch off the TV and rush downstairs.

Shireeni admitted that being caught napping or sitting in front of the TV would mean receiving a scolding. This showed the lack of space she had to form a leisure pattern. Her daily after-school timetable was taken up with attending tuition classes and doing homework. Fifteen-year-old Varsha confessed:

> I stay up late because I have to finish my homework. But I also have to get up at 5.45 AM to go to school. So by the time I get home after school, I am tired. I need to rest (giggles). I think it's catch-up time sometimes, you know, the body needs it. Because like, I have to wake up so early . . . My mum nags, like 'go study' or something like that. My dad, too, sometimes he will deprive me [from] playing [with] the iPad. I feel like I am happy when they are at work.

Such responses validate my earlier research, which found that the concept of leisure is predominantly associated with recovery from school-related activities and that any form of personalised leisure is almost completely absent (Param 2016). Donner's observations about the middle class in India also ring very true for middle-class Indians in Malaysia – that there are 'two crucial middle-class institutions which can hardly be imagined separately, namely the family and the school' (Donner 2008: 124). In separate interviews with the youths' mothers, they shared how the creation of comfort and security in the home space was their idea of 'leisure' for their children. Apart from family time (including holiday trips or weekend outings), the provision of a cosy environment that supports their children's study environment is deemed sufficient in meeting their children's 'leisure' quota. From the parental point of view, their children's schooling experiences are prized over any other aspect of their identity. And yet, what is gleaned from the responses of the youth is that they do not even have the figurative space to consider leisure beyond 'the regularities of routine family life' (Davies 2012: 15). In his study on youth culture, Arnett claims that globalisation has caused cultures previously based on collectivism to now 'become more individualistic' (2005: 30). As far as these few responses show, transgressing intergenerational norms of family time was the easy part. Rather, the desire is to have and explore various possibilities of individualised leisured space; this was missing.

The displays of ambivalence or nonchalance in the youths' answers are fragmentary pieces of information that cannot be discarded as 'nondata', as research within a qualitative lens would confirm. As a researcher, I aimed to press deeper in order to attempt to tap into what the youth were actually saying about noneducational aspirations.

Sixteen-year-old Jigna attends a private school, but the school routine is just as taxing, as she explains:

There are very few times which I can call my own. Most of the time it is tuition or homework or this or that. But when I do get the chance, I can sit in my bedroom for hours, just dancing and reading. If nobody is at home, [better still], I can just be inside there [for hours].

Seventeen-year-old Andrew says:

My mother brings me home from school, but sometimes I have to go out again for tuition. But when I am at home and there is no homework to do, my favourite place is the guest room downstairs. My Xbox is inside and I study here and I play my video games here. So my hobby is [just] being [able to be] in this room.

Sixteen-year-old Lydia speaks in a similar fashion:

I don't like it that every day I have tuition, but I know it is for my own good. But when I am free, I love my room. This is where I can just listen to music, draw, or be on my hand-phone. I also like it that I don't have to share the bedroom with my brother anymore.

Seventeen-year-old Ammresh admits:

In high school I used to hang out with friends – normally playing video games or talking about video games. Video games is [*sic*] a pretty major part of my life. Only now that I am in college I made an active decision to cut down on it. I spend more time with friends now.

Apart from seventeen-year-old Ammresh, who finds time to spend with friends, the other youths seem to complain that the time available for spontaneous activities is constantly reducing. A local study reveals how active leisure pursuits are decreasing and how passive leisure activities like the checking of Facebook are now becoming more common in Malaysia (Mustaffa et al. 2011). However, what the urban Indian youth of this study appear to be expressing, more than whether their pursuits are termed active or passive, is a desire to be left alone or to have more personal space. Their aspirations for free time are translated into seeking to have a personal time-out. This issue is also happening outside of Asia. Hasseldahl (2011) talks about how European adolescents are minimising the time they spend outdoors with nature and implies that this development is rather worrying. However, the growing disconnect with nature need not be reflective of a loss of identity. Opportunities to 'explore and create' (Skar and Krogh 2009: 343) are not only to be found in the great outdoors; such endeavours can be pursued in individuals' personalised spaces.

This preoccupation with personal space seems to be a growing reality of urban adolescents. The interview process in this research project validates this observation further, where the adolescents were very happy to talk about their longing for personal space. In fact, many of the participants were rather disappointed that they could not offer elaborations regarding leisure patterns compared to their comments on school and family life. Munro and Madigan's earlier research highlighted the 'individualistic imperatives for space and privacy' (Munro and Madigan 1999: 117). Whether in their study rooms or in their bedrooms, these youths are happy that they can just 'be' – away from 'adult-controlled, planned and organised activities' – so that they have the space to just relax (Skar and Krogh 2009: 343).

Aspirations are related to agency (Appadurai 2004) and what these youth seem to be saying is that they desire to have the capacity to aspire. This has been evident in their educational aspirations, which befits their privileged position of being middle class. However, in their limited space for noneducational pursuits, their quotidian lives seem bereft of aspirations. There also seems to be a longing for private space. In line with how globalised individuals' landscapes are influenced by other 'scapes' (Appadurai 1996), the influence of media and ideas are pertinent to this context. In other words, apart from education, these young people experience global culture only through their limited spatial practices alone, in their rooms. In this light, 'me time' or 'time-out' is something that they yearn for. This longed-for space will incorporate the creative process of them being able to shape their personal identity. This suggests that these youth would like to broaden the narrow positioning of career-based aspirations to include a frequent use of personal space that will allow them a greater opportunity to 'talk back' to parental demands and maintain a domain of personal autonomy.

Concluding Discussion

These snippets of middle-class Indian adolescents' lifeworlds speak volumes when juxtaposed against a historical backdrop of silence and invisibility. Adjusting to life in Malaysia as a diasporic ethnic minority, the grandparents or great-grand-parents of these adolescents had to work hard in order to gain their socioeconomic advantage. Although lacking symbolic advantage, they built their cultural capital through educational strategies and securing government jobs. Through kinscripts, they then preserved the intergenerational transmission of middle-classness (Stack and Burton 1994), attempting to have their children follow in established patterns of conformity. These arrangements were crucial as they had to preserve their identity as a minority group, both intra-ethnically and inter-ethnically, in multicultural Malaysia.

However, the aspirations of Indian adolescents studied in this research pose a shift in this motif. Yes, some of them aspire to follow their parents' career choices, but others aspire to *different* career options – ones that are based on their own opinions of what suits them best individually. Through mediascapes and ideoscapes, the youth are exposed to the possibilities of differences as part of reality.

Even in relation to leisure patterns, many of these middle-class Indian youth are keen to acknowledge personal space more than collective engagements with family members. Middle-class preoccupations with education can create lifestyles for school-going adolescents where there is no space for self-expression through hobbies or leisure (Donner 2008; Yeoh and Huang 2010). There has been other Malaysia-based research that reveals low leisure patterns for the Indian community (Singh 2011). This trend is corroborated in this research, where the parents of the adolescents assume that their children's extracurricular activities at school should suffice as leisure. However, when the adolescents were asked about their own definitions of leisure, their answers had nothing to do with their school-warranted engagements. Their aspirations of leisure clearly demonstrate their longing for personal space – one where they can get away from the regimens of education in their lives. From the interviews, a gap is evidently observed in the youths' responses in relation to family-based activities. None of them even commented on the 'privilege' of space, a beautiful home, a landscaped garden or a well-designed bedroom. The closest answer to this aspect of life came from Lydia, who no longer had to share a room with her younger brother. None of them referred to leisure aspirations in relation to family outings or activities. In contrast, family time was a key element of quotidian life in the interview with the mothers. The maternal parents defined leisure in terms of a beautified home space and time with the children. Most of the youth desire free time, where they can just 'be' in their own confined spaces, to do as they wish and not have to conform to controlled activities. These 'individualistic imperatives for space and privacy' are part of a global phenomenon for young people (Munro and Madigan 1999: 117).

These strains of agency contribute to a small but significant shift in attitude. This is especially meaningful within the larger context of local Malaysian research, where there is a lack of young people's voices being captured. Although there have been efforts to address narratives involving youth of the three main races of Malay, Chinese and Indian, these endeavours have so far lacked voice, detail or depth (Tien and Sim 2010; Awang et al. 2017). This chapter has been part of a larger project that seeks to address this discrepancy (Param 2016).

What is evident in the aspirations of middle-class Indian youth is an attempt to talk back to existing structures of a regimented middle-class lifestyle. In their aspirations for career-based futures, some youth demonstrate a dutiful internalisation of the existing culture of society. For these young people, the definition of future success and parental advice in the form of kinscripts is still inseparably intertwined. For other adolescents, their choices reflect an initiative of active participation in their lifeworlds. Aided by the shift of mentality in some of their parents, these youths are able to choose paths that are unpredictable in terms of generational patterns of employment. This seemingly negligible difference is again significant in light of the overwhelming preoccupation of middle-class Indians towards maintaining their privileged yet vulnerable position in society. Since their diasporic beginnings in this nation, middle-class Indians have been merely responding 'to their own real and *perceived* loss of economic access and opportunity and to their own marginalisation' (Muzaffar 2006: 226, emphasis added). A more recent study has agreed with this explicit judgement by noting that this group of people 'are unable to think out of the box' (Jayasooria and Nathan 2016: 117). Within this framework, the few expressions of alternative aspirations by middle-class Indian youth seek to penetrate existing internal impasses within the community.

The vignette of Ammresh given at the beginning of this chapter is an example of part of the actual life of a middle-class Indian youth. His aspiration is to move past the safe lifestyle of his parents, enjoy his personalised leisure and work towards a 'new' type of job away from home. Ammresh represents other middle-class youth like him, who are exposed to global scapes and yet are able to indigenise and heterogenise their experiences (Appadurai 1996). In their aspirations, they are able to experience 'the rhetoric of self-development' more than existing patterns of 'middle-class imaginations' (Donner 2008: 176–77). The findings in this chapter suggest that a small shift has occurred and a significant space for self-discovery has been created. For the middle-class Indian youth of Malaysia, this shift is an assertion of identity and prefigures that their attempt to talk back to existing norms will be a success.

Sally Anne Param's research passion as a social geographer is exploring how gender, age and/or ethnicity can make a difference in quotidian life experiences. Her international presentations have taken her to Singapore, the United Kingdom and the Czech Republic, and her latest author credit is a chapter in *Critical Perspectives on 21st Century Friendship: Polyamory, Polygamy and Platonic Affinity* (2019). When not working, she enjoys writing personal travelogues.

Notes

1. Pseudonyms have been used for the research participants mentioned in this chapter out of respect for their privacy.
2. In fact, the race towards academic excellence is so intense that a national daily newspaper called for middle-class parents to slow down their push towards private tuition, as various forms of detriments to the children's well-being were beginning to show (Perimbanayagam 2017).

References

Appadurai, Arjun. 1996. *Modernity at Large: Cultural Dimensions of Globalisation*. Minneapolis: University of Minnesota Press.

——. 2004. *The Capacity to Aspire: Culture and the Terms of Recognition*. Stanford: Stanford University Press.

Appadurai, Arjun, and David Dass. 2008. *Malaysian Indians: Looking Forward*. Selangor: Strategic Information & Research Development Centre (SIRD).

Arnett, J. J. 2005. 'Youth, cultures and societies in transition: The challenges of growing up in a globalized world', in F. Gale and S. Fahey (eds), *Youth in Transition: The challenges of generational change in Asia*. Bangkok: United Nations Economic and Social Commission for Asia and the Pacific, pp. 22–35.

Awang, M. M., A. R. Ahmad, Mumpuniarti, A. A. A. Rahman. 2019. 'Social integration practices among multi-ethnic youths', *Kasetsart Journal of Social Sciences* 40(2): 454–458. doi: 10.1016/j.kjss.2017.10.004

Beazley, Harriet, Sharon Bessel, Judith Ennew and R. Waterson. 2009. 'The Right to Be Properly Researched: Research with Children in a Messy, Real World', *Children's Geographies* 7(4): 365–78.

Bourdieu, Pierre. 1993. *The Field of Cultural Production: Essays on Art and Literature*. New York: Columbia University Press.

Burchardt, Marian, and Irene Becci. 2013. 'Introduction: Religion Takes Place: Producing Urban Locality', in Irene Becci, Marian Burchardt and Jose Casanova (eds), *Topographies of Faith: Religion in Urban Spaces*. Leiden: Brill, pp. 1–21.

Burman, Erica. 1994. 'Interviewing', in *Qualitative Methods in Psychology: A Research Guide*. Maidenhead: Open University Press, pp. 49–71.

Chen, Wei-wen, and Yi-Lee Wong. 2014. 'What My Parents Make Me Believe in Learning: The Role of Filial Piety in Hong Kong Students' Motivation and Academic Achievement', *International Journal of Psychology* 49(4): 249–56.

Corsaro, William. 2011. *The Sociology of Childhood*, 3rd edn. Los Angeles: Sage.

Daniels, Timothy. 2005. *Building Cultural Nationalism in Malaysia, Identity, Representation and Citizenship*. New York: Routledge.

Davies, Martin. 2012. *Social Work with Children and Families*. Basingstoke: Palgrave Macmillan.

Donner, Henrike. 2008. *Domestic Goddesses, Maternity, Globalization and Middle-Class Identity in Contemporary India*. Aldershot: Ashgate.

Hasseldahl, Cindy. 2011. 'Reconnecting Children with Nature: Providing Evidence and Activities for "Nature Based" Experiences in the Lutheran Learning Community', *Practicum in Early Childhood, Educ 573*, Concordia University, Nebraska.

Hopkins, Peter E. 2010. *Young People, Place and Identity*. Abingdon: Routledge.

Ismail, N., Tan Jo-Pei and Rahimah Ibrahim. 2009. 'The Relationship between Parental Belief on Filial Piety and Child Psychosocial Adjustment among Malay Families', *Pertanika Journal of Social Sciences & Humanities* 17(2): 215–24.

Jayasooria, Denison, and Nathan, K.S. (eds). 2016. *Contemporary Malaysian Indians: History, Issues, Challenges & Prospects*. Selangor: National University of Malaysia.

Kvale, S. 1996. *InterViews: An Introduction to Qualitative Research Interviewing*. Thousand Oaks: SAGE Publications.

Kumar, S. Vijaya (ed.). 1995. *Challenges before the Elderly: An Indian Scenario*. New Delhi: MD Publications.

Lim, S.P. 1971. 'Some Aspects of Income Differentials in West Malaysia', Master's dissertation. Kuala Lumpur: University of Malaya.

Mohd Ali, N.Y. 2013. 'Singapore Malay Migrants' Concepts of "Filial-Piety" and Its Support for Aged Parents to Age-in-Place in Australia', Master's dissertation. Perth: Edith Cowan University.

Munro, Moira, and Ruth Madigan. 1999. 'Negotiating Space in the Family Home', in Irene Cieraad (ed.), *At Home: An Anthropology of Domestic Space*. New York: Syracuse University Press, pp. 107–17.

Mustaffa, Normah, Faridah Ibrahim, Amizah Wan, Fauziah Ahmad, Chang Peng Kee and Maizatal Haizan Mahbob. 2011. 'Diffusion of Innovations: The Adoption of Facebook among Youth in Malaysia', *Innovation Journal* 16(3): 1–15.

Muzaffar, Chandra. 2006. 'Political Marginalization in Malaysia', in K.S. Sandhu and A. Mani (eds), *Indian Communities in Southeast Asia*. Singapore: Institute of Southeast Asian Studies, pp. 211–36.

Nair, Nevash. 2012. 'Increase in Demand for Tuition in Malaysia', *The Star*, 5 November. Retrieved 24 March 2020 from https://www.thestar.com.my/news/community/2012/11/05/increase-in-demand-for-tuition-in-malaysia.

Param, Sally Anne. 2016. 'Sustaining Middle-Classness: Studying the Lives of Indian Working Mothers and Their Children in Malaysia', PhD thesis. Kuala Lumpur: University of Malaya.

Perimbanayagam, Kalbana. 2017. 'Parents Urged Not to Overload Children with Tuition', *New Straits Times*, 24 November. Retrieved 24 March 2020 from https://www.nst.com.my/news/nation/2017/11/307030/parents-urged-not-to-overload-children-tuition.

Puthucheary, Mavis. 2006. 'Indians in the Public Sector in Malaysia', in K.S. Sandhu and A. Mani (eds), *Indian Communities in Southeast Asia*. Singapore: Institute of Southeast Asian Studies, pp. 334–36.

Qvortrup, Jens. 2005. 'Varieties of Childhood', in Jens Qvortrup (ed.), *Studies in Modern Childhood: Society, Agency, Culture*. Basingstoke: Palgrave Macmillan, pp. 1–20.

Robinson, John P., and Teresa A. Harms. 2015. 'Time Use Research: Recent Developments', in J. Wright (ed) *International Encyclopedia of Social and Behavioral Sciences (Second Edition)*. Oxford: Elsevier, pp. 383–397. doi: 10.1016/B978-0-08-097086-8.32196-1

Sandhu, Kernial Singh. 2006. 'The Coming of the Indians to Malaysia', in K.S. Sandhu and A. Mani (eds), *Indian Communities in Southeast Asia*. Singapore: Institute of Southeast Asian Studies, pp. 151–89.

Sendut, H. 1976. 'Contemporary Urbanization in Malaysia', in Y. M. Yeund and C. P. Lo (eds), *Changing South-East Asian Cities: Readings on Urbanization*. Singapore: Oxford University Press, pp. 76–81.

Singh, Shalini (ed.). 2011. *Domestic Tourism in Asia*. Singapore: Institute of Southeast Asian Studies.

Skar, Margrete, and Erling Krogh. 2009. 'Changes in Children's Nature-Based Experiences Near Home: From Spontaneous Play to Adult-Controlled, Planned and Organized Activities', *Children's Geographies* 7(3): 339–54.

Spivak, G.C. 1988. 'Can the Subaltern Speak?', in Cary Nelson and Larry Grossberg (eds), *Marxism and the Interpretation of Culture*. London: Macmillan, pp. 271–313.

Stack, Carol, and Linda Burton. 1994. 'Kinscripts: Reflections on Family, Generation and Culture', in Evelyn Nakano Glenn, Grace Chang and Linda Rennie Forcy (eds), *Mothering: Ideology, Experience and Agency*. New York: Routledge, pp. 33–44.

Swingewood, Alan. 2000. *A Short History of Sociological Thought*. Basingstoke: Macmillan.

Taylor, Gary, and Steve Spencer. 2004. *Social Identities: Multidisciplinary Approaches*. London: Routledge.

Tien, Wendy Y.M., Ponmalar N. Alagappar and Maya K. David. 2011. 'The Attitude of Filial Responsibility of Malaysian Students towards Their Elderly Parents'. Retrieved 24 March 2020 from http://eprints.um.edu.my/id/eprint/638.

Tien, Wendy Y.M., and Irene W.P. Sim. 2010. 'The Importance of Cognitive Competency in Interethnic Relations among the Youth', in Maya David, James McLellan, Ngeow Meng, Lean Yi and Wendy Mei Tien (eds), *Ethnic Relations and Nation Building: The Way Forward*. Petaling Jaya: Strategic Information and Research Development Centre, pp. 201–16.

Tsuya, Noriko, and Larry Bumpass (eds). 2004. *Marriage, Work and Family Life in Comparative Perspective, Japan, South Korea and the United States*. Honolulu: University of Hawaii Press.

United Nations Convention on the Rights of the Child (UNCRC). 1989. Retrieved 24 March 2020 from https://www.unicef.org/crc/files/Rights_overview.pdf.

Yeoh, Brenda, and Shirlena Huang. 2010. 'Mothers on the Move: Children's Education and Transnational Mobility in Global-City Singapore', in Wendy Chavkins and JaneMaree Maher (eds), *The Globalization of Motherhood: Deconstructions and Reconstructions of Biology and Care*. Abingdon: Routledge, pp. 31–54.

7

LAW STUDENTS, ASPIRATIONS AND ACCOMPLISHMENTS IN COLOMBO, SRI LANKA

Morten Koch Andersen

Introduction

> I dream of doing good for society, help[ing] people, regardless of the consequences. I know it can be dangerous, but I want to help and I want to do something for people.
>
> —Saman

When I first met Saman,[1] he did not have the appearance of an activist. He was dressed in the usual lawyer 'uniform' – white shirt and black trousers. He carried a brown leather briefcase. He apologised for being late; he did not own a car and depended on public transportation. He shook my hand, straightened his glasses and we began to talk. Over the following hours, I got to know an engaged and dedicated young professional with a strong belief in justice and the law, with high ambitions for future accomplishments and contributions to society, and a sincere consideration for respecting his family and utilising the opportunity of education – a dilemma of choice in the nexus of personal ambitions, family considerations and political contributions.

In this chapter, I investigate youth aspirations from the perspective of law students and young legal professionals in Colombo, Sri Lanka. My focus is on their professional ambitions and personal desires as students of a discipline imbued with notions of accomplishment and career, and one where they can permit themselves to foresee a middle-class life of social status, economic security and professional predictability. As such, it is a perspective from a *becoming middle class*

Endnotes for this chapter begin on page 145.

(Srivastava 2009) in a society undergoing rapid transformation in the aftermath of civil war and violent conflict.

This chapter speaks to a growing interest in the worldviews, imaginaries and aspirations of student youths in South Asia (Jeffrey 2008, 2010a, 2010b; Kumar 2012; Ruud 2014; Andersen 2016, 2018, 2019). This chapter shines a light on the aspirations of students who in time may go on to populate state institutions and administer the law. They are part of a growing urban middle class in South Asia that comprise ever more segments of the population and challenge class, caste, ethnicity and gender relations (Desai 2007; Deshpande 2003; Fernandes 2006; Gupta 2000; Harris-White and Sinha 2007; Varma 1998).

The following analysis sheds light on aspiration as a navigational capacity of social becoming amongst young lawyers-to-be in Sri Lanka. Particular attention is paid to their perspectives on future legal work and professional career paths, and to how their aspirations of becoming human rights lawyers intersect with common notions of accomplishment, in a context of heightened political tensions in the aftermath of violent conflict.

I argue that educational prescriptions, societal norms and family expecta-tions play a significant role in young people's choices, prospective anticipations and imaginings of the future. My respondents are divided between middle-class ambitions of becoming a professional by securing a job in a competitive sector and becoming respected human rights activists through assisting people in need and influencing politics and society at large. This speaks to Paolo Boccagni's (2017) dimensional framework as discussed in the Introduction to this volume, particularly addressing the specific objectives of youth aspirations – the aim of accomplishment, who this might benefit and the relation capacity of an imagined future (see the introduction by Westendorp, Remmert and Finis in this volume). If we approach aspirations as a navigational capacity, we need to pay attention to the ways in which the young people attempt to prepare and form themselves for future accomplishments, and how they navigate between personal ambitions and family responsibilities, reconciling self-development with social activism and societal expectations.

Like in other South Asian countries, lawyers have played a prominent and important role in the establishment of the Sri Lankan postcolonial independent state. Lawyers have been active in the public political debate on the transformation of laws, institutions, governance and policies in the development of the modern Sri Lankan state through law reform, public litigation and public interest cases. Lawyers have chaired numerous commissions to examine and provide advice on improvements of state institutions and legal practices. This includes permanent institutional commissions and time-bound Commissions of Inquiry.[2] Lawyers have played crucial roles in highlighting challenges and finding solutions, though historically with limited effect on national politics and state practices of human rights. For example, the most recent evocation of the role of law, legal institutions and lawyers occurred in 2015, when the long-standing ruler Mahinda Rajapaksa was rejected by the population in the parliamentary election and was defeated by a coalition of opposition parties spearheaded by the alliance of two historically competing centre-left and centre-right parties. The election brought a halt to the increasing politicisation of key legal institutions, most notably the Chief Justice's office and the Attorney General's office. The election was not just a rejection of the previous rulers and their use of state resources for private and elitist gains, but also marked the reopening of public debate, legal reform efforts and judicial accountability. This reinvigorated and rebooted legal work, and opened up political space for the legal profession to find its feet after years of targeted discouragement and the intentional deterioration of professional standards, procedures and practices. Regardless of the important role of lawyers for democracy and human rights in Sri Lanka, the young people interviewed for this study felt very alone at university. They were part of only a handful of students engaged in human rights, public litigation or constitutional issues out of approximately 200 students in their university year. Their aspirations were interweaved with notions of social becoming, of social respectability, recognition and accomplishment in society and not least within their families (Gunatilaka, Mayer and Vodopivec 2010; Arunatilake and Jayawardena 2010; Gunatilaka and Vodopivec 2010).

The young lawyers-to-be who are the subjects of this chapter are all involved in human rights work, yet to different degrees. Lawyers oriented towards human rights are a rare and dedicated minority in Sri Lanka. A small number are active in Colombo and even fewer in other parts of the country. The majority of lawyers and lawyers-to-be focus on corporate, criminal and civil law, where profits are greater and risks are lower. Many lawyers active at the courts are self-employed and live off the clients they can reach and the cases they can access. Human rights and public interest litigation are not topics that attract their full-time attention, though many lawyers and legal firms occasionally do pro bono work for individuals or organisations. For young lawyers interested in human rights, volunteering opportunities to assist individuals and human rights organisations in need are not difficult to find. There are more cases and clients than the current capacity of legal aid organisations can handle. The work not only satisfies their individual ambitions but also adds to the experiences and qualifications of the lawyer-to-be, sustaining and maintaining one public imaginary of lawyers as critical contributors to society.

During a six-month stay in Sri Lanka during the winter of 2017–18, I engaged with several institutions, civil society actors, human rights activists and legal professionals while undertaking a study of rule of law practices. This chapter is based on conversations and work relations with a number of activists and professionals working both inside and outside state institutions and civil society, including the young lawyers-to-be. It focuses on three students with ambitions of professional human rights work. At the time of our conversations, they were students of the Sri Lanka Law College in Colombo. The analysis sheds light on their aspiration(s) as lawyers-to-be in Sri Lanka, with a particular emphasis on their own perspectives of future professional career paths, in between social and familial expectations of accomplishment.

Aspirations and Youth

With regard to aspirations, I consider people as already always thinking about the future – working for a future, aspiring to a future and expressing horizons of potentialities in choices made and choices voiced. From this perspective, aspirations are about wants, preferences, choices and situated calculations of risks and gains in an attempt to foresee and control events, and steer the course of life towards opportunities and improvements in livelihood. It follows that aspirations can be approached as agency of the future and as a process of social becoming. Henrik Vigh has turned our attention to the ways in which youth navigate an incessantly moving social terrain to better their life chances on projected imaginaries of social being and becoming (Vigh 2006; Christiansen, Utas and Vigh 2006). This is equally relevant for the young lawyers, though in the case of Vigh's research, the opportunities for the young men of his analysis are relatively limited – going in and out of armed mobilisation – compared to the opportunities available to law students. Vigh's concept rests on the approach that people have multiple identities and different roles in the variety of situations in which they find themselves, based on their relations to the people and institutions that surround them. Hence, agency in aspirations is conditioned by opportunities and potentials for future accomplishment; though ambiguous and uncertain, young people try to navigate and 'stabilise' these into a coherent, predictable and realisable future.

Yet, aspirations are never simply individual (as the language of wants and choices inclines us to think); they are always formed in interactions, relations and in the thick of life. For my respondents, legal education works as an enabling and constraining social space of aspirations and of social becoming where personal desires, social status and economic solvency intersect. Hence, all people express more or less conscious ideas of future horizons in the choices they make and the choices they voice, which inevitably are tied to more general norms and axioms about 'the good life'. Choice, in this sense, is an emic concept that is formed in the intersection of societal and family expectations and young people's individual aspirations. This is not to say that young people have choices completely predetermined by the wider structural terrain of political, social and economic conditions, but that they act within a given framework – in this study, the present and future professional trajectories of becoming a lawyer, which they navigate to fit their own aims. Education and professional work open up pathways for future becoming that potentially trigger positive acceleration of desires and accomplishment, as a map of aspirations (Appadurai 2004: 70).

In the following discussion, I will show how, in order to meet their own and others' notions of accomplishment, these young lawyers think of their choices and behaviours through the lens of the future. This, the navigational aspect of the concept, is central to an understanding of young educated people's aims and life choices, in a setting of political and social transformations where political uncertainties and violence are significant life conditions.

The Lawyers-to-Be

Saman is a young lawyer and the speaker of the quote that opens this chapter. He recently graduated from the law college in Colombo and works at a law firm. He originates from the east of the country. His father is a farmer who cultivates poultry. Saman first studied agricultural science and was amongst the top students in the country. However, to the regret of his family, he did not want to continue the family business. Instead, he chose to study law in Colombo:

> My best friend suggested I should study law and work for my community and for my people. I thought, it is a colourful profession. So, I pursued what I desired but my parents did not like my decision. They said it is not a good profession in Sri Lanka – don't change your education. You will encounter too many problems. (Saman)

Saman belongs to the Muslim minority in Sri Lanka. In the beginning, his father did not support his career choice, but gradually he realised the potential of Saman's work. Though Saman is still establishing himself as a lawyer, he already financially supports his parents, who have now retired. Two sisters are already married. Saman married a girl from his home area and they have settled in Colombo, where she studies at Colombo University. Despite having moved to Colombo, Saman works voluntarily for a committee in his home area that supports people in need:

> I am well known in my community. My father is a local politician and my family own businesses in the area. I can help people because I am educated in law and I do help people. I want to be involved in politics. I already support my father and I often go back to my home town to assist people.

Even though Saman has experienced how the legal system does not safeguard people's rights, especially for those at the margins of society, he still believes in law as a means for justice: 'We have to fight in a democratic way – this is the only hope – justice can be used to fight injustices, but we can only act after violations have happened. We have to fight to establish the rule of law.' He dreams of becoming a competent lawyer who works for all citizens of the country and of developing a career in constitutional law. When this is achieved, his plan is to engage in local politics and work for his community and the people of his home area: 'There is a need for educated people to stand against corrupt politicians. However, I don't trust the established parties, I want to stand as an independent candidate.' He is already known in the constituency: 'People know me, but in five to six years I have to go back to my community if I want to be elected [an] MP.' He has realised that the toughest challenge is to earn enough money to run a campaign and at the same time to not be corrupted in the process. His family do not support these political ambitions, seeing it as a big risk to his career and life. 'Even my wife's family do not support my choice of profession or my political ambitions – I first told them after the marriage! But my wife knew.'

However, Saman's family are not strangers to politics. One of Saman's uncles, a local politician, is a representative in the municipal council as well as being a lawyer. Another uncle was a mayor and a former member of the Senate of Ceylon, which was abolished in 1971. As such, his family name is well known and well recognised by people in the constituency. For Saman, legal work and his professional career fit with his aspirations of politics and visions of changing society, against a background of heightened political tensions and violent conflict.

Kasun

My family don't want me to be a lawyer. I was supposed to be a doctor. They don't like it or support it but what can they do – I want this. My family do not support me. I don't want it. I want to make it on my own. (Kasun)

Kasun is a young man in his early twenties. When I met him for the first time, he had just returned from Diganna. He had volunteered to take part in a fact-finding investigation of the recent violent attacks on the Muslim community. He is an energetic, determined and self-assured man. He had been accepted at medical school, but instead chose a less prestigious, less secure and less predictable career path as a lawyer. His family did not support him financially, despite this being common for university students. His main motivation was to change society for the better through law and legal practice rather than just helping people through alleviating and healing injuries and sicknesses as a medical practitioner. As such, his aspirations encompassed not only his personal professional career but also the trajectory of society.

Kasun lives in Colombo. His family home is located in a rural coastal area on the eastern side of Sri Lanka. His father works as a lawyer and his mother is a schoolteacher. His mother did not support his choice of law, but rather wanted him to study biosciences. He has two younger sisters who study dental science and nutrition.

The reason for Kasun's ambition to become a lawyer was an incident that happened when he was ten years old. On their way home from a neighbouring village, he and his father had to pass through an area controlled by Tamil insurgents. They were stopped by armed men and asked to hand over their vehicle. His father explained that even though as Muslims living in a nearby village they were sympathetic to the insurgents' cause, he could not hand over the car. The armed men then put a gun to Kasun's head and asked the question again. His father immediately surrendered the car. After this incident, Kasun began to read and think about what he could do to prevent such incidents from occurring. After reading the Constitution and about the process of its writing, he discovered law and legal work. The law, for him, is the only available tool to promote changes in society. He still believes in the law, even though he has experienced an ambiguous legal system with frail hopes of justice for those on the margins of society.

In a postwar setting marked by growing hostility towards minorities and Muslims, law for Kasun stood out as the last resort against violations and the further degradation of society. His mother was worried about the possible consequences of his work, while his father accepted his choice, even though he did not support it. Kasun recalled his father's cautious words: 'It is up to you, it is your future.'

Kasun already experienced the attention of state agencies due to his volunteer work. While he was working in Diganna, the intelligence agency called him and asked about his whereabouts and residence. They called him again when he returned to Colombo in order to ensure that he had left the area. However, this attention was not a surprise. Civil activism and human rights have been dangerous for decades. During the latest war, numerous people were arrested and some were 'disappeared' in so-called 'white van' abductions. The attention of state agencies and the risk of arrest because of the work was a shared concern in the families of the young lawyers.

Harshani

I always wanted to work independently. I wanted to work on human right. I soon realised what I learned at university was very different in real life. I rarely saw high-profile fundamental rights cases, but more often everyday small cases of violations. (Harshani)

It is against this background that young people such as Harshani seek the legal profession with aspirations of *becoming* and respectability. Harshani is preparing for the bar exam, but her ambition is to work on human rights with a nongovernmental organisation (NGO). Initially she wanted to study languages and become a teacher; however, she later changed to law, to the satisfaction of her father, who works as a manager at a large company in Colombo. She explains: 'The reason that I changed discipline was to be able to assist people who can't defend themselves.' Although she does not believe that society dramatically changes for the better through law and legal institutions, especially for poor people in the rural areas, she nevertheless believes that small changes can be achieved through working in communities to help people know their rights and have access to justice: 'I would like to teach people about their rights, is this not a duty to society? – I would like to work with people, not in the courts. Even at the courts there is politics; biased judges and lawyers that are money minded – they do anything to obtain what they want!' She is already disappointed by the legal profession, but she values how her knowledge of law and the legal system can assist people to understand and perhaps access their rights. In her own way, she is combining the ambition of teaching with law and the legal profession.

Harshani's mother did not support this decision. Her mother works in corporate finance and wanted her to enter the private sector as well, never stopping in her attempts to find more suitable employment for her. Harshani's elder sister is a mathematical Ph.D. fellow in the Australia and she and her husband agree with their mother. There is a certain degree of pressure on Harshani to obtain a higher-level education and a well-paid job outside of Sri Lanka, just like her sister. However, Harshani likes to work with people, especially in the rural areas.

Harshani's mother does not support her travelling and interacting with such a variety of people, feeling that it is unsafe. In Harshani's words, 'She is just like all mothers.' Complicating things even more, Harshani's fiancé is a military officer. They met at university while he was studying political science in the same year. He likewise does not support Harshani's desire to work at the courts or travel across the country. He accepts her work on human rights because, as she reports: 'He does not really have a good understanding of it!' Considering the atrocities committed during the war and the unfulfilled transitional justice process, this is a potential issue of conflict hovering over their relationship. Such tensions may call for difficult decisions in the future. In Harshani's words: 'There are a lot of issues to think about – maybe there is a 10% chance that I will work for human rights in the future.'

War and Politics

To understand the predicaments and potentials of life and career paths in human rights work, we need to situate the young lawyers' aspirations in the wider political terrain of Sri Lankan society, which conditions and frames their choices and navigational capacity. This involves conflict, war and the politicisation of legal institutions, which influences legal work as well as the career prospects of individuals entering the legal profession.

Two independent armed conflicts have marred Sri Lanka for decades. The insurrections of left-wing mainly Sinhalese youth in the south mobilised by the JVP (Janatha Vimukthi Peramuna/People's Liberation Front), and the Liberation Tigers of Tamil Eelam (LTTE) conflict which mobilised Tamil youth in the northeast, have their roots in unfulfilled expectations and a mismatch between the aims of and opportunities for young people. During the first conflict young people were mobilised based on ideology and rebellion against the political rule of the country, while in the latter were mobilised through the demand for territorial self-determination in which religion and language played divisive roles. Both uprisings where met by a military response that ended with the complete defeat of those who challenged the uniformity of the state and the heterogeneity of nationality and religion, in which ethnonationalist and majority ideologies permeated society (DeVotta 2004; Weiss 2011; Mohan 2014; Keen 2014).

More than 65,000 people have been officially recognised as having been disappeared during the decade-long war, though the actual numbers might exceed 100,000 (Amnesty International 2017). Between 75,000 and 150,000 people were killed, including both civilians and military personal. Most of those killed during the armed conflict were youths, the majority of them young men. Although the armed conflict is over, refugees (mainly Tamils) are not returning in greater numbers, which may be an indication that fear and mistrust are still prevalent amongst large sections of the population (Azmi, Brun and Lund 2017).

The war militarised (de Mel 2008) and securitised (Spencer 2016) the Sri Lankan territory, society and economy. For example, the armed forces in Sri Lanka number more than 300,000 out of a population of 22 million. The armed forces have become an integral part of what Venugopal (2011) calls 'military fiscalism'. The state uses it to provide economic opportunities in impoverished and underprioritised rural areas through the sustained recruitment of youth, primarily young men. It has also impacted upon retail infrastructure, particularly the 99-year lease of Hambantota Port and the 99-year lease of the US $85 billion Port City project in Colombo by Chinese companies.

These parallel developments are integral to the Sri Lankan economic policy of deepening capital liberalisation and a free-market investment economy, which aimed at reconstructing the country since the end of the war in 2009 (Bastian 2013; Kadirgamar 2013a; Keerawella 2013), which nonetheless have deepened inequalities in society (Kadirgamar 2013b). Ending the war enabled the previous government to further centralise the state and consolidate its political power, arguably aggravating rather than addressing the ethnic minorities' grievances that underpinned the conflict to begin with (Byrne and Klem 2015). This situation has essentially remained unchanged during the former and current administration, with the government unable to deliver on its promises of reconciliation and transitional justice and continuing to cater for vested interests via mundane patrimonial politics.

Troubling Youths

The involvement of young people in violent organisations continues to be a special concern in Sri Lanka, more than ten years after the ending of the violent conflicts. When Muslim property, businesses and people were attacked on 5 March 2018 in Diganna in the district of Kandy, more than one hundred houses and three mosques were burnt and several people were killed. The government declared a state of emergency, imposed a curfew and blocked social media in an attempt to prevent further ethnoreligiously motivated violence by people following a Sinhala Buddhist nationalistic ideology. The violence had been stimulated through discourses of othering on a foundation of social fear, territorial supremacy, political exclusion, and societal and communal antagonisms. The attack was not considered to be a random event and nor did it come as a surprise. There had been many warning signs before the event, especially on social media. When the hate and fear that was spreading via social media transformed into violence, it had been preplanned and organised. In the days that followed the attack, the police arrested some 200 persons, the majority of whom appear to have been young men. This showed yet again the violent and destabilising potential of youth in Sri Lanka, which has marred the country for decades.

In the aftermath of the 1980s violent conflicts, a Presidential Commission on Youth Unrest (1990)[3] was established to address the causes of violent mobilisation. Ever since, youth dissociation and dissatisfaction with the state and society have been on the political agenda. Various attempts have been made to understand why young people turn to violence. The Commission itself found that these actions could mainly be explained as a response to the abuse of political power from public institutions and the inability of young people to secure employment (Presidential Commission on Youth Unrest 1990). Political exclusion, insufficient economic opportunities and lack of education were seen as causes of violent mobilisation and armed conflict. Unemployment was found to be an important destabilising factor. Conversely, employment was promoted as a viable and tangible solution that could advance political integration and create a sense of recognition and future accomplishment amongst the youth (Hettige and Mayer 2002). Sri Lankan youth were seen as an unused potential resource, and their integration into the economy through education and employment was the main avenue used for peace and stability.

Along similar lines, Ibargüen (2004) argues that youth mobilisation was intimately linked to unresolved contradictions of expanding educational opportunities and shrinking spaces for employment. When the Sri Lankan welfare state developed after independence, it facilitated prospects for social mobility by providing free education. Amongst other achievements, this opened up opportunities for rural youth to enter the ranks of the state bureaucracy with its associated higher social status. For decades, as the welfare state developed, educated youth entered the ranks of the civil service, which contributed to the expectation that educational qualifications would automatically translate into white-collar government employment (Hettige 1992; Uyangoda 2000). However, when this 'normal' progression slowed down as state positions were filled up, it created dissatisfaction and disappointment. Citing the works of Hettige (1992), Uyangoda (2000) and Mayer (2002), Ibargüen argues that 'the dissatisfaction and frustration of youth who had not been able to translate formal educational qualifications to "proper" jobs or a move up the social ladder has been advanced as one of the principal reasons for their attraction and involvement in anti-systemic movements' (Ibargüen 2014: 18). Other authors have similarly argued that attention should be directed towards a sense of relative, rather than actual, deprivation in order to better understand the array of reasons for mobilisation (Fernando 2002; Mayer 2002).

Some question 'youth' as a unified category, arguing that it glosses over the fact that this is a highly heterogeneous demographic group, divided along class, gender, political and geographical lines. Youth unrest and violent mobilisation cannot be seen in isolation from the context that has generated it. They concede that young people's grievances can be summarised as unemployment and failing economic opportunities, but contend that these are informed by social, political and cultural issues, and specific life conditions that must be understood from the perspectives of the involved individuals who are situated in particular communities and wider political ecologies (Amarasuriya, Gündüz and Mayer 2009; Amarasuriya 2010; Hughes 2017; Thiranagama 2011).

Others investigated the consequences for mental health such as *post-traumatic stress disorder* (PTSD) and depression on young people growing up under the shadow of political uncertainties, armed conflict and violence (Mollica et al. 2004; Mahoney et al. 2006; Neuner et al. 2006; Wickrama 2007; Catani et al. 2008; Elbert et al. 2009). This line of research explores how violent exposure affects society over time. For example, there may be relevant connections to the fact that nearly twenty out of every 100,000 people attempt suicide every year in Sri Lanka (Hendin et al. 2008; Siva 2010) or to causes of poverty and substance misuse (Knipe et al. 2018). It has been argued that escalating suicide rates (particularly amongst rural youth) in the 1980s and 1990s indicated the hopeless sociocultural circumstances from which both Sinhala and Tamil militant groups drew their recruits (Spencer 1990).

The above studies all attempt to understand and explain youth perspectives and motivations of their life choices. Together, they pose the question of how the recurrence of violence, such as in the Diganna incident, is connected to or can be explained by past experiences of violence, changing opportunity structures for youth, political mismanagement and the conflation of political and private interests. These are issues that influence not only the youths that become mobilised for violence, but also the choices of students, such as the young lawyers discussed in this chapter.

Contrary to the youth involved in the armed uprisings, these young lawyers do not reject law and the state; instead, their life trajectories are entangled with both. Despite this, numerous studies have shown how the judicial system has been undermined by political interference, extralegal rules and legal procedures that sustain a culture of arbitrary arrests, torture and impunity, and flawed investigations and legal proceedings (ICG 2009, 2016; Fernando 2009, 2013, 2016; Pinto-Jayawardena 2010). This has resulted in a backlog of cases, procedural delays and the inadequate administration of the courts, where lawyers and their clients often attend court only to have their case postponed to another date, often up to half a year later. Nevertheless, the client is required to pay their lawyer's fee, which means the lawyer earns money regardless of whether the case moves forward in court or not. The longer the case runs, the more money can be made, leaving a public image of lawyers as greedy and immoral, having little consideration for their clients, the law or the legal process.

Nonetheless, the young lawyers still see the law as a tool to rectify flawed decision-making and improve governance and institutional practices, including the politicisation of institutions, the slowness and arbitrariness of the judicial system, police violence to obtain confessions, private and political interference in cases and corruption. Their progression and formation as both professionals and individuals are entangled and depend on legal institutions such as the attorney general's office, the anti-corruption commission, human rights commission and the courts. For them, law and legal practice is a career choice for achieving professional accomplishment and it is an aspiration of social becoming – at the same time constituting a present practical and workable process and an imagined future of accomplishment.

Lawyers by Choice

The aspirations of the young lawyers who are covered in this chapter follow two avenues of becoming; first, by securing a job in a competitive sector and, second, by working as a human rights activist through assisting people in need and influencing politics and society at large. These avenues are situated within established norms of accomplishment in society, influencing individual career choices, based on middle-calls ambitions of economic solvency and the social respectability of altruistic activism. Still, law work and the legal profession are also somewhat defined by both common public notions of greed and a professional ethos of 'rightness' in which the lawyers-to-be find themselves.

Saman, Kasun and Harshani are well aware of lawyers' bad public reputation, yet have chosen the field with the intention of contributing to society. They specifically distance themselves from their peers in the legal profession; there is shared a recognition that 'the majority of my fellow students have no interest in human rights' (Harshani) and that 'I and a few others, less than ten out of more than 150, are the only ones that think like this, most are interested in civil law or corporate law, just to earn money' (Saman). Regardless of whether their fellow students would agree with these claims, the statements nonetheless illustrate their felt-need to distance themselves from the popular negative notions of the legal profession in general. Working as interns and juniors at private practices of law, they have already seen how senior lawyers accept cases that cannot be won and who drag out or fail to actively seek solutions to cases because they earn more money. In the words of Kasun, 'the character of the person will always be questioned when one becomes a lawyer and when one works as a lawyer'. This is also echoed in their families' understanding of the profession and their disagreement or only reluctant support of the young person's choice of career path, possibly due to not meeting middle-class understandings and recognition of respectability, solvency and accomplishment. The young lawyers navigate their own aspirations alongside the will of the families. They manoeuvre between their personal desires and the expectations or disapproval of their families, the latter of which ranging from silent acquiescence to the withdrawal of social and financial support.

However, such disapproval is not the same across gender or expected roles in the family. For example, Kasun and Saman are both the eldest sons in their respective families. They both felt the expectations within their families that they, as the eldest sons, will take care of their parents when they retire or grow older and possibly need daily assistance. Kasun chose against the will of his family to become a lawyer, but it was not an easy or straightforward decision. He tried to fulfil the expectations and traditions in his family to work in the biosciences, but was drawn towards the legal field by a strong sense of justice and dedication to help other people, especially those in his community who are unable to fend off injustices and access their rights. He knew that he would then have to manage his own life without family support and made sure that he was financially able to stand his ground and pursue his dream. He made his choice despite opposition from his family, especially his mother. Though Kasun's career choice went against the will of his family, it was not a direct challenge to the family harmony as his father is a lawyer himself. At present, Kasun is young and his parents remain active, not requiring assistance in their daily life. In time, changes to this situation might force him to confront a decision about where to settle, live and practise, but for now he is preoccupied with realising the full potential of his chosen profession.

Saman also chose the law over family expectations. He similarly abandoned a career that had the full support of his family to pursue a career in the legal profession instead. His choice was not well received within his family. There was the intention that he would take over the family's agricultural poultry business and settle in the family lands to continue developing what the family had already achieved. Saman wanted to pursue a more 'colourful' line of work than the poultry business; however, the legal profession is not the end goal of his ambitions. He dreams of becoming a local politician and of representing his constituency as an MP. However, this aspiration itself is not far from his family's experiences and expectations. If he prevails, he will join a tradition of electoral politics that his grandfather initiated and his uncle sustained. Though both Kasun and Saman somewhat challenged family expectations, at the same time their choices and future aspirations contribute to established family trajectories and recognised career paths, which work towards social respectability and accomplishment.

Similarly, Harshani chose a career to mixed family reactions. She changed from the discipline of language and the ambition to become a teacher to the field of law. Her family did not support this decision, not because she had chosen a new career, but because of the fact that the type of work was perceived to be unsafe. The family came to accept her choice, but also continue to place a degree of pressure on her to travel abroad and complete higher-level education, which would send her out of country and away from her chosen field. Another complicating issue is the fact that her fiancé is a military officer. In his line of work, relocations and transfers are a basic condition. If they are married, Harshani will traditionally be obliged to follow her husband's placement. To work independently might be a challenge in the future. Though Harshani enjoys her work, she also realises this might be a passing opportunity in her life. To some extent, she is facing two life choices: she can either follow her sister and study abroad, which might lead to permanent relocation, or she can stay working in Sri Lanka, with all the challenges this entails for her professional career, life and livelihood. For her, as for Saman and Kasun, the choice of law has opened up both opportunities and difficult life choices that unsettle and bring together family expectations, societal norms and personal desires.

Regardless of their families' concerns, all of Saman's, Kasun's and Harshani's ambitions are in the legal field – to use law to assist people and to change society to the better. However, engaging in the field of human rights work is not straightforward. Paid positions and employment opportunities are rare. Internships and volunteer work are the starting points for most young lawyers, yet there is limited scope for transforming themselves into legal professionals within these organisations. Money is scarce, jobs are few in number and the risks can be high when undertaking human rights and fundamental rights cases (often against perpetrating law enforcement agencies) in such a political heightened and tense environment. Though different in detail, Saman, Kasun and Harshani are each divided between middle-class notions of the good life (such as economic solvency and predictability), personal ambitions of performing law in the centre of politics and activist aims of contributing to improving society at large, leaving a mark in the development of the nation like the prominent lawyers who came before them. The law and legal work become the instrument and the site of personal development and accomplishment, potentially fulfilling both professional ambitions and family expectations, while at the same time contributing to society. It is a desire and it is a process in which *becoming* is the agency of future.

Conclusion

Paying attention to the ways in which the young people attempt to prepare and form themselves for future becoming illustrates how these young lawyers' choices, anticipations and notions of potential futures are produced in intersections between people, institutions and society. The choice of career and their aspirations are about opportunities and potentials for social accomplishment that reach beyond the immediate present into the prospective, yet ambiguous and uncertain, future. Each of the individuals above has made their own choice about education and career, choices which are not popular and, while not colliding with notions of respectability, solvency or status, rarely attract the full support of their families. Nonetheless, their choices encapsulate their ambitions and their imagined futures, based on a capacity to navigate social norms and family expectations, aiming for social recognition, professional achievement and political contributions. It is a process that intersects self-development and social consciousness, combining professionalism and activism, navigating between the different expectations and responsibilities, while reconciling clashing imaginaries and expectations, and confronting contradictions of uncertain, yet possible, futures.

These young people work to prepare and form themselves for future accomplishments, notwithstanding their families' concerns. This work on the self is based in their continued ambitions of doing good for others. They actively navigate between personal ambitions and family responsibilities, to use law to assist people and to change society to the better, while establishing themselves in the field of human rights legal activism, which they anticipate will provide sought-after respectability and commendation.

This agency of the future shows aspirations as a relational process and imaginary, formed in the intersections between people, imaginaries and (educational and legal) institutions, forming their aims, ambitions and desires. However, these are not static, but are constantly changing in their interactions with people, families and society, as a moving terrain that conditions and is conditioned by emerging and receding conflicts, contradictions, opportunities and potentialities.

Intrinsically, aspirations reconcile and project hope – for the lawyers-to-be, for their families and for society.

Morten Koch Andersen specialises in the study of the interdisciplinary nexus of violence, human rights and corruption, with a special focus on the administration of justice, legal reform and institutional practices, mainly in South Asia. His current research interests are rule of law practices, violent exchanges, accidental citizenship and violent social orders, and their effects on individuals, institutions and societies. He has researched youth and urban violence and human rights documentation. He has previously managed preventive and rehabilitative interventions programs on violence, war trauma and torture for a decade. He researches at the Centre for Global Criminology, Anthropology, University of Copenhagen, Denmark.

Notes

I would like to thank the editors and the reviewers for their valuable comments and critique.
1. Pseudonyms have been used for the research participants mentioned in this chapter out of respect for their privacy.
2. This includes permanent institutions such as the Human Rights Commission, the National Police Commission, the Commission to Investigate Allegations of Bribery or Corruption and the Public Service Commission, newer ones such as the Office in Missing Persons and the Right to Information Commission, as well as several time time-bound Commissions of Inquiry – for example, the 1946, 1970, 1995 and 2004 inquiries into police institutions and practices, the Lessons Learnt and Reconciliation Commission, Commissions of Inquiry into the Involuntary Removal or Disappearance of Persons and the International Independent Group of Eminent Persons.
3. The National Youth Policy of Sri Lanka defines youth as those within the age group of fifteen to twenty-nine. It is estimated that there are approximately 4 million individuals in that age category, which represents nearly a fifth of the total population of twenty-one million (Department of Census and Statistics Sri Lanka, retrieved 7 June 2018 from http://www.statistics.gov.lk/PopHouSat/VitalStatistics/MidYearPopulation/Mid-year%20population%20by%20age%20group.pdf).

References

Amarasuriya, Harini. 2010. 'Discrimination and Social Exclusion of Youth in Sri Lanka', in Ramani Gunatilaka, Markus Mayer and Milan Vodopivec (eds), *The Challenges of Youth Employment in Sri Lanka*. Washington DC: World Bank, pp. 199–216.

Amarasuriya, Harini, Canan Gündüz and Markus Mayer. 2009. *Rethinking the Nexus between Youth, Unemployment and Conflict: Perspectives from Sri Lanka*. London: International Alert.

Amnesty International. 2017. *Only Justice Can Heal Our Wounds: Listening to the Demands of Families of the Disappeared in Sri Lanka*. London: Amnesty International.

Andersen, Morten Koch. 2016. 'Time-Use, Activism and the Making of Future', *South Asia: Journal of South Asian Studies* 39(2): 415–29.

——. 2018. 'Thresholds of Mobilization: Coercion and Opportunity', in Henrik Vigh and Steffen Jensen (eds), *Sporadically Radical: Ethnographies of Organized Violence and Militant Mobilization.* Copenhagen: Museum Tusculanum Press, pp. 91–118.

——. 2019. 'Everyday Routines and the Making of Youth Politics in Bangladesh', *Contemporary South Asia* 27(3): 342–57.

Appadurai, Arjun. 2004. 'The Capacity to Aspire: Culture and the Terms of Recognition', in Vijayendra Rao and Michael Walton (eds), *Culture and Public Action.* Stanford: Stanford University Press, pp. 59–84.

Arunatilake, Nisha and Jayawardena, Priyanka, 'Labor Market Trends and Outcomes in Sri Lanka', in Ramani Gunatilaka, Markus Mayer and Milan Vodopivec (eds), *The Challenges of Youth Employment in Sri Lanka.* Washington DC: World Bank, pp. 19–48.

Bastian, Sunil. 2013. *The Political Economy of Post-war Sri Lanka. Research Paper no 7.* Colombo: International Centre for Ethnic Studies.

Boccagni, Paolo. 2017. 'Aspirations and the Subjective Future of Migration: Comparing Views and Desires of the "Time Ahead" through the Narratives of Immigrant Domestic Workers', *Comparative Migration Studies* 5(4): 1–18.

Byrne, Sarah, and Bart Klem. 2015. 'Constructing Legitimacy in Post-war Transition: The Return of "Normal" Politics in Nepal and Sri Lanka?', *Geoforum* 66: 224–33.

Catani, C., Jacob, N., Schauer, E., Kohila, M., & Neuner, F. 2008. 'Family violence, war and natural disaster: A study of the effect of extreme stress on children's mental health in Sri Lanka', *BMC Psychiatry*, 8:33. doi:10.1186/1471-244X-8-33

Christiansen, Catrine, Mats Utas and Heinrik Vigh. 2006. 'Introduction: Navigating Youth, Generating Adulthood', in Catrine Christiansen, Mats Utas and Henrik Vigh (eds), *Navigating Youth – Generating Adulthood: Social Becoming in an African Context.* Uppsala: Nordic Africa Institute, pp. 9–30.

De Mel, Neloufer. 2008. *Militarizing Sri Lanka: Popular Culture, Narrative and Memory in Sri Lanka.* New Delhi: Sage.

Desai, S. 2007. 'The Middle Class', in Kaushik Basu (ed.), *The Oxford Companion to Economics in India.* Oxford: Oxford University Press, pp. 345–57.

Deshpande, Satish. 2003. *Contemporary India: A Sociological View.* London: Penguin.

DeVotta, Neil. 2004. *Blowback: Linguistic Nationalism, Institutional Decay and Ethnic Conflict in Sri Lanka.* Stanford: Stanford University Press.

Elbert, Thomas, Maggie Schauer, Elisabeth Schauer, Bianca Huschka, Michael Hirth and Frank Neuer. 2009. 'Trauma-Related Impairment in Children: A Survey in Sri Lankan Provinces Affected by Armed Conflict', *Child Abuse and Neglect* 33(4): 238–46.

Fazeeha, Azmi, Cathrine Brun and Ragnhild Lund. 2017. 'Young People's Recovery in Eastern Sri Lanka: From War to Postwar and Beyond', in Christopher Harker, Kathrin Hörschelmann and Tracey Skelton (eds), *Conflict, Violence and Peace.* Singapore: Springer, pp. 169–86.

Fernandes, Leela. 2006. *India's New Middle Class: Democratic Politics in an Era of Reform.* Minneapolis: University of Minnesota Press.

Fernando, Basil. 2009. *Recovering the Authority of Public Institutions: a Resource Book on Law and Human Rights in Sri Lanka.* Hong Kong: Asian Human Rights Centre.

——. 2013. *Narrative of Justice in Sri Lanka.* Hong Kong: Asian Legal Resource Centre.

——. 2016. *Undermining of the Legal and Political Systems.* Colombo, Sri Lanka: Wijesooriya Grantha Kendraya.

Fernando, Gaithri, Kenneth Miller and Dale Berger. 2010. 'Growing Pains: The Impact of Disaster-Related and Daily Stressors on the Psychological and Psychosocial Functioning of Youth in Sri Lanka', *Child Development* 81(4): 1192–210.

Fernando, L. 2002. 'Youth and Politics: Why They Rebel?', in Siripala Hettige and Markus Mayer (eds), *Sri Lankan Youth: Challenges and Responses*. Colombo: Friedrich Ebert-Stiftung Foundation, pp. 121–41.

Gunatilaka, R. Mayer, M. and Vodopivec M. (eds). 2010. *The challenge of youth employment in Sri Lanka*. Washington, DC: World Bank.

Gunatilaka, Ramani and Vodopivec, Milan. 2010. 'Labor Market Institutions and Labor Market Segmentation in Sri Lanka', in Ramani Gunatilaka, Markus Mayer and Milan Vodopivec (eds), *The Challenges of Youth Employment in Sri Lanka*. Washington DC: World Bank, pp. 49–68.

Gupta, Dipankar. 2000. *Mistaken Modernity: India between Two Worlds*. Delhi: HarperCollins.

Harris-White, Barbara, and Anushree Sinha (eds). 2007. *Trade Liberalization and India's Informal Economy*. Oxford: Oxford University Press.

Hendin, Herbert, Michael Philips, Laskhmi Vijayakumar, Jane Pirkis, Hong Wang, Paul Yip, Danuta Wasserman, José Bertolote and Alexandra Fleischmann (eds). 2008. *Suicide and Suicide Prevention in Asia*. Geneva: World Health Organization.

Hettige, Siripala. 1992. 'Introduction', in Siripala Hettige (ed.), *Unrest or Revolt: Some Aspects of Youth Unrest in Sri Lanka*. Colombo: Goethe Institute, pp. v–xxv.

Hettige, Siripala, and Markus Mayer (eds). 2002. *Sri Lankan Youth: Challenges and Responses*. Colombo: Friedrich Ebert Stiftung Foundation.

Hughes, Dhana. 2017. 'Violence of Youth and the Youthfulness of Violence', in Christopher Harker, Kathrin Hörschelmann and Tracey Skelton (eds), *Conflict, Violence and Peace*. Singapore: Springer, pp. 1–17.

Ibargüen, Claudia. 2014. Youth in Sri Lanka: A review of Literature Working paper on Poverty and Youth, The Centre for Poverty Analysis (CEPA), Colombo, Sri Lanka.

ICG. 2009. *Sri Lanka's Judiciary: Politicised Courts, Compromised Rights (Report No. 172)*. Brussels: International Crisis Group.

——. 2016. *Sri Lanka: Jumpstarting the Reform Process (Report No. 278)*. Brussels: International Crisis Group.

Jeffrey, Craig. 2008. 'Kicking away the Ladder: Student Politics and the Making of an Indian Middle Class', *Environment and Planning D: Society and Space* 26: 517–36.

——. 2010a. 'Timepass: Youth, Class and Time among Unemployed Young Men in India', *American Ethnologist* 37(3): 465–81.

——. 2010b. *Timepass: Youth, Class and the Politics of Waiting*. Stanford: Stanford University Press.

Kadirgamar, Ahilan. 2013a. 'Second Wave of Neoliberalism: Financialisation and Crisis in Post-war Sri Lanka', *Economic and Political Weekly* 48(35). See https://www.epw.in/journal/2013/35/web-exclusives/second-wave-neoliberalism-financialisation-and-crisis-post-war-sri.

——. 2013b. 'Rebuilding the Post-war North', *Economic and Political Weekly* 48(43). See https://www.epw.in/journal/2013/43/web-exclusives/rebuilding-post-war-north.html.

Keen, David. 2014. 'The Camp and "the Lesser Evil": Humanitarianism in Sri Lanka', *Conflict, Security & Development* 14(1): 1–31.

Keerawella, Gamini. 2013. *Post-war Sri Lanka: Is Peace a Hostage of the Military Victory? Dilemmas of Reconciliation, Ethnic Cohesion and Peace-Building*. Colombo: International Centre for Ethnic Studies.

Knipe, Duleeka, D. Gunnell, Melissa Pearson, Shaluka Jayamanne, Ravi Pieris, Chamil Priyadarshana, Manjula Weerashinghe, Keith Hawton, Flemming Konradsen, Michael Eddleston and Chris Metcalfe. 2018. 'Attempted Suicide in Sri Lanka: An Epidemiological Study of Household and Community Factors', *Journal of Affective Disorders* 232: 177–84.

Kumar, Satendra. 2012. 'Ethnography of Youth Politics: Leaders, Brokers and Morality in Provincial University in Western Uttar Pradesh', *History and Sociology of South Asia*, 6, pp. 41–70.

Mahoney, J., Chandra, V., Gambheera, H., De Silva, T., & Suveendran, T. 2006. 'Responding to the mental health and psychosocial needs of the people of Sri Lanka in disasters', *International Review of Psychiatry* 18(6): 593–97.

Mayer, Markus. 2002. 'Violent Youth Conflicts in Sri Lanka: Comparative Results from Jaffna and Hambantota', in Siripala Hettige and Markus Mayer (eds), *Sri Lankan Youth: Challenges and Responses*. Colombo: Friedrich Ebert-Stiftung Foundation, pp. 216–256

Mohan, Rohini. 2014. *The Seasons of Trouble: Life amid the Ruins of Sri Lanka Civil War*. London: Verso.

Mollica, R. F., Cardozo, B. L., Osofsky, H. J., Raphael, B., Ager, A., & Salama, P. 2004. 'Mental health in complex emergencies', *Lancet*, 364, pp. 2058–2067.

Neuner, F., Schauer, E., Catani, C., Ruf, M., & Elbert, T. 2006. 'Post-tsunami stress: A study of posttraumatic stress disorder in children living in three severely affected regions in Sri Lanka', *Journal of Traumatic Stress* 19(3): 339–47

Pinto-Jayawardena, Kishali. 2010. *Still Seeking Justice: Rule of Law, the Criminal Justice System and Commissions of Inquiry since 1977*. International Commission of Jurists. Geneva, Switzerland.

Presidential Commission on Youth Unrest. 1990. *Report of the Presidential Commission on Youth*. Colombo: Government Publication Bureau.

Ruwanpura, Kanchana. 2016. 'Post-war Sri Lanka: State, Capital and Labour and the Politics of Reconciliation', *Contemporary South Asia* 24(4): 351–59.

Ruud, Arild. 2014. 'The Political Bully in Bangladesh', in Anastasia Piliavsky (ed.), *Patronage as Politics in South Asia*. Delhi: Cambridge University Press, pp. 303–25.

Siva, Nayana. 2010. 'Sri Lanka Struggles with Mental Health Burden', *The Lancet* 375(9718): 880–81. http://dx.doi.org/10.1016/S0140-6736(10)60370-4.

Somasundaram, Daya. 2002. 'Child Soldiers: Understanding the Context', *BMJ* 324(7348): 1268–71.

Spencer, Jonathan. 2007. *Anthropology, Politics and the State: Democracy and Violence in South Asia*. Cambridge: Cambridge University Press.

——. 2016. 'Securitization and Its Discontents: the End of Sri Lanka's Long Post-war', *Contemporary South Asia* 24(1): 94–108.

——. (ed.). 1990. *Sri Lanka: History and the Roots of Conflict*. London: Routledge.

Spencer, Jonathan, Jonathan Goodhand, Shahul Hasbullah, Bart Klem, Benedikt Korf and Kalinga Tudor Silva. 2015. *Checkpoint, Temple, Church and Mosque: A Collaborative Ethnography of War and Peace*. London: Pluto Press.

Srivastava, Sanjay. 2009. *Urban Spaces, Disney-Divinity and Moral Middle Classes in Delhi*. New Delhi: Routledge.

Thiranagama, Sharika. 2011. *In My Mother's House: Civil War in Sri Lanka*. Philadelphia: University of Pennsylvania Press.

Uyangoda, J. 2000. 'Southern Insurgency and the Future of Insurrectionist Politics in Sri Lanka', in J. Uyangoda (ed.), *Sri Lanka's Conflict: Context and Options*. Colombo: CHA, pp. 49–73.

Varma, Pavan. 1998. *The Great Indian Middle Class*. New Delhi: Penguin Books.

Venugopal, Rajesh. 2011. 'The Politics of Market Reform at a Time of Civil War: Military Fiscalism in Sri Lanka', *Economic & Political Weekly* 46(49): 67–75.

Vigh, H. 2006. *Navigating Terrains of War: Youth and Soldiering in Guinea-Bissau*. Oxford: Berghahn Books.

Weiss, Gordon. 2011. *The Cage: the Fight for Sri Lanka and the Last Days of the Tamil Tigers*. London: Bodley Head.

Wickrama, K. A. S., & Wickrama, K. A. T. 2007. 'Family context of mental health risk in tsunami affected adolescents: Findings from a pilot study in Sri Lanka', *Soc Sci Med*, 64, 713–23.

8

Cosmopolitan Coffee Aspirations in Contemporary Vietnam

Sarah G. Grant

One way for an aspiring young barista to make it in the Vietnamese specialty coffee industry is to pour exceptional latte art, yet a rosetta design or a layered heart with perfect balance, symmetry and texture of milk is easier said than done. In August 2017, nearly three dozen Vietnamese baristas registered for an amateur latte art competition on the outskirts of Ho Chi Minh City. The competitors were a mix of men and women, mostly between the ages of eighteen and twenty-five and from the city or an immediately neighbouring province. Some competitors drove at least two hours simply for the opportunity to compete. The competition itself was hosted by a local coffee enthusiast, Duc,[1] who regularly opens his home and ground floor café to promising baristas – he provides the expensive, high-end espresso machines, tampers and milk jugs, and baristas bring their own coffee and milk to practise with.

On this particular day, Duc was live-streaming and narrating the competition on social media and encouraging competitors to support each other with enthusiastic cheering, clapping and words of encouragement. The goal of the event was to collegially introduce amateurs to the world of professional coffee, where creativity, skill and aspiration all seemingly matter. The competition itself was only open to first-time competitors, each representing the café at which they worked. They each created personalised performances, but also represented a larger collective of Vietnamese coffee professionals who aspire to create a community through regular competitions, sponsorships and support of the kind they often see in specialty coffee cultures in Japan, Europe and the United States.[2] During the event,

Endnotes for this chapter begin on page 167.

competitors were required to produce several free-pour lattes in a designated amount of time, present them to a panel of judges and wait to hear the results of each round. At the end of the seven-hour single-elimination tournament, a winner was declared, modest awards were distributed and advice was shared with those who failed to advance. Defeated and dripping with sweat, all but a handful of the young competitors hopped on their motorbikes and sped off to work at various cafés across the city. At the end of the day, each of these coffee enthusiasts must still 'make a living' and provide for someone, whether it is themselves, their immediate family or their friends (see Sasges 2013).

Although an amateur competition like this might be considered informal, the competitors themselves reveal something much deeper about young adult aspirations in urban Vietnam. In a country where cafés line streets, alleyways, upper levels of high-rise buildings and the front porches of rural houses, serving coffee is not unique or new. Nor is conspicuous consumption and the use of brands to perform a middle-class sensibility (Earl 2014; Truitt 2008; Vann 2012). However, the aspiration to serve coffee for a living is indeed new among young adults in Vietnam. Unlike the 'class-based aspirations that are framed by a state-sponsored notion of development that promotes internal strength and self-reliance' shared by rural agricultural enterprises (Nguyen 2018: 109), the aspirations of young coffee professionals are rooted in a desire to foster global community that calls into question the boundaries of class distinctions. If becoming cosmopolitan necessitates experience with Ho Chi Minh City and global virtual communities, it does not necessarily come to fruition in middle-class status. In fact, few young coffee professionals discuss their class status, although the anecdotes that follow suggest their financial struggles and inability to afford living in a city, let alone travel abroad for coffee competitions. While rural coffee farmers often express their aspirations in terms of social and economic mobility, young baristas expressed their aspirations in terms of a desire to find their creative selves, whether their selves existed in the city, a small town or abroad.

Having a middle-class sensibility or identifying with perceived middle-class cultural activities and forms of consumption is a common thread across coffee professionals. However, this sensibility materialises in ways that are distinct from those identified in the other chapters in this volume. Aspirations for socioeconomic mobility, even among university-educated Vietnamese coffee professionals, are rarely mentioned in conversations about *why* someone pursues a career in coffee or seeks community in coffee culture. Although class distinctions may be visible from the outside, few young adults aspiring in the coffee industry take note of or measure each other's worth and value by standards of living or other class signifiers. Harms examines the Ho Chi Minh City public facing streetside cafés of the late 1990s and early 2000s, where 'friends from all social classes, ranging from poor rural migrants and economically strapped university students to business professionals and university professors' came together before the area transformed to 'something of an upper middle class domain' (Harms 2009: 185). In the 2010s, specialty coffee in the Vietnamese city presents something of a dilemma – the ways in which Vietnamese negotiate the preservation of Vietnamese coffee style with global coffee culture suggests that exploring urban aspiration as a process of negotiation is a generative way to understand what it means to be a young adult in a perpetually developing Asian metropolis.

Aspiration in Contemporary Vietnam

This chapter is situated at the seams of an ethnographic research project conducted over 20 months across 2011 and 2012 with several return visits since 2014. Although my longer-term research focuses on the Vietnamese coffee industry and how various actors across this space navigate state bureaucracy, multinational commodity coffee corporations and efforts to develop a domestic 'coffee identity' and brand, many interviewees, acquaintances and friends within the Vietnamese coffee industry are young adults who have tacked back and forth between the small highland town of Dalat and urban Ho Chi Minh City 300 kilometres to the south. As the coffee industry in Vietnam expands into the arena of global specialty coffee, these young adults are making a concerted effort to produce spaces that can accommodate this nascent culture. Producing these spaces requires a form of cosmopolitan knowledge that comes from experience with urban Vietnam and familiarity with the global specialty coffee community via social media platforms, participation in coffee 'pop-ups' or internationally sponsored coffee trade shows and competitions.

These young adults offer an especially informative glimpse into how urban Asia – in this context Vietnam – is conceptualised, desired and experienced as these coffee enthusiasts and entrepreneurs succeed, fail, embrace and reject the city. The 'prospect of being elsewhere' (Bunnell et al. 2018) is indeed a way to understand the aspirations of Hong, Thinh and Duc, the three young adults who are the subjects in this chapter. Each of them certainly imagines a future in which an elsewhere exists for them, although they each embrace this prospect and come to understand themselves in different ways. Scholars of urban Vietnam are careful not to chalk emerging categories up to neoliberalism as a blanket process that operates in predictable ways (Schwenkel and Leshkowich 2012). As a recent work by Schwenkel and Leshkowich on neoliberalism in Vietnam demonstrates, 'state-sponsored notions of "quality" – in the realm of commodities, aesthetics and knowledge practices – become aspirations for individuals and families, although often with implications for class and other hierarchies' (2012: 329). In the context of coffee, thinking beyond what the state might qualify as quality, Vietnamese coffee professionals are attempting to challenge state ideas of quality that are driven by an export market and international commodity prices. Aspiring towards a coffee quality defined by an international body that informally governs quality benchmarks for the specialty coffee industry nonetheless has implications for individuals, their families and communities.

In contemporary Vietnam, where the desire for material goods not only signifies one's class but also marks future socioeconomic mobility, young adults are 'classing up through consumption' (Leshkowich 2014: 181). Anthropologists examining urban Vietnam frequently address the concept of social mobility through the meandering category of the Vietnamese middle class – how middle-classness is produced and experienced in everyday Vietnam. This is taken up ethnographically by exploring the urban Vietnamese marketplace (Leshkowich 2014), the financial landscape (Kim 2008) and the experience of urbanisation on the city's edge (Harms 2011). Scholars of Vietnam have also offered many ways to think about social mobility through the material. As Truitt (2013) demonstrates, conceptually disentangling money with place, social mobility, longing and the Vietnamese state is no easy task. The visibility of capitalism in Ho Chi Minh City transcends material, conspicuous consumption. Truitt shows that money itself is shaping economic citizenship and what it means to be Vietnamese at an especially interesting moment in which social stratification becomes a lived experience and a product of a post-Đổi Mới market-oriented socialist economy. The concept of aspiration and futurity is certainly present in each of these works, albeit in different ways. Using aspiration as a framework to understand everyday life opens up new conceptual possibilities for thinking about urban Vietnam and the young adults living within it.

Bayly (2013) explores the 'achievement experience' from the context of late-socialist Hanoi, in the process revealing 'achievement as continually evolving, contested and reconceptualised' and the 'often painful moral concerns inflecting Vietnamese understandings of achievement' (2013: 159). In this context, she is exploring achievement from the context of 'achievement disease' (*bệnh thành tích*) and a particular kind of patriotic 'achiever-citizen'. This model and the work it does to unpack social and state dimensions to achievement also encourages further understandings of how aspiration is linked to achievement and what happens when aspirations are not met.

Following the introduction by Westendorp, Remmert and Finis in this volume, I am concerned less with defining aspiration and thinking through what constitutes urban Asia than with positioning aspirations as a cultural category for young adults in Vietnam. Ethnography seems to be an effective methodological approach to achieve this, as aspirations are neither fixed nor easily identifiable. Aspirations reveal themselves at the seams of everyday life where moments stitch together and young adults see or hear something that alters their perception of the future. For example, attending a 'latte art throwdown' (latte art competition) with a small group of coffee enthusiasts may lead to a conversation about why a young man may pass up employment opportunities to focus on coffee training and national competitions. One time, simply watching YouTube videos about climate change and coffee with a small group of interlocutors allowed me to hear why a young coffee professional left the city to intern for a project on an 'eco-friendly' sustainable and experimental coffee farm. Rarely did aspiration come up as a subject of discussion, except in the context of higher education, yet the capacity to aspire and the ways in which young adults aspired became increasingly obvious as they moved through their daily lives and discussed the possibility of crafting a career in coffee.

Specialty Coffee and Crafting a Career

Locally grown commodity-grade coffee that much of the country produces and consumes is relegated to 'Vietnamese-style coffee', often roasted commercially or chemically processed into soluble instant coffee crystals. Specialty coffee, however, is roasted lightly and brewed via a 'pour-over' method, and baristas in the specialty industry often note their training and careful attention to global specialty coffee consumption styles.[3] There is rarely sweetened condensed milk at these new 'specialty' cafés and baristas' efforts focus on the 'pure' quality of specialty coffees grown in Vietnam without the adulteration that often masks Robusta coffees from neighbouring provinces. Despite the rising production rates of specialty coffee varieties in Vietnam and the growing popularity of specialty cafés and consumption styles, these cafés are still few and far between in Vietnam.

In particular, becoming cosmopolitan is part of a larger aspiration to achieve professional and thus financial stability while simultaneously tapping into a national and international network of like-minded coffee enthusiasts who share similar interests and struggles in the industry. For example, one young man who was eliminated in the first round of the tournament shared that he was working in a café with no espresso machine, so he had limited opportunities to practise. He had moved to the city from a neighbouring province not necessarily for the opportunity to make more money, but in order to surround himself with like-minded baristas who cared about the industry. If he stayed at home with his family, he could have lived rent-free and made a similar wage, but the notion of serving regular coffee (*cà phê bình thường*) like everyone else or working to please his parents without following his passion seemed insufferable. Inspired by recent media attention on the specialty coffee industry in Vietnam, he ignored his family's wishes to work outside of an industry that few consider a legitimate career.

Work in specialty coffee is a relatively new occupation in Vietnam and thus a risky but malleable one with a steep learning curve and many potential career paths to follow. For example, one may begin as a barista and climb the ranks to become a roaster, a quality control specialist and grader or a café owner. The attention to quality at all stages of the specialty coffee spectrum reflects a turn towards quality control and a response to food safety scares and scandals related to coffee in Vietnam (see Uyên 2015). The emergence of specialty cafés also reflects an anxiety about a strong association between Vietnam and low-quality commodity coffees and an ambition to showcase the high-quality Arabicas that do exist in Vietnam. This is part of Duc's mission and the larger specialty coffee community's attempts to differentiate quality coffee from commodity coffee. One can aspire to something ostensibly great in the specialty industry, but commodity coffee work relegates the average Vietnamese youth to agricultural work. With agricultural work comes proximity to family and the obligations and limitations that may come with living at home.

The specialty coffee industry in Vietnam sheds light on what Appadurai (2004) refers to as the 'capacity to aspire', namely in the ways in which this industry illuminates how the process of realising and failing to realise aspirations is a collective experience for Vietnamese young adults across different educational and socioeconomic backgrounds. For many competitors, the end goal is a successful career in the coffee industry that, aspirationally, peaks at a shot for the national competition and an opportunity to compete on the global stage – a global stage that necessitates a nerve-wracking fifteen-minute performance in English in front of thousands of viewers. Rather than aspiring to wealth or social mobility, the Vietnamese baristas who train for years to compete on the national stage do so to represent what they view as a traditionally underrepresented country in the global coffee industry, despite being the second-largest coffee producer in the world. Ostensibly nationalistic, the aspirations of Duc and other young coffee professionals should not be reduced to a sentimental expression of national identity. Rather, it reflects pride in and commitment to a larger community of young Vietnamese who rely on each other and a global virtual network of friends and colleagues for support and creative influence in the industry. Duc's latte art competition was just the start for baristas who want to move forward and establish themselves as serious professionals within these real and community-based networks.

Cosmopolitan Café Culture

There are cafés everywhere in Ho Chi Minh City and the vast majority of them serve unbranded commodity-grade coffee from the Central Highlands region of the country, brewed in what has come to be known as a traditional Vietnamese style. A *cà phê sữa đá* is simply coffee brewed through a delicate metal filter and chamber with a sizeable serving of sweetened condensed milk served over ice.

This style of coffee, whether served on the street, at a park, in a sit-down café or perhaps at a *phở* restaurant in Chicago or Berlin, is ubiquitous. It is also synonymous with Vietnamese coffee, as popular international media outlets write about the surprise that is Vietnamese coffee and the 'treat' that the traditional brewing method results in (Spiegel 2017).[4] Although there is no shortage of cafés in the city, specialty coffee roasters and cafés are relatively few in number and range from small takeaway counters in the city centre of District 1 to multimillion dollar build-outs across the Saigon River. These specialty cafés reflect a cosmopolitan and trending style, modelled after spaces in international magazines and social media feeds.

Cafés aside, specialty coffee culture also exists in virtual spaces where baristas, coffee media companies and roasters construct and promote their respective brands. The Instagram feeds of many Vietnamese specialty cafés are not populated by simple photos of coffee cups and lattes; rather, the feeds are choreographed, carefully framed and sometimes captured with professional-grade cameras. The captions are often bilingual in Vietnamese and English or skip text altogether in favour of commonly used hashtags within the specialty coffee community (e.g. #farmtocup, #singleorigin and #kalitawave). Regardless, specialty coffee culture becomes a space for creative expression and identity-crafting for many young adults working in the industry, and it is positioned squarely against 'corporate brands' (Foster 2007) that are widely recognised with extensive distribution networks. As such, specialty coffee is a space where Vietnamese youths can simultaneously participate in and shape the future of Vietnam's reputation in a larger global industry.

Urban, cosmopolitan and virtual spaces are a way to understand the aspirations of young Vietnamese coffee enthusiasts specifically and Vietnamese young adults more generally. The specialty coffee industry provides a particularly timely and useful lens for exploring young adult aspirations because of its relationship to other cosmopolitan subcultures – a nascent farm-to-table food scene, creative graphic design and branding, music and burgeoning environmental activism. The newness of specialty coffee in Vietnam engenders an optimistic sense of possibility and generates a 'navigational capacity' (Appadurai 2004) that intersects with Vietnamese youths across the spectrum of the industry. This chapter also considers aspiration as a framework for thinking through contemporary Vietnam and the diverse ways in which aspiration is realised, practised and conceptualised among young adults within the nation. Notably, and in spite of the significant social media and photography presence in specialty coffee, the three young Vietnamese studied here all share a desire for a type of analogue existence that harkens back to a Vietnam before conspicuous consumption and branding (Vann 2005) shaped their young adult counterparts working in other industries across the country.

An ethnographic approach to specialty café culture brings into relief the complicated ways in which these small Vietnamese communities think beyond the nation and imagine lives as global coffee citizens with many aspirations. Vietnamese baristas and other coffee professionals are wittingly branding themselves as urban global citizens through their style (e.g. fashion and music) and use of English, while simultaneously redefining what it means to be local.[5] Some young baristas aspire to remain geographically situated outside of the city and they do so in a way that frames urban Ho Chi Minh City as a sort of repellent to creative possibilities – although cosmopolitan, an urban environment might cause one to forget where coffee is grown and what constitutes good-quality coffee. On the other hand, young baristas from the city and those who choose to migrate to the city conceptualise it as a sort of incubator for creative possibilities and community in coffee. Regardless, baristas from urban and rural Vietnam alike adopt specialty coffee and its cultural tributaries to develop and express a set of global aspirations. Here, belonging is about knowing where one comes from and having a deep knowledge and passion for one's career choice. Home and a sense of belonging exists in shared experiences, understandings and aspirations (see the chapters by Westendorp, Remmert and Finis in this volume).

It is important to point out that many Vietnamese young adults do conceptualise aspiration as something that comes to fruition only after graduation from university (*nguyện vọng của sinh viên*). Indeed, the anxiety around access to higher education in Vietnam is a complex landscape that certainly reveals the aspirational desires of young adults and the lived consequence of a student not fulfilling their role in a larger state project (Duong 2017). However, not all Vietnamese young adults place higher education at the forefront of their aspirations. Thinking about aspirations as a future-oriented category that does not always revolve around education allows us to explore questions of self-worth and motivation that exist outside of nation-building frameworks. Unlike young adults in Asia who may migrate because they seek new opportunities and a different lifestyle (see the chapter by Suzuki in this volume), these Vietnamese young adults seek to cultivate these opportunities for each other in Vietnam. A focus on specialty café culture in urban Vietnam illuminates cosmopolitanism as a concept that transcends higher education and socioeconomic status, while remaining ostensibly achievable to many Vietnamese baristas with the proper dedication and opportunities. Although some of the coffee professionals working in Vietnam are university-educated and middle class, many are not and recognise that accessing a cosmopolitan coffee community does not require a degree.

The stories of Hong and Thinh are parallel stories that never quite converge. Each of these emerges from a larger ethnographic research project about the rise of the Vietnamese coffee industry and how risk, uncertainty and the future are conceptualised and mitigated by a diverse community of Vietnamese and international coffee actors. Although this was not a project about aspiration, understanding risk as productive (Zaloom 2004) is an opportunity to explore aspiration as a product of risk. Risk is experienced in uneven ways across Vietnam. Moving beyond risk in the context of 'at-risk' communities or 'vulnerable' communities makes it possible to conceptualise risk as a category that creates possibilities. For Vietnamese young adults experiencing social mobility that comes with English-language fluency and access to higher education, opting for a career as a barista rather than pursuing a more 'traditional' career constitutes a risky endeavour. Becoming part of a global coffee community necessitates weighing up risks and subsequently aspiring towards something larger in scope and reach than working in a local café. In some ways, each of these anecdotes reveals aspiration as a productive effect of risk, and the 'capacity to aspire' across the coffee industry might serve as an alternative framework for understanding the success, failure and lived experiences of young adults in Vietnam as they navigate an inherently global specialty coffee culture.

Hong is a 24-year-old ethnic minority-identifying woman from a coffee-producing village. She aspires to share Vietnamese coffee culture with a wider audience through her family's history, anecdotal stories about educating consumers to 'taste specialty coffee', knowledge exchange and a positive outlook on life and the future of Vietnamese coffee. Thinh is a young coffee roaster and co-owner of a small delivery-based coffee company and occasionally works as a professional photographer. He aspires not only to share the specialty coffee industry in Vietnam with outsiders, but also to establish a positive reputation for the coffees he works with by moving beyond traditional methods of roasting and consuming Vietnamese coffee. According to him, this is an uphill battle and he understands the risks he is taking in developing his roasting business. Duc is a 33-year-old small café owner who opens his doors for free training opportunities – young baristas can bring their own milk and coffee and he will provide the equipment and know-how for developing latte art and brewing skills – and amateur competitions. Of course, there is some overlap between these three young adults. They each highlight the hard work that young Vietnamese coffee professionals are putting into their community's growth and culture, while underscoring the fears and limitations that come into existence through the process of aspiring. Each of their stories reveals a categorical understanding and experience of what it means to aspire and in what cultural spaces aspiration can happen. The intersecting and occasionally clashing ideologies across these three young adults reveal the murkiness of aspirations and the lessons we can learn from exploring how aspirations come to be. The newness of specialty coffee and the ways in which each of these three professionals came to the industry allow us to think about aspiration as a framework in the context of young adults in Vietnam and generally open up the possibility for understanding everyday experiences of uncertainty and how aspiration is practised among young adults in contemporary Vietnam.

Hong's Local Aspirations

The first time I met Hong, she insisted on driving thirty minutes into town, on her day off, to show me the café where she worked. Although I had been to the same café countless times before and interviewed many people affiliated with the café, this was different. She gave me a thorough behind-the-scenes tour and introduced me to all the staff as well as a few regular customers. Her enthusiasm for coffee was obvious, but not unique. Many young adult baristas in Vietnam share this enthusiasm at work, in latte art and brewing competitions, and across social media platforms, where they share their latest pours, coffee tattoos or equipment procured from a friend living abroad. However, Hong has little experience in the coffee competition arena and little in the way of personal brewing equipment – the intermittent electricity and water access in her village would make this difficult in any case. She prefers to hone her skills at work, in a community of like-minded young Vietnamese who share a common passion, although their aspirations may be quite different. Some of Hong's coworkers and coffee enthusiast friends perpetually muse about life in the city, with its ubiquitous specialty cafés and latte art competitions to participate in and thus, by extension, the possibility of one day becoming Vietnam's National Barista Champion and travelling to the World Barista Championships. These young baristas and coffee roasters also speak about a cosmopolitan life that for them can only exist in a place like Ho Chi Minh City. As one young man told me: 'I take the bus to the city when I can . . . because that's where you can find the most people who like this kind of coffee and visit a different café every day or have Ethiopian natural processed coffee . . . sometimes I will take the bus overnight just for one day, drink coffee all day and then take the overnight bus back here.' Hong, however, aspires to 'share coffee culture from her hometown' in the highland producing region where she grew up. By cultivating a specialty coffee community at origin, she hopes to bridge the urban divide with her own collection of coffee brewing equipment, roasting expertise and specialty coffee aesthetic. The city lacks a connection to origin and environmental sensibility, and Hong aspired to nurture that connection with local residents and visitors from the city.

Hong eventually left her job at the café where we originally met in order to develop a short-lived coffee 'project' in her village and start a YouTube channel and blog for specialty coffee tutorials in Vietnamese. Her decision coincided with several major developments in the Vietnamese specialty coffee industry, namely the first national barista champion representing Vietnam on a global stage at the World Barista Championships in 2016. Media attention in national newspapers and television stations quickly spread to international media outlets and several widely read popular coffee magazines and blogs, and Hong felt an energy around the Vietnamese specialty coffee industry. Several years later, she invited me to visit her new place of employment. She sent me the address of an 'eco-homestay/café' about 15 kilometres outside of the town centre and upon my arrival gave me a tour of the minimalist, open-air space. The space was indeed fantastic, but it surprised me to see Hong working at what was essentially a boutique hotel. She made a cup of coffee and explained what had happened in the year since we had met:

Sarah (S): What happened to your café project and the YouTube channel?

Hong (H): Well, the café project was too hard for me to do alone but the YouTube channel is still up. We haven't posted any new videos because we are all busy with our other jobs right now.

S: So, why did you make a change to this homestay job? Are you thinking about jobs outside of coffee now?

H: Actually, I think this job is focused on coffee. It's a way to introduce specialty coffee to people in a natural environment. I think people may come to see the lake or even spend the night in a unique place, but then they can try local coffee that is different from traditional Vietnamese coffee and I can be the person to explain the history, to tell them that the coffee comes from my home area and that I know everything about how it was processed and roasted. (Conversation with the author, 12 January 2018)

This conversation reminded me that since the day we met, Hong espoused a desire to introduce Vietnamese specialty coffee to a broader public that includes domestic Vietnamese tourists, foreign tourists and a virtual community of specialty coffee enthusiasts (including potential investors and buyers), but to do so from the coffee 'origin'.[6] This origin, although 'home' for Hong, has little to do with her kin ties and more to do with her desire to belong in the Vietnamese highland mountain coffee-producing region. Although she recognised the value of the coffee community and opportunities in Ho Chi Minh City, she felt very strongly that she could carve out her space in the specialty coffee world by staying close to the community that produces it. Only by doing so could she create her ideal environmentally friendly café that serves high-quality coffee grown in her community. She was also acutely aware that not everyone in her own community has access to the specialty coffee she served – indeed, the price point for specialty coffee excludes many rural Vietnamese and the very farmers who grow it.

On the surface, this aspiration seems to simply convey a fondness for the mountains and for Hong's own community and background growing up in a coffee village, but it also hints at a resistance to an urban lifestyle. Hong, after all, has travelled to the city many times and she is acutely aware of the cost of living, traffic, pollution and dearth of green space compared to the highlands. Familiarity with these very qualities of urban living created the capacity for her to aspire to something different. Urban living may encourage an itinerant community of coffee travellers who regularly visit the highlands to experience coffee producing areas and bring imported coffee, ideas and inspiration from the city. Hong's aspiration is especially interesting precisely because it creates other spaces for aspiration among urban coffee professionals who desire geographical mobility via the worldly experience of travel, even if it is a mere seven-hour bus ride away from their door. These aspirations are only possible because of this particular moment in which Vietnam is emerging as a potential rising origin for specialty coffee and where there is a new focus on quality rather than the quantity of low-grade commodity coffee that was characteristic of the 1990s Vietnamese coffee boom.

Rather than focusing on Hong's processual journey as a way to define aspiration, I focus on what her aspirations may reveal about similar young adults in Vietnam who desire the cosmopolitanism of an urban environment without the city itself. Hong's aspirations are enabled by dichotomies in the global coffee market (commodity/specialty) and an emerging interest in Vietnamese coffee as an object of significance within the specialty coffee community (*Sprudge* 2013). However, her aspirations are also limited by that same dichotomy and by the Vietnamese state. King et al. suggest that in post-Đổi Mới Vietnam, 'the market economy has created "winners" and "losers" together with social class divisions in this socialist state' (2008: 792). Although I do not think about Hong as a winner or a loser, her ability to aspire as a young, educated middle-class woman is overshadowed by the everyday lived experience of occupying a precarious social space as a member of an ethnic minority community from a poor village. Why does she aspire to participate in a global coffee community from this small town in Vietnam and is her capacity to aspire limited to conversations with visitors from the city and engagement on social media? What do her aspirations reveal when understood in contrast to other Southeast Asian migration patterns?

Thinh's Creative Venture

Thinh wants to distinguish himself from his counterparts by embracing specialty coffee standards for roasting and by developing a unique brand and logo. By promoting his coffee and photography skills through his respective social media platforms, he sees himself as working towards his larger aspirations related to global connectivity, travel and reputation. While he does not actively participate in the small Vietnamese coffee competition circuit, he still views himself as part of a larger coffee community built upon the exchange of ideas and cosmopolitan sensibilities – he is from Ho Chi Minh City, speaks fluent English and identifies strongly as someone who could never live outside of a city environment. He is deeply motivated by global (albeit virtual) relationships and this is highlighted through his carefully choreographed Instagram feed, which sometimes advertises his slick black-and-white urban wedding photos, distinct portrait style and coffee-roasting sessions. He is yet to travel abroad due to financial limitations and the arduous visa process but is fully aware of the global specialty coffee circuit.

In late 2016, Thinh had something of a big break. If one element of his aspiration was to be part of a larger global coffee community through his photography skills and careful social networking skills, he certainly came close to achieving it. A series of portraits he had composed of Vietnamese specialty coffee baristas and the specialty coffee scene in Ho Chi Minh City graced the cover and feature story of a widely read, international industry magazine. When I asked him what that meant for his future, he simply acknowledged that it was a great opportunity and said that he was looking forward to distributing his most recent sample roast and saving up for a new camera lens. As it turns out, his aspiration is a continually moving target, as the next big moment for Vietnamese coffee is yet to be captured through his camera and vision. His local notoriety is further advanced through his connections to international coffee photographers, content managers and digital media companies. For all intents and purposes, he has realised his aspirations, but in doing so, he re-navigates them accordingly, ebbing and flowing with the specialty coffee culture.

Thinh is also connected to many other industry experts, including Vietnam's first national barista champion and others who facilitate the training of young baristas. Tran Han, Vietnam's National Barista Champion, despite her notoriety, shares many of the attributes of other young Vietnamese. After dropping out of university, she realised that her calling was elsewhere, choosing to focus instead on developing her craft, professionalism and English-language skills. Although her parents disagreed with this nontraditional plan, they eventually came around to support her when they saw her first barista performance and realised that this is a career and not 'making coffee'. Despite this success, she still wonders what her future holds and keeps an open mind while aspiring to be an ambassador of and for Vietnamese coffee. Other coffee professionals are taking up this task at a local level.

Duc, the latte art competition host, is married and settled in a small house that operates as a café for young baristas to hone their skills in a supportive and welcoming environment. He talks about his future with more certainty than some of his colleagues – he sees it fixed squarely in his small alleyway neighbourhood, his regular coffee gatherings and position as a sort of informal mentor of Vietnamese latte art. I knew about him through baristas based in Ho Chi Minh City, long before I met him in person at the amateur latte art competition. Several young baristas working for less than US$125 per month at cafés around the city had told me about some of the underground events he had hosted and about his openness to mentoring young baristas.

One young man recounted to me how he was not accepted into university, but had been able to make decent latte art, even though it was not appreciated by his boss at a small hotel restaurant. When he finally secured a job as a barista, he knew that he was not simply 'making coffee' anymore and had to find a space to train. Word of mouth introduced him to Duc and other baristas who frequent the space. Duc has carved out a space for baristas to connect and compete in the city while simultaneously encouraging Vietnamese youths to develop their craft by watching English-language broadcasts of global competitions and how-to videos. Inspiring youth to get into coffee for the challenge but to have fun while doing so is one way of legitimising the barista as a profession in Vietnam. Although he could not say for sure, he mused that explaining barista culture and 'career baristas' to parents and friends who do not care about coffee must be a challenge everywhere in the world. It is a challenge to explain that working as a professional barista is a creative and potentially rewarding and fulfilling career outside of Vietnam, admittedly one that is just recently tapping into fair salaries and health and retirement benefits for workers. Of course, there are many other young adults in Vietnam facing the same challenges – to explain a nontraditional career to one's family or have to justify choices is something many Vietnamese face regardless of their education level. Even if a young barista fails to become a national or global barista champion, the by-product of their aspiration is something that many Vietnamese baristas may aspire to generally; putting Vietnam on the global coffee map of high-quality specialty production is a topic nearly every specialty coffee professional in Vietnam feels strongly about. Unlike the 'transnational orientations' that Vietnamese in the diaspora occupy (Small 2019), these baristas are forging urban Vietnam as its own global coffee culture, simultaneously Vietnamese and cosmopolitan. Vora (2011) considers the ways in which Indian merchant diaspora belonging is negotiated in the shadow of shifting development projects and economic focus in Dubai. Seemingly global but ultimately 'centered on forms of economic freedoms and cosmopolitanism that were specific to an Indian Ocean mercantilism', belonging is contingent on the complexities of the Indian diaspora and the 'global city' (Vora 2011: 315). While citizenship does not factor into whether a Vietnamese coffee professional can participate in or belong to a global community, belonging is inseparable from a larger state project of international development and the post-Đổi Mới policies, and many foreign development projects and transnational relationships in Vietnam that make cosmopolitanism appealing for young adults. The aspiration to 'put Vietnam on the map' is not rooted in class mobility or even nationalism. Instead, it reflects a desire to belong to a larger global community that ultimately has little to do with coffee and much to do with belonging and a like-minded desire to participate in cosmopolitan urban life or to cultivate an intimate relationship with nature in precarious times of urban development in Asia.

Conclusion

The aspirations of young adult coffee professionals transcend the rural/urban divide and extend to an imagined overseas experience. Like Huang (see Chapter 2 in this volume), the transborder networks that exist within the global specialty coffee community play a significant role in shaping the future aspirations of these young adults. However, the difference is that many of these transborder networks exist not in the physical migration experiences of Vietnamese, but in a cosmopolitan Southeast Asian city and in the virtual spaces of social media and image exchange. The ability to interact with other young professionals who share similar aspirations to be their creative selves and connect with other like-minded coffee enthusiasts is facilitated by these platforms. Global social media platforms also introduce Vietnamese young adults to other cosmopolitan spaces (e.g. a café in London) and even small towns (e.g. a café in Wisconsin) where baristas, roasters and other coffee professionals work with the same espresso machines and a similar desire to belong. Globalisation and the virtual worlds that global processes spawn become a platform for young adults to explore, learn, experiment and ultimately aspire. As noted by the authors of the other chapters in this volume, aspiring is a process that is not fixed in time or space.

As specialty coffee develops, it becomes an industry rooted in a global community. Transnational conversations about climate change, sustainability practices in the industry, café and packaging design, diversity, inclusion and harassment in the coffee industry and the LGBTQ coffee community are all taking shape on social media and other content platforms. These virtual coffee communities may seem specific to the coffee industry, but the dialogue generated within these spaces transcends coffee, engendering larger conversations about cosmopolitan Vietnamese youths who are grappling with the Vietnamese state's relationship to sustainability initiatives, climate change discourse and the national and global future of coffee. As Vietnamese coffee professionals read extensively about the implications of climate change on coffee, some take to Instagram to share what this may look like on the ground in Vietnam. For instance, a sickly coffee tree on a drought-ridden farm in the Central Highlands becomes a dialogue for a larger conversation about the Ministry of Natural Resources and Environment or Association of Southeast Asian Nations (ASEAN) initiatives to address climate change nationwide and regionwide. Here, young coffee professionals connect with other young Vietnamese around a common cause.

In the wake of rapid economic development and still in the midst of larger urban privatisation processes, the ways in which Vietnamese individuals experience the once streetside but increasingly indoor private café and public space more generally signals a shift in how the Vietnamese state regulates space and property (Harms 2009). Mapping on to a shift in Vietnam's socioeconomic profile, the formation of specialty cafés capitalises on a moment in which the consumption of media and global brands may create a consumer base that leads to personal entrepreneurial achievement. Earl (2014) examined such notions of aspiration in the context of urban social mobility and an emerging Vietnamese middle class. Although young adult coffee professionals in Ho Chi Minh City may not best reflect middle-class status, they do grapple with how their expendable income can best be spent on fashioning a desire for global belonging in a specialty coffee community. As one young barista told me, 'I think photography and coffee have a very similar feeling because . . . anyone can take a photograph or make coffee but to do it well, they both require a lot of practice and skill'. What this barista failed to mention is that purchasing a professional camera and coffee equipment amounts to more than the entire monthly salary of a Vietnamese barista living in Ho Chi Minh City. Although increased wealth is not at the root of these aspirations, it is a by-product of realising them and creates the 'capacity to aspire' that brings the socioeconomic limitations of a coffee career into stark relief (Appadurai 2004). With a growing middle class especially prominent in Ho Chi Minh City and the process of 'classing up through consumption' (Leshkowich 2014: 181) becoming increasingly visible, young professionals in the coffee industry are saving up to consume products and brands that do not conspicuously mark them out as socioeconomically stable. Instead, they are consuming brands that mark them out as coffee industry-savvy and familiar with the global landscape of specialty coffee.

What stands out most in Hong's, Thinh's and Duc's respective stories is their desire to identify as individuals while also placing themselves within a collective global coffee community – sometimes struggling, but justifying their struggle with the motivation inherent in aspiration. In the process, they demonstrate an open willingness and desire to promote Vietnam and its specialty coffee as a legitimate player within this global community. Despite their ongoing efforts to shed conspicuous markers of 'traditional' Vietnamese culture, they clearly embrace and defend Vietnam when it comes to judgement imposed by 'experts' within the global industry and their peers' critiques. By doing so, they render possible aspirations towards a future in which young adults can occupy multiple cultural spaces at once – spaces that are simultaneously cosmopolitan, global, virtual and uncertain.

While chatting over coffee with Thinh one day, he mentioned that a foreigner had complained about the quality of Vietnamese specialty coffee on a social media platform. Thinh was visibly angry, defensive and muttered 'Vietnamese coffee is difficult and we are doing the best we can, learning every day, alone with only a little bit of support but look at what we have done so far'. He waved his hand, broadly calling out the café we were in, but also referencing the full scope of specialty coffee in Vietnam. The 'we' here included the Vietnamese coffee community at large and constructed their aspirations as driven less by an imagined 'good life' (Fischer 2014) and more by a desire for respect within the global industry. Even in his dejection, an optimistic silver lining ('look at what we have done so far') shone through. Thinh's aspirations reflect those of a much larger community of Vietnamese young adults who are at the nexus of a postreform coffee crossroads in which Vietnam, as a producing country, can move into the global specialty coffee arena.

As Appadurai reminds us, 'aspirations are never simply individual . . . they are always formed in interaction and in the thick of social life' (2013: 187). The lives of Thinh, Hong and their coffee peers are intertwined with each other as they read interviews with Vietnam's first National Barista Champion, attend impromptu latte art training sessions and design coffee tattoos for each other. Even seemingly individual aspirations (e.g. to win the Vietnam National Barista Championships) are embedded in community aspirations tinged with a hint of national pride (e.g. to represent Vietnam on the global coffee stage at the World Barista Championships). None of these aspirations reflect an overt desire for a wealthy lifestyle; despite many baristas having moved from rural areas to the city and needing to share small apartments with several friends, none of them mentioned a desire to move into a new place. Rather, visiting other coffee origins, iconic cafés and travelling to see coffee competitions make for a worthy way to spend one's limited money. While some Vietnamese coffee professionals lament their inability to travel because they cannot afford it and the visa process is quite difficult, their aspirations are being worked towards if not achieved – one cannot possibly become a barista champion without developing the requisite skills, including fluency in English. Aspirations are processual and thus call attention to the shifting ways in which young adults experience change, pressure and the sometimes stark realisation that they may not travel abroad anytime soon. A constant checking-in and re-evaluation of one's aspirations and how they may come at the expense of family norms and societal obligations is all part of the process. The global aspirations of young adults in the Vietnamese specialty coffee scene are obscured at times by the complex nature of what it means to be a young adult in Vietnam, but the process of aspiring is nonetheless a productive endeavour.

Sarah G. Grant is Assistant Professor of Anthropology at California State University, Fullerton, United States. Her research investigates the cultural and economic politics of Vietnam's rapidly growing commodity coffee industry and the expanding specialty industry. She examines the coffee industry as a space for local Vietnamese farmers, traders, government officials, multinational corporations and international organisations to navigate market-oriented socialism and the complexities of contemporary Vietnam. She is the current multimedia editor for the *Journal of Vietnamese Studies*. Her work has been supported by the University of California Pacific Rim Research Program and the Fulbright IIE.

Notes

1. Pseudonyms have been used for the research participants mentioned in this chapter out of respect for their privacy.
2. Specialty coffee is a reference to green coffee that is predominantly defect-free while offering a distinctive taste that reflects rigorous tasting and visual inspections. In addition to these industry standards, a more popular understanding of specialty coffee may include notions of traceability down to the farm, careful processing and Arabica varietals of coffee that meet a standardised criteria of quality by the international Specialty Coffee Association (SCA). This distinction is necessary to understand because the coffee itself is valued (monetarily and culturally) and traded differently from 'commodity coffee', and it is one of the fastest-growing coffee markets. Specialty coffee is also part of a larger 'specialty coffee culture' in which cafés and consumption are marked by a particular design aesthetic, global community and minimalistic menus that foreground coffee rather than additives (e.g. artificial flavours and sugar). In practice, specialty coffee is viewed by Vietnamese coffee professionals as a relatively new concept, with attention to a larger culture that distinguishes itself from soluble, 'cheaper' and lower grades of commodity coffee regularly consumed across Vietnam. For more on the industry definition of specialty coffee, see Rhinehart (2017).
3. Pour-over is a standard brewing method in the specialty coffee industry that involves a controlled pour of near-boiling water over freshly roasted and ground beans into a paper filter and a 'brew cone'.
4. Spiegel's article, entitled 'What Vietnamese Coffee Culture Gets Right', seems to imply the following question: what does Vietnamese coffee culture get wrong? Considering this, how does 'coffee culture' beget any sort of 'right' or 'wrong' and who gets to decide? As it turns out, young baristas working at specialty cafés in Vietnam have plenty to say about what Vietnamese ('traditional') coffee culture gets right and wrong.
5. See Luvaas (2009) for more on Southeast Asian youth, global citizenship and localization in the Indonesian indie rock scene.
6. The term 'origin' is commonly used in the specialty coffee industry to reference where a coffee is produced. Origin may refer to a specific country (e.g. Vietnam) or a region (e.g. Sidamo), or in the context of 'single-origin' coffees to a particular farm and single varietal. Within the industry, the term is also commonly used to reference 'origin trips' or what is happening 'at origin'.

References

Appadurai, Arjun. 2004. 'The Capacity to Aspire: Culture and the Terms of Recognition', in Vijayendra Rao and Michael Walton (eds), *Culture and Public Action*. Stanford: Stanford University Press, pp. 59–84.

———. 2013. *The Future as Cultural Fact: Essays on the Global Condition*. London: Verso.

Bayly, Susan. 2013. 'For Family, State and Nation: Achieving Cosmopolitan Modernity in Late-Socialist Vietnam', in Nicholas J. Long and Henrietta L. Moore (eds), *The Social Life of Achievement*. New York: Berghahn Books, pp. 158–81.

Bunnell, Tim, Jamie Gillen and Elaine Lynn-Ee Ho. 2018. 'The Prospect of Elsewhere: Engaging the Future through Aspirations in Asia', *Annals of the American Association of Geographers* 108(1): 35–51.

Duong, Phuoc M. 2017. 'Unpredictable Agency: An Analysis of Youth and Educational Practices in Times of Political and Economic Precarity in Contemporary Đà Nẵng City, Việt Nam', Ph.D. dissertation. Riverside: University of California, Riverside.

Earl, Catherine. 2014. *Vietnam's New Middle Classes: Gender, Career, City*. Copenhagen: NIAS Press.

Fischer, Edward F. 2014. *The Good Life: Aspiration, Dignity and the Anthropology of Wellbeing*. Stanford: Stanford University Press.

Foster, Robert J. 2007. 'The Work of the New Economy: Consumers, Brands and Value Creation', *American Anthropologist* 22(4): 707–31.

Harms, Erik. 2009. 'Vietnam's Civilizing Process and the Retreat from the Street: A Turtle's Eye View from Ho Chi Minh City', *City and Society* 21(2): 182–206.

———. 2011. *Saigon's Edge: On the Margins of Ho Chi Minh City*. Minneapolis: University of Minnesota Press.

Kim, Annette Miae. 2008. *Learning to Be Capitalists: Entrepreneurs in Vietnam's Transition Economy*. New York: Oxford University Press.

King, Victor T., Phuong An Nguyen and Nguyen Huu Minh. 2008. 'Professional Middle Class Youth in Post-reform Vietnam: Identity, Continuity and Change', *Modern Asian Studies* 42(4): 783–813.

Leshkowich, Ann Marie. 2014. *Essential Trade: Vietnamese Women in a Changing Marketplace*. Honolulu: University of Hawaii Press.

Luvaas, Brent. 2009. 'Dislocating Sounds: The Deterritorialization of Indonesian Indie Pop', *Cultural Anthropology* 24(2): 246–79.

Nguyen, Minh T.N. 2018. *Waste and Wealth: An Ethnography of Labor, Value and Morality in a Vietnamese Recycling Economy*. Oxford: Oxford University Press.

Rhinehart, Ric. 2017. 'What is Specialty Coffee?', *SCA News*, 17 March. Retrieved 25 March 2020 from http://www.scanews.coffee/2017/03/17/what-is-specialty-coffee.

Sasges, Gerard (ed.). 2013. *It's a Living: Work and Life in Vietnam Today*. Singapore: National University of Singapore Press.

Schwenkel, Christina, and Ann Marie Leshkowich. 2012. 'Introduction: How Is Neoliberalism Good to Think Vietnam? How Is Vietnam Good to Think Neoliberalism?', *Positions: East Asia Cultures Critique* 20(2): 379–401.

Small, Ivan V. 2019. *Currencies of Imagination: Channeling Money and Chasing Mobility in Vietnam*. Ithaca: Cornell University Press.

Spiegel, Alison. 2017. 'What Vietnamese Coffee Culture Gets Right, Beyond Sweetened Condensed Milk', *Huffington Post*, 6 December. Retrieved 25 March 2020 from https://www.huffingtonpost.com/2014/12/08/vietnamese-coffee_n_6275576.html.

Sprudge. 2013. '"A Template for Life": Will Frith and Specialty Coffee in Vietnam'. Retrieved 25 March 2020 from http://sprudge.com/interview-will-frith-43112.html.

Truitt, Allison J. 2008. 'On the Back of a Motorbike: Middle-Class Mobility in Ho Chi Minh City', *American Anthropologist* 35(1): 3–19.

———. 2013. *Dreaming of Money in Ho Chi Minh City*. Seattle: University of Washington Press.

Uyên, Kh. 2015. 'Cà phê làm từ đậu nành và hoá chất', *VNExpress*, 20 January. Retrieved 25 March 2020 from https://vnexpress.net/tin-tuc/thoi-su/ca-phe-lam-tu-dau-nanh-va-hoa-chat-3136437.html.

Vann, Elizabeth F. 2005. 'The Limits of Authenticity in Vietnamese Consumer Markets', *American Anthropologist* 108(2): 286–96.

——. 2012. 'Afterword: Consumption and Middle-Class Subjectivity in Vietnam', in Van Nguyen-Marshall, Lisa B. Welch Drummond and Danièle Bélanger (eds), *The Reinvention of Distinction: Modernity and the Middle Class in Urban Vietnam*. New York: Springer, pp. 157–70.

Vora, Neha. 2011. 'From Golden Frontier to Global City: Shifting Forms of Belonging, "Freedom" and Governance among Indian Businessmen in Dubai', *American Anthropologist* 113(2): 306–18.

Zaloom, Caitlin. 2004. 'The Productive Life of Risk', *Cultural Anthropology* 19(3): 365–91.

9

TRANSCENDING ASPIRATIONS

Buddhism and the Quest for Belonging in Urban Hong Kong

Mariske Westendorp

In June 2015, Teresa,[1] a doctor and Buddhist in her thirties, shared with me her perception of the prospects for her future in her hometown Hong Kong:

> Hong Kong has such an unclear future from the perspective of local Hong Kong people that I am considering buying a flat elsewhere, maybe Bangkok, so that I can stay there when Hong Kong changes just like other Chinese cities . . . Hong Kong's houses are expensive, yet the space is small. And politically, Hong Kong will become a communist region. Also, my lifestyle is simple and I will not have lots of money, so I want to go to a cheaper place.

At the time of writing, Teresa still lives in a rental apartment in Hong Kong. However, she is thinking of leaving the city in the near future in search of another home.

On the surface, Teresa's speculations might not seem out of the ordinary. As multiple chapters in this volume have shown, moving to another city or even another country can almost be regarded as a characteristic of the lives of many of Asia's contemporary young adults who aspire to another or a better future (see e.g. the chapters by Huang and Suzuki in this volume). However, knowing Teresa, the current housing situation in Hong Kong and its political developments, I regard the above comments as indicative of a larger issue at play, namely the quest to belong.

Endnotes for this chapter begin on page 185.

In this chapter I explore this aspiration through the narratives of Teresa and other Buddhists currently living in Hong Kong. These narratives are presented here as exemplary accounts of young, middle-class Hong Kong residents who feel out of place in their own city. In the accounts, I highlight the tensions inherent in the perceived difficulty of the material aspiration to own a home and young people's spiritual reflections on the difficulty of achieving this. My aim in doing this is to argue for a more encompassing understanding of the concept of aspirations, namely one that takes the transcendent into account: that which lies beyond a person's current life and relates to larger frameworks of meaning – in this case, the religious.

As indicated by Arjun Appadurai (2004, 2013) and other scholars, aspirations concern ideas, wants and desires for the future. This focus on the future is the reason why people do certain things and hold certain values in life. As such, aspirations relate to who a person is or wants to become (Fischer 2014). Often, studies of aspirations focus on wants and desires that arise within an individual's lifetime and consequently give meaning to a particular timespan and place of living. However, certain aspirations transcend such individual timeframes and localities by including ideas of the past and the future and features of the local, global and universal all at the same time. This is especially the case when aspirations relate to religious beliefs. Religions can provide meaningful rubrics for people, guiding and helping them understand their place in their city, in the world and in the universe, both during and beyond their lifetimes. In addition, religions provide people with networks that similarly extend beyond specific times and places. Consequently, religions can inform the ways in which aspirations are constructed and reflected upon.

In this chapter, I will discuss the possible spatial and temporal transcendental nature of aspirations by highlighting the aspirations of Hong Kong Buddhist residents to find a home, either in their city or elsewhere. People make homes in cities through processes of physical constructions, modifications and meaning-making; in other words, by transforming abstract spaces into concrete, meaningful places (Jaffe and De Koning 2016). Homes are often the places where one can be at ease and be oneself, and from where one can further one's aspirations. They are related to memories and attachments. They are, in the words of geographer Yi-Fu Tuan (1977), related to expressions of 'topophilia', or place-love.

One can feel at home in a neighbourhood, a city or a country. Often, our home is seen as the place to which we belong or to which we want to belong. This reasoning is apparent in studies that align questions of where people feel a sense of belonging with issues over homeownership – that is, having a place to call 'home'. For instance, studies on migrant communities emphasise the relationship between symbolically feeling at home in a new country and having a physical place to call as such (see e.g. Duyvendak 2011; Ralph and Staeheli 2011;

Salih 2003). The connection between having a home and belonging is similarly expressed in one of the most famous sayings in the English language: 'home is where the heart is'. Having a place to call 'home' inherently relates to the question of where one belongs.

However, homes can extend beyond these concrete places and one can feel at ease in global communities, cosmic universals or (religious) traditions. Furthermore, the wish to own a home can extend beyond having a physical property to call 'mine'. As we will see, the narrative of Teresa alludes to this in two ways: first, the larger geopolitical forces at play in the city of Hong Kong make the aspiration to own one's own home difficult to achieve; and, second, the question of where one's home is and how one deals with the (im)possibilities of owning a physical home can relate to religious beliefs. These beliefs may guide a person's actions towards the making of a home, as well as to the value they place on owning a home in the first place. Religion as such can provide believers with an alternative 'home', namely one that extends beyond the borders of lives and the city (see Westendorp 2017).

Hence, the narratives presented in this chapter allude to an antagonism between aspirations for a physical home and the quest to have a spiritual, transcendental home. When seen from a broader perspective, they engage with a possible disconnect between aspiring for material self-development on the one hand and spiritualism on the other. In this chapter I argue that nowadays the aspiration to own one's own home is becoming increasingly difficult to achieve for middle-class people in Hong Kong. In this situation, Buddhism – with its heavy emphasis on personal accountability through, amongst other things, the prominence of karma – offers a belonging that transcends this particular Hong Kong context both geographically and transcendentally, providing adherents with a sense of home that the city by itself cannot.

The Hong Kong Middle Class

Before elaborating on the aspirations of my informants, I will first offer a quick note on what is meant by their status as 'middle-class residents'. The Hong Kong middle class is a prominent group in academic and journalistic writing. It is often described as being very large. For example, Siu-kai Lau states that in 2013, 'more than 70% of Hongkongers consider themselves as belonging to the "middle strata"' (2013: 108). However, figures differ drastically, indicating that in a society where there is no longer a manufacturing industry and in which the working class is no longer only 'blue collar' (Ng 2009), it is hard to define what constitutes the middle class.

Regardless, members of the younger generation of the Hong Kong middle class in particular have a few characteristics in common. They have generally all finished their tertiary education, most of them in Hong Kong, but some of them abroad. Most, but not all, are confident regarding their respective levels of English. As self-proclaimed members of the middle class, they differentiate themselves from the upper class – those they see as affluent people living in apartments in the Mid-Levels (Hong Kong Island) or close by. They also tend to differentiate themselves from people they see as belonging to the lower ranks of Hong Kong's population, those who live in areas such as Sham Shui Po (Kowloon) or deep in the New Territories (e.g. Yuen Long). Finally, they show the aspiration of being part of a hardworking and professional class and of being able to identify with the 'Hong Kong Dream'. In addition, most aspire to own property and other assets.

Much has been written about middle classes in Asia (see e.g. Chua 2000; Robison and Goodman 1996), including in Chinese regions such as Taiwan, China, Hong Kong and Macao (Hsiao 2014). Research into Hong Kong's middle class has so far been mainly sociological, a notable exception being the research undertaken by Hong Kong-born anthropologist Helen Siu (2009, 2011; Siu and Ku 2008). Siu's work offers great insights into the Hong Kong middle class and the macro-processes its members find themselves confronted with. However, it does not deal with individual socioeconomic, political or spiritual aspirations. In this way, Siu's research differs from my own approach, as mine focuses on individual perceptions, aspirations and religious orientations.

Despite the emphasis on this individuality, two additional aspects of the Hong Kong middle class need to be taken into account. According to Loïc Wacquant, classes 'are constantly organised, disorganised and reorganised as an effect of struggles – economic, political and ideological – that are partly indeterminate from the standpoint of the structure' (1992: 51). Classes are contested and fluid categories that come into being the moment people begin to articulate their needs and interests in relation to other classes or the state (So 2014). This has been the situation in Hong Kong, where a middle class developed in reaction to the capitalist and the working classes in the mid-twentieth century and developed into a politically active class critical of both the government of the People's Republic of China and of the Hong Kong Special Administrative Region. Second, 'class' is not merely based on narrow economic interests, as once suggested by Max Weber (So 2000). Classes not only reflect material desires, such as property and capital, but also specific lifestyles, values, ethics and even religious beliefs, as I will show in this chapter.

Being Buddhist in Modern Hong Kong

I met Teresa through the Leadership and Communication Skills Programme offered by a Hong Kong Buddhist monk, which aimed at providing young professionals with the tools to deal with the stress of their jobs using Buddhist concepts.

At the time when Teresa attended the course, she was working as an anaesthesiologist in one of Hong Kong's busiest hospitals. In addition to a workload that regularly consisted of over 50 hours a week, she affiliated herself with Buddhism, a religion that she felt 'makes sense if you look at the world and everything. It explains what happens around us and to us'. Prior to attending the Leadership and Communication Skills Programme, Teresa's Buddhist learning started in Hong Kong's Chi Lin nunnery, where she attended a foundational course every Sunday for half a year. Over the past ten years, she has regularly visited a small Buddhist temple on Lantau Island and once attended a retreat on Cheung Chau Island. She joined several local meditation camps, held at different places and led by international masters, including the Australian Theravāda monk Ajahn Brahm and the Vietnamese Zen master Thich Nhat Hahn. However, her Buddhist path stretches beyond the borders of Hong Kong. Sometimes she travels to other countries and Buddhist organisations – for example, to Taiwan for the Dharma Drum Foundation or to monasteries in Bhutan, where she enjoys teachings that capture her interest. Teresa is not unique in the way she practices Buddhism. Many others her age who are interested in Buddhism also travel around Hong Kong and overseas to listen to Buddhist masters and join retreats, while also using different social media platforms for their Buddhist development.

Teresa is one of the many informants who took centre stage in my research, which was conducted in Hong Kong between 2012 and 2014. During this period, I talked to over ninety Hong Kong Buddhist and Catholic laity and clerical members, whose experiences and reflections I explored in over 120 interviews and additional meetings. Regarding my Buddhist informants, a minority of them defined themselves as belonging to Mahāyāna or Vajrayāna Buddhism; most of the Buddhists I met identified as Theravāda Buddhists. In contemporary Hong Kong, as in virtually all Chinese contexts, Mahāyāna Buddhism (mainly Pure Land, but also Chan and Taintai) is the most popular form of Buddhism practised, with Theravāda the least popular. However, Theravāda Buddhism is gaining popularity amongst the younger generation of Hong Kong Buddhists (Yeung and Chow 2010). It has also become the most popular form of Buddhism amongst the Hong Kong middle class and is increasingly influenced by Buddhism as practised in other Asian and, to a lesser degree, Western countries (see Mak 2012). For my informants, it has also become a key element in the expression of their Hong Kong middle-class identity.

Instead of defining them as Theravāda Buddhist, I refer to Teresa and others as 'modern Buddhists'. Modern Buddhism emerged in the late nineteenth century in different Asian countries (Crosby 2014; Lopez Jr. 2002). It encompasses all Buddhist schools and is branded as a demythologised, psychologised and rationalised expression of the Buddhist tradition, making it better adjusted to 'modern' tastes and values (McMahan 2008, 2012). It is also characterised by a wish to recover the original Buddhist tradition as a reaction to 'the dominant problems and questions of modernity' (McMahan 2008: 5). As I argue elsewhere (Westendorp 2021), this claim to go back to the true, original tradition of Buddhism is a very specific, consciously modern and predominantly middle-class claim.

Other characteristics of modern Buddhism are it being socially engaged, almost not ritualistic or hierarchical and more focused on the individual rather than the deified Buddha. These features are reflected in the increasing importance attached to the role of the laity in modern Buddhist practices (see Gombrich 2006). For example, the aspiration to reach enlightenment is no longer solely associated with monastic vocation, but can equally be aspired to by the laity. To attain such enlightenment, personal experience has become central. Commenting on 'Reformist Buddhism' in contemporary Singapore, Kuah-Pearce Khun Eng (2009) concludes that members of a new generation of local Chinese Buddhists in the city 'are not only interested in the functional aspects of religion, but rather are intent on seeking solutions to their individualised religious needs and personalised spiritual fulfilment. As with other modern religious trends, they see their religious needs as *personal*, no longer tied to religious needs of their families or community' (2009: 6, emphasis added).

This later aspect is also prominent in the values Hong Kong modern Buddhists attach to their religion. Often in conversation with these Buddhists, an emphasis was placed on personal accountability. Most notable in my Theravāda Buddhist informants' narratives were their descriptions of Buddhism as an individually practised religion and their strong individual commitments to Buddhism. Even though my informants go to centres to listen to Buddhist masters and to practise mediation with others, their ultimate practice is done individually.

Moreover, each person alone is thought to be held accountable for their actions and to have their own agency to influence life and karma. In Buddhism, accountability is closely related to the notion of karma or the principle of cause and effect. A popular understanding of karma is that 'each deed has its consequences, either in this life or a future one; good and evil deeds will eventually come back to you' (Palmer 2011: 94). Various Buddhist schools have different understandings of how karmic merits can be gained, whether and how they can be transferred to others, and at what point karma will take effect (van der Velde 2016). In Theravāda Buddhism, karma is the sum of merit created by an individual in their present and past lives. In order to secure a good rebirth, preferably in the human world, one has their own ability to create positive merit. Karma is thus created by and for oneself (Cassaniti 2012), through one's own agency. It follows from this that each individual is to be held accountable for their own karma and, by extension, for what happens to them.

Consequently, many of my Hong Kong modern Buddhist informants picture their religion as an individually practised one. For example, Emily, a Tibetan

Buddhist in her mid-thirties, chooses not to practise with her mother, who is also a Tibetan Buddhist. When I questioned her about this, she replied: 'Religion is something that is really individual and you've got your own way to act on it.' Individuals are thus themselves accountable for practising, calming their own mind and accumulating positive karma. Regardless of the many Buddhist centres present in Hong Kong today, attaining Buddhist understanding through practice is something that each individual needs to do for themselves. Teresa similarly showed this emphasis on personal accountability when describing the many different places she visited to enhance her Buddhist development, both in and outside of Hong Kong. By travelling to different places, she was able to personally seek out the teachings and practices that she thought reflected the true nature of Buddhism.

In addition, and central to the argument of this chapter, all the Buddhist places Teresa visited gave her the feeling of belonging to a larger Buddhist network. She expressed belonging not to a specific place or community, or even country, but to a master or a practice that she could learn at that certain place. Travelling gave her access to diverse teachings by international masters and attended by an international audience. This created for her a sense of belonging to a global world, while at the same time providing her with a spiritual community of which to feel a part.

In summary, what is most apparent in discussions with modern Hong Kong Buddhists is the emphasis they place on personal accountability and the accumulation of good karma. Through this focus, they find in their faith an answer to their quest for belonging. As I will show in the next section, this emphasis on accountability relates well to the specific economic wants and desires of my middle-class informants in shaping their everyday lives, from homeownership and a reasonable income to having enough time to spend with friends and families. Taken together, these wants and desires may be summed up as their socioeconomic aspiration to the Hong Kong Dream, as I will explain in the next section.

Aspiring to Belong

As the chapters throughout this volume have shown, urban youth and young adults all aspire. People aspire to certain things and take actions to make those aspirations a reality. They aspire to a desired career and will travel all over the country, or even the world, to obtain their preferred job. They aspire for a family of their own or the ability to support the family into which they were born. They aspire perhaps for a middle-class lifestyle, including fashionable clothes, healthy food, the latest technological devices or homeownership.

The young adults I met in Hong Kong are in many respects not different from the other young adults mentioned in this volume. They too aspire to a middle-class lifestyle and seek to take the necessary steps to achieve it. They study and work hard, they save and spend their money, some of them actively try to influence the political climate in the city and they make sure to look after their families.

However, there is one aspect that sets my particular Hong Kong informants apart. This is the combination between their modern Buddhist beliefs, as outlined in the previous section, and their aspiration to achieve what is called the 'Hong Kong Dream'. This dream, which originated in the 1970s, builds on the confidence that one can become successful through one's own merits, achievements and hard work (Mathews, Ma and Lui 2008). In the 1970s and 1980s, many Hong Kong residents (mainly from worker and peasant family backgrounds) were able to achieve this dream due to economic opportunities and improvements in education (Baker 1983; So 2014). They came to be seen as possessing the 'Lion Rock Spirit', named after a popular TV series broadcast from 1974 to 1994. The series portrayed the life stories of Hong Kong people from different strata against a backdrop of historical happenings in the city and showed 'how people had survived even tougher times in the old days of relative poverty with a strong will and a spirit of community and self-help' (Lee 2005: 304). The people who achieved the Dream grew up to become part of Hong Kong's middle class and perceived themselves as the backbone of Hong Kong's postwar affluence. They had facilitated the city's engagement with the industrialised world and worked hard to produce vocationally trained children to fuel the post-industrial service economy (Siu and Ku 2008).

Within this Hong Kong Dream, homeownership has always played a crucial role in determining success. Since the mid-twentieth century, many local residents have become rich and famous through speculation on the property market, making a fortune out of Hongkongers' eagerness to acquire their own properties (Mathews and Lui 2001). More importantly, homeownership has also always been related to a sense of connectedness to the Hong Kong city. In the 1980s, scholar Hugh Baker argued: 'Ownership . . . gives a sense of permanence to the home and in a society as volatile and mobile as Hong Kong the security and tolerance of the family counts for much' (1983: 473). The dream of owning a home is thus not only related to the aspiration to own a good investment, but is likewise a way for individuals and families to secure both a home and a feeling of belonging in the city of Hong Kong.

Unfortunately, it is exactly this part of the Dream that is felt to be threatened by larger geopolitical forces at play in the city, especially since the 1997 Asian financial crisis (Chua 2000). Since then, Hong Kong society has been roughly divided into two groups of people: those who own property and those who do not (Ng 2014). One of the more current geopolitical forces making this distinction even sharper is the increasing influx of mainland Chinese tourists, traders and talented professionals into the city. Consequently, confidence that the Hong Kong Dream can be achieved is rapidly declining, being replaced by a feeling of incapability and a lack of confidence in the future, especially amongst the middle class. This has led some scholars to conclude that this middle class 'has morphed from a self-confident and complacent social class into an anxious, impetuous and discontented social class since the handover' (Lau 2013: 107).

One informant who succinctly expressed this was Winston, a Buddhist in his early thirties who recently bought a small apartment in the newly built Bellagio apartment complex in Sham Tseng, on the southwest coast of the New Territories. His apartment is small and very far removed from Hong Kong Island, where he initially wanted to live, but it was all he could afford. In conversations, Winston often reflected on factors that for him signalled 'the end of the Hong Kong fairy tale, or our version of the American Dream':

> There aren't going to be any more Li Ka-shing rags-to-riches stories told to inspire anymore. It is extremely hard to grow a business from a family-owned start-up to a multinational conglomerate. You will likely keep struggling in small businesses, while already huge groups like Jardines [Jardine Matheson Holdings] and the real estate companies continue to gobble up more companies and real estate . . . Not only is the rags-to-riches tale over (except for the occasional miracle that the media seizes on) but the middle-class aspirational narrative of 'study hard, get your well-earned rewards after' is also almost broken. Look at how Hong Kong students break their backs and have such a miserable life. For what? Think also of all the things Hongkongers associate with the middle class; homeownership, a comfortable office job in either suit or smart casual clothes, a family with two or more kids. This Dream is becoming bankrupt in Hong Kong.

In a different conversation, Winston further observed:

> The lavish lifestyle is shouted at your face every day. CCTV has changed. Look at their sitcoms: they talk about the everyday life of Hong Kong people, but their apartments and homes are Mid-Levels apartments, of more than 1,000 square feet! It's brainwashing, their message that this is the average Hongkonger. No wonder people are unhappy! They look at that and think: I'm middle class, why don't I have that life and those possessions? The sad thing is, even if they work 50 hours a week, they will still not get it. Of course there are always people with the right circumstances, who strike it lucky and become wealthy: we shouldn't deny their story. I'm just saying that the average Hongkonger is not like that.

As Winston's reflections clearly indicate, for most Hong Kong residents, owning a house is strongly aspired to, but it is an aspiration that is difficult to achieve. Property prices on Hong Kong Island are the third most expensive in the world, after Monaco and London. On average, families of four live in apartments of less than 50 square metres. The average housing size is around 45 square metres, one of the smallest in the world (*Global Property Guide* 2019; Pak 2013). Some people live as though in 'cages', as 'human battery hens' in small square apartments, or in single beds surrounded by bars on which to attach their personal belongings. Recently built flats have even been referred to as 'mosquito homes' due to their minimal size.

The issues over who does or does not own property and what this means for achieving success in life is likewise prevalent in the narratives of other Hong Kong Buddhists. As indicated at the start of this chapter, Teresa also seemed to have lost confidence in her city's future. She similarly aspired to own her own place, but fully realised the difficulty of making this happen. These difficulties are often related to the increase of immigrant Chinese mainlanders coming to the city. First, the increase in population has led to a scarcity of housing. One of my informants reflected:

> The Hong Kong Government is influenced by Mainland China. Look at the houses in the New Territories. They are built near the border. They are built for mainlanders. When that part of the New Territories is developed, it will be for mainland people from Shenzhen, not for us.

Second, Chinese developers are perceived to be driving the housing prices up. Elsie, a Buddhist housewife in her mid-thirties, commented:

> I see a lot of mainlanders who are very wealthy. They want to spend their black money, so they buy a lot of properties here. That is why our housing prices are up sky-high.

Even though there are no official data supporting such opinions, these public narratives are popular in Hong Kong, expressed in both conversations and popular (social) media.

These reflections can make one ponder the following question: if owning one's own home is such an important part of the Hong Kong Dream and, more importantly, relates to feelings of belonging to the city, what will happen when local Hong Kong residents are no longer able to buy properties? In the remainder of this chapter, I indicate how for my informants these aspirations to the Hong Kong Dream and homeownership are partly dependent upon Buddhist notions regarding personal accountability and karma. In this, I show that the ways in which my Buddhist informants deal with their frustrations or despair over the Hong Kong Dream might be different than expected.

Transcended Belonging

The stress placed on personal accountability and karma by my Buddhist informants not only affects their religious life, but also shapes their ideas about how they can actively control and change the world around them. In Buddhist thought, the environment is a reflection of a person's inner self and state of mind. By changing oneself, one changes the world. Following up on this is a second Buddhist perspective: the impermanence of the world. Because the world is a reflection of the sadness and happiness within an individual, it is at the same time impermanent and fluid. In the words of one of my informants, life should be taken 'like a river that comes and goes'. This idea of impermanence affects how Buddhists perceive the world around them and their position in that world. It is important to remember here that a change in the world is believed to be not merely a perception of change, but actual change itself. Following on from this is the belief that each individual can be held accountable for the condition of the world. As I have already shown, it is this empowering agency (expressed in sayings such as 'Be the change you want to see in the world' or, as one of my informants put it, 'It is a transformation of one's ideas on life and thus life itself') that features predominantly in how my modern Buddhist informants view their religion, as well as their capacity to aspire to homeownership and belonging. This agency helps them transcend their current situation, both spatially and temporally.

As already indicated, for Teresa (and similarly for other Hong Kong Buddhists), the world in which she makes her home is for the most part constituted by the large Buddhist network to which she feels she belongs. Instead of defining herself as a member of a particular community located at a specific site, she feels she belongs to a larger global Buddhist community. Her 'home' is not necessarily in Hong Kong, but rather in a Buddhist network that transcends contemporary Hong Kong.

The localisation of Buddhism in Hong Kong thus relates to the question of what it means to be local in a globalised world. From their local contexts, my informants connect to wider, global networks. These networks and the ways with which they are lived through practices, movements and the exchange of ideas become part of the everyday lives of my informants. Being Buddhist thus offers adherents a way to belong to the world and find their homes therein; participating in that world becomes an integral part of one's identity as a Buddhist.

Simultaneously, being Buddhist is also a way to relate the temporal to the spiritual, the present to the past and future, and the here and now to the what comes after. A forty-year-old Buddhist interlocutor, who works for a major Buddhist temple in the city, indicated: 'In Buddhism, I found the answers. There is only karma, cause and effect . . . And since you are creating your own karma right now, you must start working on your future in the here and now.' He emphasised his personal role in learning about, understanding and practising Buddhism, while at the same time highlighting his personal accountability for a future that extends beyond his present life.

Being Buddhist and the aspirations of belonging that come with this thus transcend the 'secular' by including the 'spiritual'. This can also be described as an 'alternative belonging', in the sense of 'offering or expressing a choice . . . existing or functioning outside the established cultural, social, or economic system' (*Merriam Webster Dictionary* 2019). This 'alternative' refers to what people choose for themselves and what they are thus personally accountable for. Even though the aspiration for belonging is coloured by the wider geopolitical circumstances of the city, my informants express their individual agency in aspiring to belong to an alternative, spiritual network that transcends both geography and temporality.

These understandings shape the values Hong Kong residents attach to certain aspirations, such as the Hong Kong Dream. This again relates to the emphasis on personal accountability described above; the question of who or what is responsible for a given situation. As I will indicate, rather than simply debating the perceived increasing difficulty of owning one's own home, my Buddhist informants attempt to change their attitudes towards it, by extension changing the nature of their hopes, discontents and anxieties. Considering that my informants place heavy emphasis on personal accountability and on the idea that the world is a reflection of one's personal mind, it comes as no surprise to learn that they consider each individual personally responsible for changing their personal situation. Consequently, they do not necessarily view the growing 'aspiration gap' regarding homeownership (Ray 2006) as a factual issue; instead, they reflect on their own selves as powerful agents capable of changing these issues. Teresa explained to me how Buddhism made her look at the world in a different way:

> The external environment reflects your own heart. Therefore, the solution is always in yourself. You can clean up your own heart and then the environment, instead of asking for the external to change.

Teresa observed how the generation of the 1970s and 1980s (those who possessed the so-called Lion Rock Spirit) 'only focused on earning money to raise their children'. As long as there was food on the table, they were satisfied. Part of the issue in contemporary Hong Kong, according to her, is that these aspirations have changed. It is no longer enough to simply earn sufficient money to buy food;

instead, the full Hong Kong Dream must be realised, including homeownership. Yet, as she sees it, this leads people to become attached to too many material things:

> In Hong Kong, money is the main value. That's why people work like madness [*sic*]. People of the middle class sometimes don't realise that they can just concentrate on loving their families and friends and be happy. They want society to change. But if you want something to change, you need to change yourself.

Teresa emphasised that in order to acquire a goal, the goal itself and one's attitude towards that goal should be changed. She thereby stressed each individual's own accountability in the world.

A person who experienced this first-hand is William, a Buddhist in his early forties. He is a wealthy upper middle-class Hong Kong resident, working as a professional mediator. He discovered Buddhism a few years ago and since then has tried to lead a more basic lifestyle. During his career, he met a number of 'wealthy businessmen' and he was not impressed:

> In my career, I have seen all these so-called business leaders; I have been rubbing shoulders with the elite in our society. I don't find them respectful ... When you are in the middle management, you want to be the senior of the firm. Then you want to be the managing director, then the CEO, then a board member and in the end a chairman of a charitable organisation. But these are all ulterior motives; they don't come from within.

William thus reflects negatively on the focus on aspiring to materiality, even when this involves working for a charitable organisation.

Despite William and Teresa's emphasis on nonmaterialism, both participate in the material world. Just like other Buddhist informants, they have not retreated from the world by becoming monks or nuns (although William has expressed an interest in doing so). Somewhat significantly, I met William in the Foreign Correspondents' Club and Teresa on multiple occasions in expensive Western-style cafés and restaurants. Also, as indicated, Teresa does aspire to own her own home one day. The difficulty for my Buddhist informants is to strike a correct balance between nonattachment to materialism on the one hand and securing a decent lifestyle for themselves on the other hand.

My interlocutors did not necessarily give up their hope to succeed materially in Hong Kong because of their religious identities. Instead, they altered their perception on aspirations and their capacities to aspire. The Buddhist way of thinking about attachment and nonattachment, coupled with the emphasis on personal accountability, leads to a particular reflection on the growing difficulties impeding the achievement of the Hong Kong Dream. However, whether the Dream becomes impossible to achieve depends upon how attached one is to the particularities of this Dream; that is, how much one should earn, at which high-quality university one should study and in which part of Hong Kong one should own a house. Thus, although my Buddhist informants recognise and acknowledge the severity of the issues at hand in contemporary Hong Kong, they also feel that they themselves are accountable for the gravity of these issues. They see themselves as having the personal ability to change the situation, either by becoming less attached or by changing their perspectives towards the perceived problem. Modern Buddhism teaches them to be active agents who are personally responsible for the existence of setbacks, the manner in which these are experienced and consequently the ways in which one should respond to them.

This does not mean that Buddhism for my informants is merely a project of self-improvement that provides meaning in light of material insecurities. The concluding discussion of this chapter will make this clearer.

Concluding Discussion

This chapter alludes to antagonisms between aspirations for a physical home and a feeling of being spiritually at home in a particular city, the world or even the universe. The narratives presented above portray a tension between materialistic aspirations (homeownership) and the desire to acquire a spiritual home – or, in a broader sense, between material self-development and spirituality. This last desire emerges from a highly individualised form of 'modern Buddhism', stressing an individual's own responsibility to achieve their goals. What I have argued by presenting these narratives is a need to transcend a secular view on aspirations, in this case of homeownership.

This leads me to wonder about three things in relation to the urban aspirations of young people in Asia. First, the emphasis on aspirations as presented in this chapter questions the apparent dichotomy between 'worldly' goals, such as homeownership, and 'other-worldly' goals, such as salvation. According to Marian Burchardt, 'religious vitality emerges from and must be situated within, the broader social context of the challenges that people . . . face in their everyday lives . . . The question is thus how practices of acting upon these challenges shape and are shaped in the religious field' (2013: 169–70). I have tried to relate challenges concerning homeownership to my informants' aspirations in order to show that aspirations can extend beyond particular timeframes.

Buddhism, as with all religions, is not something separate from 'normal' or 'ordinary' life, but rather is very much a part of it. Because all religion is lived, it is fluid and creative and, by extension, it is adjustable to particular socioeconomic and political circumstances. By relating religion to aspirations, I have indicated the unique ways in which Hong Kong Buddhism becomes a meaningful grid for guiding my informants and helping them understand their place in Hong Kong and in the world.

As shown in this volume, a study of aspirations directs our attention to the future, as aspirations are future-oriented cultural capacities related to wants, preferences, choices and calculations (Appadurai 2004). Such a focus on the future might provide us with insights into urban Asian cultures, especially when seen from the viewpoint of younger generations. Often, aspirations are studied and constructed within the timeframe of one's own life. However, a focus on religion shows that aspirations can transcend particular timeframes and localities and can include history and future and the local, the global and the transcendental all at the same time. What then might this focus on aspiring to a home and the combination between aspirations and religious beliefs tell us about young adults finding a place to belong in Hong Kong?

I started this chapter with the musings of Teresa, a young Buddhist whose sense of belonging to a wider world appears to underlie her willingness to consider moving overseas in the face of domestic pressures in order to make a home for herself. As I have argued, perhaps Teresa belongs to the world instead of to her particular city. As indicated, having a place to call 'home' is often regarded as vital for a feeling of belonging to a particular place. However, in the case of Hong Kong, owning property is at the same time crucial and relatively difficult to achieve. What then will happen to the feelings of local Hong Kong residents when they are no longer able to buy properties and create homes? What will the future of Hong Kong be when aspirations extend beyond local homeownership to feelings of home in (religious) communities or the world at large? Will homeownership in the future be just as important as it is today or, in these globalised, modern times, will it perhaps be replaced by the aspiration to seek belonging elsewhere?

This chapter has been a call to explore in more depth the concept of 'aspirations' beyond temporal and spatial boundaries. It has attempted to broaden the concept of aspirations to include those that are informed by issues literally larger than life and also to question whether we, as scholars, should ourselves transcend the concept in order to extend our gaze beyond the boundaries of the lives of ourselves and our research participants.

Mariske Westendorp is an anthropologist and religious studies scholar. She was awarded her Ph.D. in anthropology in 2016 from Macquarie University, Australia. Her research interests include the anthropology of religion, urban anthropology, Buddhist and the study of death in contemporary urban societies.

Note

1. Pseudonyms have been used for the research participants mentioned in this chapter out of respect for their privacy.

References

Appadurai, Arjun. 2004. 'The Capacity to Aspire: Culture and the Terms of Recognition', in Vijayendra Rao and Michael Walton (eds), *Culture and Public Action*. Stanford: Stanford University Press, pp. 59–84.

———. 2013. *The Future as Cultural Fact: Essays on the Global Condition*. London: Verso.

Baker, Hugh. 1983. 'Life in the Cities: The Emergence of Hong Kong Man', *China Quarterly* 95: 469–79.

Burchardt, Marian. 2013. 'Belonging and Success: Religious Vitality and the Politics of Urban Space in Cape Town', in Irene Becci, Marian Burchardt and José Casanova (eds), *Topographies of Faith: Religion in Urban Spaces*. Leiden: Brill, pp. 167–87.

Cassaniti, Julia. 2012. 'Agency and the Other: The Role of Agency for the Importance of Belief in Buddhist and Christian Traditions', *Journal of the Society for Psychological Anthropology* 40(3): 297–316.

Chua, Beng-huat. 2000. 'Consuming Asians: Ideas and Issues', in Beng-huat Chua (ed), *Consumption in Asia: Lifestyles and Identities*. London: Routledge, pp. 1–34.

Crosby, Kate. 2014. *Theravada Buddhism: Continuity, Diversity and Identity*. Chichester: Wiley Blackwell.

Duyvendak, Jan Willem. 2011. *The Politics of Home: Belonging and Nostalgia in Western Europe and the United States*. Basingstoke: Palgrave Macmillan.

Fischer, Edward. 2014. *The Good Life: Aspiration, Dignity and the Anthropology of Wellbeing*. Stanford: Stanford University Press.

Global Property Guide. 2019. 'World's Most Expensive Cities'. Retrieved 25 March 2020 from http://www.globalpropertyguide.com/most-expensive-cities.

Gombrich, Richard. 2006. *Theravāda Buddhism: A Social History from Ancient Benares to Modern Colombo*, 2nd edn. London: Routledge.

Hsiao, Hsin-huang (ed.). 2014. *Chinese Middle Classes: Taiwan, Hong Kong, Macao and China*. London: Routledge.

Jaffe, Rivke, and Anouk De Koning. 2016. *Introducing Urban Anthropology*. London: Routledge.

Kuah-Pearce, Khun Eng. 2009. *State, Society and Religious Engineering: Towards a Reformist Buddhism in Singapore*, 2nd edn. Singapore: Institute of Southeast Asian Studies.

Lau, Siu-kai. 2013. 'The Middle Class and Politics in Hong Kong since the Handover', *East Asian Policy* 5(4): 107–16.

Lee, Eliza. 2005. 'The Regeneration of the Social Pact in Hong Kong: Economic Globalisation, Socioeconomic Change and Local Politics', *Journal of Social Policy* 34(2): 293–310.

Lopez Jr., Donald. 2002. 'Introduction', in Donald Lopez, Jr. (ed.), *A Modern Buddhist Bible: Essential Readings from East and West*. Boston: Beacon Press, pp. vii–xli.

Mak, Bill. 2012. 'Theravāda Teachings and Buddhist Meditation Training in Hong Kong', *International Journal for the Study of Humanistic Buddhism* 3: 19–38.

Mathews, Gordon, and Tai-lok Lui. 2001. 'Introduction', in Gordon Mathews and Tai-lok Lui (eds), *Consuming Hong Kong*. Hong Kong: Hong Kong University Press, pp. 1–22.

Mathews, Gordon, Eric Ma and Tai-lok Lui. 2008. *Hong Kong, China: Learning to Belong to a Nation*. London: Routledge.

McMahan, David. 2008. *The Making of Buddhist Modernism*. Oxford: Oxford University Press.

———. 2012. *Buddhism in the Modern World*. Abingdon: Routledge.

Merriam Webster Dictionary. 2019. 'Alternative'. Retrieved 25 March 2020 from https://www.merriam-webster.com/dictionary/alternative.

Ng, Janet. 2009. *Paradigm City: Space, Culture and Capitalism in Hong Kong*. Albany: State University of New York Press.

Ng, Jason. 2014. *No City for Slow Men: Hong Kong's Quirks and Quandaries Laid Bare*. Hong Kong: Blacksmith Books.

Pak, Jennifer. 2013. 'Hong Kong Copes with Tight Living Spaces', *BBC News*, 11 April.

Palmer, David. 2011. 'The Body: Health, Nation and Transcendence', in David Palmer, Glenn Shive and Philip Wickeri (eds), *Chinese Religious Life*. Oxford: Oxford University Press, pp. 87–106.

Ralph, David, and Lynn Staeheli. 2011. 'Home and Migration: Mobilities, Belongings and Identities', *Geography Compass* 5(7): 517–30.

Ray, Debraj. 2006. 'Aspirations, Poverty and Economic Change', in Abhijit Banerjee, Roland Bénabou and Dilip Mookherjee (eds), *Understanding Poverty*. Oxford: Oxford University Press, pp. 409–21.

Robison, Richard, and David Goodman. 1996. *The New Rich in Asia: Mobile Phones, McDonald's and Middle-Class Revolution*. London: Routledge.

Salih, Ruba. 2003. *Gender in Transnationalism: Home, Longing and Belonging among Moroccan Migrant Women*. London: Routledge.

Siu, Helen. 2009. 'Positioning at the Margins: The Infra-power of Middle-Class Hong Kong', in Deeborah Madsen and Andrea Riemenschnitter (eds), *Diasporic Histories: Cultural Archives of Chinese Transnationalism*. Hong Kong: Hong Kong University Press, pp. 55–76.

———. 2011. 'Returning a Provincialized Middle Class in Asia's Urban Postmodern: The Case of Hong Kong', in Ananya Roy and Aihwa Ong (eds), *Worlding Cities: Asian Experiments and the Art of Being Global*. Malden, MA: Wiley-Blackwell, pp. 129–59.

Siu, Helen, and Agnes Ku (eds). 2008. *Hong Kong Mobile: Making a Global Population*. Hong Kong: Hong Kong University Press.

So, Alvin. 2000. 'Changing Patterns of Class and Status-Group Struggles in Hong Kong: A World-Systems Analysis', *Development and Society* 29(2): 1–21.

———. 2014. 'The Making of Hong Kong's Middle Class in the 1997 Transition and Beyond: A Conflict Perspective', in Hsin-huang Hsiao (ed.), *Chinese Middle Classes: Taiwan, Hong Kong, Macao and China*. London: Routledge, pp. 249–60.

Tuan, Yi-Fu. 1977. *Space and Place: The Perspective of Experience*. Minneapolis: University of Minnesota Press.

Van der Velde, Paul. 2016. *De Oude Boeddha in een Nieuwe Wereld: Verkenningen in de Westerse Dharma*, 2nd edn. Nijmegen: Vantilt.

Wacquant, Loïc. 1992. 'Making Class: The Middle Class(es) in Social Theory and Social Structure', in Scott McNall, Rhonda Levine and Rick Fantasia (eds), *Bringing Class Back in: Contemporary and Historical Perspectives*. Boulder: Westview Press, pp. 39–64.

Westendorp, Mariske. 2017. 'Belonging to a Global Family of God in Hong Kong: The Relevance of Religion in Facing an Uncertain Future', *Asian Anthropology* 16(2): 116–32.

———. 2021. 'Doing Good: Local and Global Understandings of Buddhism in Hong Kong's Umbrella Movement', *Global Religions (Special Issue: Bad Buddhism)*.

Yeung, Gustav, and Wai-yin Chow. 2010. '"To Take up Your Own Responsibility": The Religiosity of Buddhist Adolescents in Hong Kong', *International Journal of Children's Spirituality* 15(1): 5–23.

CONCLUSION

The Future of Urban Asia

Mariske Westendorp

Aspirations of Young Adults in Urban Asia

This volume contains nine ethnographic narratives of young adults living and designing a life for themselves in a variety of urban Asian contexts. The chapters range from East Asia (Beijing, Taipei, Shanghai, Seoul, Tokyo, Osaka and Hong Kong) to Southeast Asia (Kuala Lumpur and Ho Chi Minh City) and South Asia (Colombo and Dhaka). The actors presented in the chapters express economic, political, social, cultural, educational, physical, national, transcendental and familial aspirations.

Taking all these chapters together, we obtain a unique picture of the theory of aspirations at play. The collection of chapters in this volume has presented us with empirical evidence to understand changing aspirations and lifestyles in various Asian contexts that are at different stages of economic development and integration into global capitalism and consumerism. They also grant us the possibility of examining the cultural and ideological discourses behind aspirations, which are related to divisions between classes, generations and ethnicities.

At first glance, it seems as if the chapters all deal with a wide and perhaps dissimilar variety of aspirations. They are economic, political, religious or social in nature. They are variously material and immaterial, subjective and communally constructed, practical and idealistic, individual and universal. These aspirations are sometimes national, related to the state or a state apparatus such as the educational system; other aspirations are transnational, global or even transcendent in nature. Moreover, as the ethnographers of these chapters show, they are neither fixed nor always easily identifiable. Each country's context is different, as are the ways in which the actors described engage with direct local, national and international networks. The chapters thus contain a diversity of experiences, filled with cultural and contextual differences.

However, upon closer analysis, we can uncover a number of commonalities between the chapters, which can help us to better understand the theoretical concept of aspirations as *lived practice*, as well as the context of the wider Asian region. Let us therefore in this conclusion try to formulate an answer to the main question behind this book: when using the concept of aspirations as an analytical framework, what can we learn about the concept and its use in explaining the behaviours of present-day adolescents and young adults in urban Asian contexts?

Following Boccagni (2017), in this conclusion we analyse the aspirations presented in this book along the lines of three characteristics. While Boccagni used this framework to study migrant aspirations, we believe it can be applied to the study of aspirations in general. The first focus will be on the *content* of the aspiration – what it is that people aspire to. Aspirations are specific and subjective meaning-making tools. They include ideas about the 'modern self' (Giddens 1991) and the future. Specific to this volume are aspirations constructed by youth and young adults. Their particular life-course position shapes their aspirations in crucial ways. Second, we analyse the *relational references* of these aspirations. Who are the aspirations focused on and whom do they (or should they) benefit? While some actors hold aspirations that are subjective and self-focused (although not necessarily self-ish), others express aspirations related to the common good. As we will see, both agency and structure play a crucial role here: an individual decides who their aspiration and subsequent actions aim to benefit, although always in communication with the wider context. Lastly, we look at the *space-time horizons* of the aspirations: whether the content of the aspirations are directed towards places close to home or far away and whether they are concentrated on a short-term or long-term future. Here we will especially see the particular challenges that young adults in contemporary Asia face. While previous generations might have aspired to a life close to home and tradition, the aspirations of younger people living in global Asian contexts seem much more explorative, with increasingly wider horizons.

We add to these three characteristics a fourth one: *context*. The contents, relational references and horizons of the aspirations at hand are constructed by young adults who are (or aspire to be) members of the middle class and who live in, wish to live in or deliberately move away from twenty-first-century Asian urban contexts. The fact that they are young, middle class and urban impacts upon their future outlooks in ways that not only make sense of their personal navigational capacities and maps, but perhaps also help us to better understand and foresee the future of Asia in more general terms.

The Content of Aspirations

Aspirations are future-oriented and people who aspire are 'future-makers' (Appadurai 2013: 285). Aspirations revolve around 'imaginings' of other places, other times, other traditions or other selves. The chapters in this volume show how these imaginings dialectically relate to two ideals: that of the good life and that of self-realisation.

In her chapter, Carolin Landgraf aptly describes how young adults in Seoul desire a valuable life; a good life in which the they can develop their full potential. Likewise, Suborna Camellia shows how young girls in Dhaka aspire to a 'good future', which is defined as having a successful career and becoming economically independent. In a certain way, Mariske Westendorp in her chapter also alludes to the desire for a good life, if not in the here and now, then in the transcendental future. These ideas can be captured by what Edward Fischer describes as 'the good life', 'not a state to be obtained but an ongoing aspiration for something better that gives meaning to life's pursuits. In this view, striving for the good life involves the arduous work of becoming, of trying to live a life that one deems worthy, becoming the sort of person that one desires' (2014: 2). Aspiring to develop one's full potential, to be economically successful, to construct a new identity or to find a place to belong can all be seen as part of this 'arduous work of becoming' in an immanent or faraway future.

The aspirations towards this idea of the good life are related to the 'prospects of being elsewhere' (or, as we will indicate below, of 'being somebody else'). This 'elsewhere' is a space that can be reached by using navigational maps and by taking choices that can help us negotiate the complex terrains of life. The 'prospect of being elsewhere' (Bunnell, Gillen and Ho 2018) is indeed a way to understand the aspirations of the young adults described by Landgraf, Camellia and Westendorp in their chapters. Each of them imagines a future in which an elsewhere exists for them, wherever and whenever this might be. Whether this good life is ultimately achieved or whether the aspirations towards this good life are even probable is not always significant; what matters instead is that the *prospect* of this elsewhere exists as nurturing tool (2018).

This aligns closely with the desire for self-realisation. Sarah Grant shows how young baristas in Ho Chi Minh City desire to uncover their creative selves. Désirée Remmert describes the struggle of young women in Chinese contexts with their dual identity of being good daughters and being independent women. Ayako Suzuki illustrates something similar by narrating the lives of young Japanese women in Dublin, who do not orient their lives based on filial piety towards older generations, but rather on the question of when and how to enter motherhood themselves. Chia-Yuan Huang and Sally Anne Param illustrate the need to construct a new identity in more general terms. For Huang, it is about the construction of an identity that makes sense for young Taiwanese adults in Shanghai in their new national context; Param describes the identity search of Malaysian Indian youth in Kuala Lumpur in terms of both rebelling against and falling in line with the expectations and pathways of an older generation. Finally, Morten Koch Andersen describes the aspiration of law students in Colombo to become middle class, meaning constructing an identity that is characterised by a certain social status, economic security and professional predictability.

These quests for self-realisation can be equated with what Giddens terms 'the reflexive project of the self' (1991: 75) or one's ongoing processes of 'becoming'. According to Giddens, in modern societies 'the self is not a passive entity, determined by external influences' (1991: 2). Instead, the self is reflexively made by individuals in their respective contexts. Moreover, it is both an embodied and a psychological identity. For example, Camellia shows how the self of her participants is for the most part constructed by ideas of appearance and beauty. Huang describes her participants' need to construct an identity that is recognised by oneself as well as by others. Lastly, the self is reflexively made 'amid a puzzling diversity of options and possibilities' (Giddens 1991: 3). Each individual who lives in a modern and global world is confronted with a plethora of choices. Based on these choices, one designs lifestyles that accommodate the construction of the self that one aspires to. The self in this case is self-representational or 'the individual's mental representation of his own person' (Ewing 1990: 109).

These two components of aspirations (i.e. imaginings of the good life and of self-realisation) are informed by two crucial characteristics of the actors described in this book: they are young and they find themselves in urban contexts. The designation 'youth' is here used as a group, not a category. The actors in this book are too different to categorise into one 'type'. What it means to be a young adult is different in each cultural context. Regardless, the actors presented in this book seem to be 'in the process of being recognised as youth and struggling to train themselves for their eventual entry into the adulthood with participation in the economy and establishing their own family of procreation' (Atal 2005: 12). They are members of society on the cusp of adulthood, struggling with questions of career, leisure time, familial obligations, relationships and self-identities. To make matters even more complicated, they find themselves in urban contexts characterised by large populations, density and heterogeneity. In cities, individuals encounter many different socialisation groups. One has the chance to socialise not only with family, but also with classmates, members of different racial and ethnic backgrounds, people with diverse sexual orientations and members of different occupational, economic and social classes. All these groups have an impact upon the formation and development of an individual's self-realisation and self-formation (see also Proshansky 1978). Taking these characteristics together, one could argue that the actors presented in this volume are situated within contexts and encounters that make them particularly prone to aspire.

Relational References of Aspirations

All chapters in this volume share a clear emphasis on the individual agencies of the actors introduced. According to Fischer, aspirations '[give] direction to agency – the power to act and the sense of control over one's own destiny' (2014: 207). At the same time, we argue, a sense of agency can in turn give direction, content and context to aspirations. Agency and agentive capacities make realising aspirations seem viable. To develop aspirations involves first having the capacity to aspire and then making choices about the form these aspirations take, who such aspirations aim to benefit, and when and where the aspirations can or need to be achieved.

Aspirations are almost always directed towards people. The question of who the aspirations benefit is – just like the context of aspirations – answered from a subjective, agentive position. The actors themselves decide to whom their ideas of the good life or their self-realisation apply. In some cases, the aspirations seem to be specifically oriented towards the self. Suzuki and Huang both describe how their research participants construct aspirations that primarily affect themselves in a hopefully positive way. Interestingly, in both cases, the actors decide upon migrating internationally to pursue these aspirations. Camellia describes the embodied aspiration of looking attractive, a delicate balance between being too conservative and too progressive. Westendorp also describes aspirations that are primarily oriented towards the individual, the main difference being that these aspirations are described in transcendental terms. In other cases, like those given in the chapter by Param, aspirations seem to be almost solely focused on the community. The young people introduced by Param are constantly searching for ways in which to be 'successful' according to their families' agendas.

The other chapters illustrate aspirations that reference both the self and others to varying degrees. The young adults described by Landgraf desire a fully developed life, mostly for themselves, but always in consideration of surrounding ethical ideals. Remmert places the personal aspirations of her research participants on maps of filial obligation, highlighting the struggle between wanting to be free from these obligations while at the same time being a good daughter. Andersen's and Grant's respondents place even more emphasis on the other by describing how their aspirations aim to help change not only the lives of the individuals themselves, but also their wider political, social and economic contexts.

While the relational references thus differ throughout the chapters, two commonalities can be detected. The first is, as noted before, the agentive power of the individual to construct the contents and references of the aspirations pursued. As to the second, the chapters demonstrate the significance of the surroundings in which these aspirational characteristics are constructed. Aspirations are both personal and collective. They are not only constructed by and reflected in maps of personal aspirations, but also by maps of obligations and expectations, such as family agendas, nation-building incentives, religious ideals or understandings of gender, ethnicity and class. Hence, while aspirations can reflect individual aims and ideals, they are always accompanied by shared principles and ethics. They are collective experiences, shaped and negotiated within networks of family, ethnicity, nationality, gender and transnationality – in other words, in the thick of life. Again, the particular flavours of aspiration described in this book are informed by the fact that the actors presented are young and live in urban contexts full of possibilities and challenges.

Emphasising the agency present in these individuals offers an interesting picture of life in Asian cities, namely one that identifies creativity, dynamism and fluctuation. The chapters in this book thus highlight a positive agentive approach. They show, in the context of urban middle-classness, the different creative ways in which aspects of country of origin, family, community, gender, class, ethnicity, schooling and so forth provide key conditions that encourage young people to explore their future yearnings. While this is often done in relation to traditional establishments and forms, it can be seen to also occur at a certain remove that seeks to escape the constraints of conventional discourses and disciplines.

Space-Time Horizons of Aspirations

Aspirations have contents that have referential qualities, but that are also aimed at particular places and times. People can hold desires that they aim to fulfil in the here and now, or wishes that can only be achieved by movement to another place or timeframe (i.e. the future). Aspirations can be pursued in the present lifetime and stage of life, or towards later ages or even later lifetimes. They can be mundane as well as transcendent. This is all exemplified by the order of the chapters in this book (see the Introduction in this volume).

The research of Remmert shows how aspirations, such as having a fulfilling career and family life, can be directed towards 'home', whether this home is the place where one grew up or a new place where one now lives. The research participants in Huang's chapter likewise express more short-term and everyday aspirations, but with the higher aim of identity transformation. Landgraf shows how such mundane aspirations can be placed on an even wider temporal horizon: for her research participants, aspirations are related to what 'should be' and are therefore never to be fully reached. Similarly, Camellia's research participants express horizons that are both within reach and extended towards a future further away: the career path might be clear, while the aspiration for independence might be more difficult to reach. The same applies to the actors in Suzuki's chapter, who want both freedom (which they have already achieved through migration) and self-fulfilment (which is potentially a goal uncertain to be reached). For them, the space horizon is clearly extended further than in the earlier chapters of this volume: the young women described have moved to another country, of which they had previously only dreamed.

In the final four chapters of the volume, the 'space' to which the aspirations allude is not clearly defined. The aspirations can be directed towards a town, a city or the nation, or can be transborder and transcendent. Param describes her participants' wish for a new identity, which will be gained the moment they achieve greater freedom after leaving school. Andersen describes how young lawyers in Sri Lanka have both an aspiration that is short-term and relatively clear to achieve (becoming lawyers) and a desire that is more long-term (effecting change in their society). Finally, Grant's and Westendorp's analyses both extend the horizons beyond the temporal and geographical by including the digital and transcendent. Like Andersen, Grant's research participants depict a horizon with socioeconomic spaces. Her cosmopolitan participants move through global, imagined networks. The actors in the final chapter by Westendorp likewise travel on global as well as universal horizons.

The space-time horizons of the young adults described are informed by the global contexts in which they live. The young adults presented are global agents who analyse, evaluate and present themselves in and from Asian urban contexts. Consequently, many of them are forced to developed bicultural identities, 'one part of their identity rooted in their local culture while another part stems from an awareness of their relation to the global culture' (Arnett 2004: 185). Giddens (2000) observes that in our global world, traditional ways are eroded and identities need to be created and re-created on a more active basis than ever before. Consequently, the horizons on which aspirations are focused are only sometimes a continuation of the present. Individuals may aim to stay in the same place (both geographically and temporally) or the same position as their parents; they remain middle class, like their parents or others from previous generations, and perform the duties that are expected and desired of them. However, at other times, discontinuities arise, especially when young individuals (partly encouraged by their cosmopolitan worldliness) actively choose to pursue other aspirations and navigational maps. This does not always come easy, as the chapters in this volume attest.

In each chapter, a certain degree of challenge and tension comes to the fore. We read how actors need to navigate between different responsibilities, reconcile clashing ideologies and confront possible contradictions between the local and the global, the 'traditional' and the 'modern'. For example, Remmert describes how actors struggle between wanting to be mobile and being close to their parental homes. Huang illustrates the tensions between economic opportunity and socio-political commitments. Camellia and Suzuki both describe frictions between different notions of what it means to be a woman. Landgraf focuses on the dilemma between self-development and stability, while Andersen illustrates the dilemma between self-development and social activism. Param shows difficulties to reconcile the need for personal space and leisure time with family obligations and affiliations. Lastly, Grant and Westendorp focus on the double binds and disassociations between the local and the global.

Ways to negotiate these challenges are complex and diverse, and come with a certain level of risk. To change what can seem a set future, one often has to break away from the past. This can be done by moving towards a different, unknown place (see the chapters by Remmert, Huang and Suzuki), by cutting oneself loose from existent imposing structures or parental influences (see the chapters by Param, Camellia, Andersen and Westendorp), by changing one's ethics (see the chapter by Landgraf) or by choosing a path other than tradition as the way forward (see the chapter by Grant). As such, aspirations are paths of sacrifice and paths towards the unknown.

In some cases, this might lead to a gap between generations or gaps in space and time. These gaps can be experienced as a loss of relations, traditions or identifications. However, they can also be viewed as a strategic resource or as opportunities to reflect and re-evaluate who individuals are and the aspirations they have for themselves, their families and their wider communities. In this way, aspirations can be positive and empowering.

Context and Aspirations

Lastly, the aspirations as illustrated above are constructed within a particular situation: that of being young and middle class (or aspiring middle class) in urban Asian contexts. This situation impinges on both the particular types of aspirations that are constructed, as well as on the capacities one has to construct these and pursue them to fruition. Fischer notes how 'the effectiveness of aspirations and agency is often limited by available opportunity structures (the social norms, legal regulations and market entry mechanisms that delimit, or facilitate, certain behaviours and aspirations)' (2014: 6). Imaginations and the probability to make these aspirations a reality are clear signs of particular times and places. They are reflections of changing economic, political and social circumstances, as well as ideas of empowerment and of personalised ideals and ethics. In other words, there should not only be a will, but also a way.

The people presented in this book are not just people 'in Asia', but primarily people 'of Asia'. The aspirations described in this book are not just ones that happen to take shape in Asian cities and that might just as well take shape elsewhere; they are the result of the dynamic engagements of the lives of young adults with the specific features of Asian industrial and post-industrial cityscapes and social conditions. In these engagements, the actors in this book are agents who have their own versions of who they are and what and where they want to be, and they take advantage of opportunities to enact this. They creatively use multiple global locations and connections (either within or outside of Asia) to create a new self and a new life.

According to Ananya Roy and Aihwa Ong (2011), Asian cities have their own 'art of being global', meaning that amongst other things, they have their own distinctive forms of aspirations and agencies that are incredibly diverse and increasingly significant and that differ from aspirations and agencies in non-Asian urban contexts. These differences can perhaps best be explained by the major economic changes that have occurred in East and Southeast Asia in the twentieth century.

In 1968, the economist and sociologist Gunnar Myrdal published *Asian Drama: An Inquiry into the Poverty of Nations*. Based on a ten-year study of poverty in Asia, Myrdal argued that population growth in the continent would stunt economic growth. He characterised Asian countries as ethnically, culturally, linguistically and religiously diverse; as being led primarily by local beliefs and practices; as having religious systems that are more concerned with the other-worldly than the mundane; as having systems that favoured the family above national institutions; and as having a mixture of functional and personal patron–client relations. All these characteristics, in addition to high population growth, would hinder Asian countries from developing economically.

Only twenty-five years later, a World Bank policy research report entitled *The Asian Miracle: Economic Growth and Public Policy* was published, which stated that:

> East Asia has a remarkable record of high and sustained economic growth. From 1965 to 1990 the twenty-three economies of East Asia grew faster than all other regions of the world. Most of this achievement is attributable to seemingly miraculous growth in just eight economies: Japan; the 'Four Tigers' (Hong Kong, the Republic of Korea, Singapore and Taiwan); and the three newly industrialized economies (NIEs) of Southeast Asia, Indonesia, Malaysia and Thailand. (Page 1994: 219)

Arguably, this economic growth has now extended to almost all countries in South, Southeast and East Asia. Contrasting these two publications makes clear how the economic growth of different Asian countries, starting with the 'Four Tigers', was unprecedented and unexpected. It is reasonable to suggest that this growth took place not only *in spite of* the characteristics described by Myrdal, but more importantly perhaps even *because of* them. Development in Asia has primarily been on its own terms and with its own characteristics, and has occurred along a different trajectory from that of the West (specifically Europe and the United States).

Regardless of the specific dynamics that make Asia's increasing progress possible, the economic development and subsequent political and social changes it has brought forth has impacted the lives of each of the individuals presented in this book. They are all part of, or aspire to be part of, the 'new rich' (Robison and Goodman 1996): a middle-class group of people that emerged and that continues to increase in size due to these rapid changes. This middle class is diverse. It involves both the bourgeoisie and the professional middle classes; owners of capital as well as those with managerial and technical skills. In comparison to much of the middle classes in the West, these new rich 'appear as likely to embrace authoritarian rule, xenophobic nationalism, religious fundamentalism and *dirigisme* as to support democracy, internationalism, secularism and free markets' (Robison and Goodman 1996: 3). This mirrors the description Yeung and Alipio (2013) give of young adults in Asia as people who have a later entry into the workforce, live for longer periods with their parents and delay their age of marriage. According to them, 'deep-seated traditions regarding gender and intergenerational relations remain prevalent in moral teachings and in religious decrees' (2013: 12). Because of this, the family is still a stronger socioeconomic unit than, for example, in Western countries and the gender divide is still more strict. These cultural aspects, determined by public policies, religion, tradition and other factors, influence the aspirations of young adults and the trajectories chosen to bring these aspirations to life. In other words, in constructing and working on their aspirations, young adults in Asia may be both inclined to follow ways that are more 'traditional', as well as those that are often associated with the 'modern'.

The diversity of the middle-class group and the difficulties that arise when trying to classify their aspirations as either 'traditional' or 'modern' also clearly come to the fore in the chapters in this volume. The contributors all describe the middle class in different terms, either implicitly or explicitly and as resulting from a diverse range of specific historical and contemporary experiences. For some, being middle class means having had the best education, being able to attend some of the top-tier high schools and universities (for example, as described in the chapters by Remmert, Landgraf, Suzuki and Andersen). For others, it means having the possibility to be mobile, both in terms of geographical mobility (see the chapters by Remmert, Huang and Suzuki) and in terms of socioeconomic mobility (see the chapter by Grant). In almost all chapters, being a member of the middle class means either having or being able to secure a certain career and the economic stability and independence that comes with that (see the chapter by Camellia). In his chapter, Andersen describes how a career may come with a sense of social status, economic security and stability. Interestingly, being a successful middle-class professional in the case of his research participants can seem contradictory to being a human rights activist. In other chapters, most notably those by Param and Suzuki, it is exactly the possibility to make individual choices that defines the middle class.

Despite this diversity in the meaning of the concept of 'middle class', in all the chapters it becomes clear that being part of the middle class is both a subjective and a relational identity. Being member of the middle class means not being a member of the lower class or belonging to the wealthier higher classes. It is also something that cannot be measured objectively. The actors in this book all express a certain understanding of what it might mean, without being able to support this with definitive statements or objective evidence. Being a member of the middle class comes with a certain level of income. It means being educated in universities, or at least having the opportunity to be highly educated. It is related to the possibility to be mobile, both in geographical and mental terms. Notably, being a member of the middle class comes with a certain degree of consumerist behaviour and a level of independence from otherwise imposing structures such as the family or the nation-state.

The growing impact of the middle class may differ from one country to another, and so will the consequences of different conflicts of interest and the varying aspirations of its members. Perhaps this is especially so as the middle-class individuals presented here are young adults – those who may have the capacity to shape their local and national contexts. As Amartya Sen (1999) has observed, there is a direct link between lack of opportunity, restrictions on economic opportunities and poverty. As members of the more wealthy middle class, the actors of this volume might have greater opportunity to influence the development of the cultural, social, economic and political life of the societies of East, Southeast and South Asia. How exactly this may play out in the future is hard to predict, although some initial observations might be made based on their narratives.

Ethnographies of the Future

In the introduction to this book, we introduced questions which the different chapters in this volume seek to answer. In Asian urban contexts, what are young adults' aspirations? How do young adults and youth engage in local and global economic, political, or sociocultural markets in the pursuit of these aspirations? And what does this tell us about the cultural lifeworlds in which they grow up, start families and build careers? We also introduced young adults in different Asian urban contexts as global citizens who are being confronted with possible futures involving uncertainties, unpredictability, ecological catastrophes and the threat of political or economic crises. Social change, urbanisation and globalisation are factors that shape and inform these dilemmas, making these tensions a timely prism for understanding Asian young adults and Asian development.

The actors presented in this book all articulate aspirations emerging within the specific timeframes and spaces in which they were situated at the time that the research in question was undertaken. As such, analysing their aspirations not only tells us something about their present individual lives, but might also give us ideas about future developments in twenty-first-century Asian contexts; the opportunities, challenges and negotiations expressed in the nine chapters of this volume are signs of the present and future Asia.

For a long time, anthropology has not seemed overly interested in the study of the future; the future was a domain of investigation for other social sciences, like geography or sociology (Bryant and Knight 2019; Persoon and van Est 2000). Anthropological enquiry mainly considered the past by focusing on the continuity and discontinuity of tradition and culture. Since the beginning of the twenty-first century, this has started to change. The study of the future is an emerging field in anthropology, in line with an increase in global challenges and features such as diverse financial crises, political and religious uprisings, climate change and an increasing presence of digital and social media.

Another development within the study of anthropology is the shift from 'dark anthropology' towards an anthropology of good and hope (Ortner 2016). In the imaginings of the future, such as those illustrated in this book, people aspire, imagine, desire, speculate, anticipate and expect (Appadurai 2013; Bryant and Knight 2019). Concepts of the future, either mundane or utopian, are constructed in present-day life and influence this life in particular ways. Looking at aspired-to futures therefore shows us the present and the ways in which people construct and live their everyday lives. These futures are, in other words, 'contemporary futures' (Wallman 1992). A study of these contemporary futures improves our understanding of the present, as 'our concept of the present *as present* derives from the future' (Bryant and Knight 2019: 16).

The future orients us in the present and, at the same time, the present influences the possibilities of the future. This interrelationship is also reflected in the chapters in this book. The contributors show how each new generation re-creates, reshapes or rejects the world of its elders, mostly not through overt political action, but rather through a myriad of personal choices – for example, by having a career instead of being a housewife or by migrating to other cities or countries. The chapters show the particularities of the young, the wishes and needs they have, the constraints they face and the varied paths forward.

The imagined future is thus shaped by and in the present. Following Appadurai (2013, 2016) and Clammer (2012), we believe that an anthropological or ethnographic approach is particularly suited to create a richer understanding of the affective orientations that shape shared and differing notions of the present and the future. As anthropologists and ethnographers, we seek to delve beneath the externalities of people. Through long-term contact, deep conversations and being open to the thick of life, we get to know these individuals and their hopes, dreams, fears and wishes, the risks they take and the opportunities they make for themselves and their communities. We hope that this book has shown these ways in which anthropology can contribute to a study and understanding of the future.

One last comment needs to be made here. Change in Asia is fast-paced, especially in its urban centres. Cities are growing rapidly and an increasing number of people migrate to cities from rural areas looking for housing, jobs and perhaps to make new selves and possibilities. At the same time, economic, political and social inequalities, both within and between Asian countries, are growing. It is important to note that the narratives presented in this book are time-specific snapshots of Asian urban contexts in this particular period only. The futures alluded to in the chapters are unforeseen futures, based on desires that change perhaps as swiftly as the lives of the individuals themselves. In addition, as alluded to by some authors in this volume, digital social spaces are important and will become increasingly so in the future. How these and other influences affect the aspirations of subsequent generations of urban Asians, as well as the futures of the contexts in which they live, remains to be seen – and should therefore be the subject of continued ethnographic investigation.

Mariske Westendorp is an anthropologist and religious studies scholar. She was awarded her Ph.D. in anthropology in 2016; her dissertation was entitled 'In the Eye of the Typhoon: Aspirations of Buddhists and Catholics in Turbulent Hong Kong'. Her research interests include the anthropology of religion, urban anthropology, Buddhist and the study of death in contemporary urban societies.

References

Appadurai, Arjun. 2013. *The Future as Cultural Fact: Essays on the Global Condition.* London: Verso.

———. 2016. 'Moodswings in the Anthropology of the Emerging Future', *Hau: Journal of Ethnographic Theory* 6(2): 1–4.

Arnett, Jeffrey Jensen. 2004. *Adolescence and Emerging Adulthood: A Cultural Approach.* Upper Saddle River, NJ: Prentice Hall.

Atal, Yogesh. 2005. 'Youth in Asia: An Overview', in Fay Gale and Stephanie Fahey (eds), *Youth in Transition: The Challenges of Generational Change in Asia.* Canberra: AASSREC, pp. 9–35.

Boccagni, Paolo. 2017. 'Aspirations and the Subjective Future of Migration: Comparing Views and Desires of the "Time Ahead" through the Narratives of Immigrant Domestic Workers', *Comparative Migration Studies* 5(4): 1–18.

Bunnell, Tim, Jamie Gillen and Elaine Lynn-Ee Ho. 2018. 'The Prospect of Elsewhere: Engaging the Future through Aspirations in Asia', *Annuals of the American Association of Geographers* 108(1): 35–51.

Bryant, Rebecca, and Daniel Knight. 2019. *The Anthropology of the Future*. Cambridge: Cambridge University Press.

Clammer, John. 2012. *Culture, Development and Social Theory: Towards an Integrated Social Development*. London: Zed Books.

Ewing, Katherine. 1990. 'The Illusion of Wholeness: Culture, Self and the Experience of Inconsistency', *Ethos* 18(3): 251–78.

Fischer, Edward F. 2014. *The Good Life: Aspiration, Dignity and the Anthropology of Wellbeing*. Stanford: Stanford University Press.

Giddens, Anthony. 1991. *Modernity and Self-Identity: Self and Society in the Late Modern Age*. Cambridge: Polity Press.

———. 2000. *Runaway World: How Globalization is Reshaping Our Lives*. New York: Routledge.

Myrdal, Gunnar. 1968. *Asian Drama: An Inquiry into the Poverty of Nations, Volume 1*. New York: Pantheon.

Ortner, Sherry. 2016. 'Dark Anthropology and Its Others: Theory since the Eighties', *Hau: Journal of Ethnographic Theory* 6(1): 47–73.

Page, John. 1994. 'The East Asian Miracle: Four Lessons for Development Policy', in Stanley Fisher and Julio Rotemberg (eds), *NBER Macroeconomics 1994*. Cambridge, MA: MIT Press, pp. 219–82.

Persoon, Gerard, and Diny van Est. 2000. 'The Study of the Future in Anthropology in Relation to the Sustainability Debate', *Focaal* 35: 7–28.

Proshansky, Harold. 1978. 'The City and Self-Identity', *Environment and Behavior* 10(2): 147–69.

Robison, Richard, and David Goodman. 1996. *The New Rich in Asia: Mobile Phones, McDonald's and Middle Class Revolution*. New York: Routledge.

Roy, Ananya, and Aihwa Ong. 2011. *Worlding Cities: Asian Experiments and the Art of Being Global*. Chichester: Blackwell.

Sen, Amartya. 1999. *Development as Freedom*. New York: Random House.

Wallman, Sandra (ed.). 1992. *Contemporary Futures: Perspectives from Social Anthropology*. London: Routledge.

Yeung, Wei-Jun Jean, and Cheryll Alipio. 2013. 'Introduction', in Wei-Jun Jean Yeung, Cheryll Alipio and Frank Furstenberg (eds), *Transitioning to Adulthood in Asia: School, Work and Family Life*. Philadelphia: Sage, pp. 6–27.

INDEX

academic, vii, 21, 54, 110, 172
  academic achievement(s)/success, 16, 20, 21, 76, 79, 80, 85
  academic activities, 81, 85
  academic ambitions, 24
  academic credential(s), 21
  academic education, *see* education
  academic excellence, 16, 18, 126n2
  academic performance, 21
  academic life, 15, 23
  academic result(s), 71
access, 5, 6, 35, 40, 41, 44, 49, 60, 71, 72, 73, 77, 85, 86, 87, 95, 101, 103, 104, 116, 121, 126, 132, 137, 142, 157, 158, 159, 160, 176
accomplishment(s), 11, 97, 130, 131, 132, 133, 134, 139, 141, 142, 143, 144
accountability, 132, 172, 175, 176, 180, 181, 182, 183
adolescence, *see* youth
adulthood, 24, 37, 38, 64, 110, 190
adult(s), 81, 93, 111, 116, 124
  adulthood, 24, 37, 38, 64, 110
  adulteration, 154
  adult daughter(s), 17, 18, 21
  nonadult(s), 115
  young adult(s), 2, 9, 10, 11, 15, 17, 18, 22, 23, 29, 30, 34, 35, 36, 40, 50, 91, 151, 152, 153, 155, 156, 157, 158, 159, 160, 161, 163, 164, 165, 166, 170, 176, 184, 187, 188, 189, 190, 191, 193, 195, 196, 197, 198
agency/ies, 7, 22, 27, 65, 102, 104, 111, 121, 124, 125, 133, 136, 143, 144, 175, 180, 181, 188, 191, 192, 194, 195
ambition(s), vii, 6, 16, 24, 43, 119, 120, 130, 131, 132, 133, 135, 136, 137, 141, 143, 144, 155
anthropology, 3, 4, 32, 166, 198, 199
  anthropological, 4, 6, 69, 73, 198
antisocial, 83, 86
anxiety/ies, 58, 66, 82, 87, 155, 157, 181

Appadurai, Arjun, 4, 5, 6, 7, 9, 17, 22, 23, 30, 31, 55, 58, 66, 67, 72, 73, 86, 95, 111, 112, 113, 114, 115, 121, 124, 126, 134, 155, 156, 165, 166, 171, 184, 189, 198
appearance, 11, 25, 70, 71, 74, 76, 78, 79, 81, 83, 85, 130, 190
  physical appearance, 74, 76, 81, 83
Asia(n), vii, 1, 2, 7, 8, 9, 42, 46, 110, 111, 119, 123, 157, 164, 170, 173, 174, 177, 183, 188, 194, 195, 196, 198, 199
  AESAN, 164
  Asian cities, 2, 3, 9, 10, 35, 70, 152, 192, 195
  East Asia(n), 3, 56, 57, 187, 195, 197
  South Asia(n), 71, 72, 88n6, 111, 131, 187, 195, 197
  Southeast Asia(n), 56, 112, 161, 164, 167n5, 187, 195, 197
  urban Asia(n), vii, 1, 2, 3, 10, 15, 121, 152, 153, 184, 187, 188, 193, 195, 197, 199
aspiration(s), 3–8, 8–10, 11, 14, 15, 16, 17, 18, 20, 22, 23, 25, 30, 35, 36, 39, 40, 41, 43, 44, 48, 50, 54, 55, 57, 58, 59, 60, 61, 64, 65, 66–68, 69, 70, 71, 72, 73, 74, 79, 80, 81, 84–86, 87, 91, 93, 94, 95, 96, 98, 99, 101, 102, 103–104, 110, 111, 112, 114, 117, 119, 121, 122, 123, 124, 125–126, 130, 131, 132, 133–134, 135, 136, 137, 141, 142, 143, 144–145, 150, 151–152, 152–154, 155, 156, 157, 158, 159, 160, 161, 162, 163, 164, 165, 166, 170, 171, 172, 173, 175, 176, 177, 178, 179, 181, 182, 183–184, 187–197, 198, 199
assimilation, 39
attachment(s), 171, 182
attractive, 35, 45, 48, 72, 78, 86, 95, 101, 191
  attractiveness, 78, 86
authority/ies, 3, 7
  authoritarian, 196
  authority, parental, 7, 17, 19, 24, 26
  authority, state, 2

www.ingramcontent.com/pod-product-compliance
Lightning Source LLC
Chambersburg PA
CBHW070621030426
42337CB00020B/3875